# Avant-Garde Nationalism at the Dublin Gate Theatre, 1928–1940

Irish Studies

Kathleen Costello-Sullivan, *Series Editor*

SELECT TITLES IN IRISH STUDIES

For a full list of titles in this series, visit https://press.syr.edu/supressbook
-series/irish-studies/.

# AVANT-GARDE NATIONALISM
## AT THE
# DUBLIN GATE
# THEATRE, 1928-1940

## Ruud van den Beuken

Syracuse University Press

∞ The paper used in this publication meets the minimum requirements of the American
National Standard for Information Sciences—Permanence of Paper for Printed Library
Materials, ANSI Z39.48-1992.

For a listing of books published and distributed by Syracuse University Press,
visit https://press.syr.edu.

ISBN: 978-0-8156-3625-0 (hardcover)      978-0-8156-3643-4 (paperback)
        978-0-8156-5471-1 (e-book)

**Library of Congress Cataloging-in-Publication Data**

Names: Beuken, Ruud van den, author.
Title: Avant-garde nationalism at the Dublin Gate Theatre, 1928–1940 /
    Ruud van den Beuken.
Description: First edition. | Syracuse : Syracuse University Press, 2021. | Series: Irish
    studies | Includes bibliographical references and index. | Summary: "While the
    Dublin Gate Theatre (est. 1928) has become renowned for introducing experimental
    foreign drama to Ireland, this study is the first to analyse how the Gate also sought
    to become a site of avant-garde nationalism and to contribute to Irish identity
    formation in the nation's first post-independence decades"—Provided by publisher.
Identifiers: LCCN 2020028199 | ISBN 9780815636250 (hardcover) |
    ISBN 9780815636434 (paperback) | ISBN 9780815654711 (ebook)
Subjects: LCSH: Dublin Gate Theatre. | Experimental theater—Ireland—Dublin—
    History. | Theater—Ireland—Dublin—History—20th century. | Theater and
    society—Ireland—History—20th century.
Classification: LCC PN2602.D82 D83 2021 | DDC 792.09418/35—dc23
LC record available at https://lccn.loc.gov/2020028199

*Manufactured in the United States of America*

# Contents

# Acknowledgments

While doing research on the Dublin Gate Theatre's early years, I enjoyed the encouragement, support, and good advice of many wonderful scholars, including Hans Bak, Helleke van den Braber, Daniel Carey, Mary Clark, Christopher Cusack, Tracy C. Davis, Joan FitzPatrick Dean, Mark Fitzgerald, John Flood, Adrian Frazier, Virginie Girel-Pietka, Katherine Hennessey, Lindsay Janssen, José Lanters, Patrick Lonergan, Radvan Markus, Anna McMullan, Trish McTighe, Chris Morash, Justine Nakase, Siobhán O'Gorman, Connal Parr, Emilie Pine, Richard Pine, Ondřej Pilný, Liedeke Plate, Alexandra Poulain, Paige Reynolds, Elaine Sisson, Grace Vroomen, Clare Wallace, Ian R. Walsh, and Feargal Whelan. A special word of thanks is due to Marguérite Corporaal and Odin Dekkers, who guided my first steps and kept my course steady, and to David Clare, Barry Houlihan, and Des Lally, whose encyclopedic knowledge about the Gate has been almost as inspiring as their generosity and good company over the years.

I also had the pleasure of working with many staff members at the National Library of Ireland, the Charles Deering McCormick Library of Special Collections at Northwestern University, the Manuscripts and Archives Research Library at Trinity College Dublin, and the James Hardiman Library at the National University of Ireland Galway. I am very grateful for their assistance and expertise, as well as their permission to publish from the sources that I consulted. In this respect, I specifically thank the Board of Trinity College Dublin and the Mary Manning Estate. I am also greatly obliged to the Moore Institute for the Humanities and Social Studies (National University of Ireland Galway) for awarding me a research fellowship in 2018, which enabled me to work on this book in a stimulating and—as we say in Dutch—*gezellige* environment.

I would like to note that several sections of this book have previously appeared in *Irish Studies Review* (23, no. 1, 2015); *Irish Studies and the Dynamics of Memory* (edited by Marguérite Corporaal, Christopher Cusack, and Ruud van den Beuken, 2017); *The Gate Theatre, Dublin: Inspiration, and Craft* (edited by David Clare, Des Lally, and Patrick Lonergan, 2018); *Études irlandaises* (43, no. 2, 2018); and *Navigating Ireland's Theatre Archive: Theory, Practice, Performance* (edited by Barry Houlihan, 2019). I thank the respective editors and publishers for allowing me to also incorporate my analyses in this book; the relevant information appears on the first pages of the respective chapters and in the bibliography. I am also grateful to Deborah Manion, my editor at Syracuse University Press, for her support and patience in working on this project.

My final remark here concerns Micheál mac Liammóir's name, which has appeared in numerous variants over the years. I have adhered to what Michael Travers, the executor of the Edwards–mac Liammóir Estate, has identified as mac Liammóir's own preferred spelling. I also express my great thanks to the Estate for granting me permission to quote from mac Liammóir's work and to reproduce mac Liammóir's original design for the Gate Theatre's logo on the cover of this book.

# Avant-Garde Nationalism at the Dublin Gate Theatre, 1928–1940

# Introduction

*"Ireland is one long unending problem"*

In 1938, the Abbey Theatre celebrated its thirty-fifth anniversary by organizing a two-week festival, which offered lectures in the mornings and plays in the evenings, including the premiere of *Purgatory*, W. B. Yeats's final play. The speakers included such luminaries as Denis Johnston, T. C. Murray, Frank O'Connor, and Micheál mac Liammóir, who had been asked to give a lecture on the topic of Irish problem plays. The cofounder of the Dublin Gate Theatre admitted to his audience that he faced a conundrum, since he felt that it was impossible to demarcate the genre:

> The first conclusion I come to on reviewing my own thoughts on the subject is, bewilderingly enough, that every Irish play that I know is what I would call a problem play, that Irish life has a startling propensity to produce problems from nowhere as a conjurer produces rabbits out of a hat, that the Irish people are possibly the most problematic creatures in Europe or even, it may be, out of it, and that Ireland is one long problem whose solution may conceivably be lying in the womb of time.[1]

It is revealing that, within a single sentence, mac Liammóir's attempt to identify a subset of Irish drama escalated into a darkly comical reflection on the very nature of the Irish nation and its people. At the same time, however, mac Liammóir's conflation of Irish playwriting with the strictures of national identity formation did offer an explanation as to why "from a country like this, torn . . . by inner turmoils and furrowed with introspection, should spring a literature and a drama whose main

I

preoccupation is with the various presentations of the problems that beset its life."[2]

In many ways, mac Liammóir's struggle underlines the persistence—albeit in a defeatist vein—of the nineteenth-century mode of national identity formation that Joep Leerssen describes as "attempt[ing] to distil such an invariant and universally shared awareness out of a contentious and conflict-ridden past, transcending thereby the violent vicissitudes of history and extracting from them an essential and unchanging principle of Irishness."[3] However, during his lecture, mac Liammóir refrained from explicitly articulating the nation's fraught history of famine, diaspora, religious tensions, anticolonial struggle, and civil war, despite their importance to the construction of Irish identities—and this illustrates at least one part of the mimetic problem.

While mac Liammóir's lecture only addressed "Irish life" in a cursory manner, then, his comments exemplify what Richard Kearney calls the "transitional paradigm" between tradition and modernity, which has provided a pertinent—if contested—critical discourse in Irish Studies.[4] In this sense, the Irish model is distinctive, for if, as Luke Gibbons has asserted, "the sense of disintegration and 'unconditional presentness' (Simmel) which exerted such a fascination for writers from Baudelaire to Benjamin was pre-eminently spatial, the result of a new topology of social relations in the metropolis," it is remarkable that Irish modernity is primarily "bound up with *temporality*, as the endless preoccupation with ruins and remnants of ancient manuscripts in cultural nationalism made all too evident."[5] This fixation on commemoration tends to be consolidated as a "politics of identity" that is progressive rather than contemplative: as Barbara A. Misztal, for example, observes, "Memory is used strategically: not merely to explain the group past but also to transform it into a reliable identity source for the group present."[6]

In the postcolonial context of the Irish Free State, dramatic expressions of such cultural memories thus offer engagements with the various sociopolitical tensions that dominated the nation's public sphere, which, of course, also comprised its cultural products. Yet, in examining Irish drama in the first postindependence decades, conventional theatrical historiography has focused mostly on the Abbey Theatre and its importance as Ireland's national playhouse. Not in the least due to this official status, theater scholarship on the first half of the twentieth century has generally focused on the Abbey's seminal productions, which have overshadowed the existence of equally important, if not more innovative, engagements with national history and identity on other Irish stages.

In order to contribute to a more pluralistic historiography of Irish theater, then, this book will focus on the Dublin Gate Theatre, the avant-garde playhouse that mac Liammóir founded with Hilton Edwards in 1928. From its inception, the Gate served as a cultural counterweight to the Abbey's ostensible hegemony as Ireland's official national theater—a role for which the Gate received due praise in its heyday, if less so from the 1960s onward. Accordingly, this study analyzes how the Gate's directors and playwrights sought to contribute to Irish identity formation during the years leading up to World War II, as they articulated their own views on a colonial past that had to be reassessed, on the one hand, and a postcolonial future that still had to be molded, on the other. These processes will be clarified by examining a twofold corpus: this book will both discuss the ways in which the Gate's founders and associates reflected on their theater's role in facilitating Ireland's cultural development in various publications, and it will show how a new generation of playwrights engaged with contested collective memories in a corpus of original Irish plays that premiered at the Gate.

In fostering such initiatives, the Gate's founders adopted a markedly cosmopolitan approach, creating a performative forum that facilitated onstage and offstage discussions of cultural nationhood in an explicitly international context. Edwards and mac Liammóir thus consolidated the precursory efforts of Edward Martyn's Irish Theatre Company (1914–20) and W. B. Yeats and Lennox Robinson's Dublin Drama League (1919–29) to introduce foreign influences to the Irish stage, and their playhouse would quickly become renowned for producing stylistically and dramaturgically innovative plays in a uniquely avant-garde setting. Indeed, Christopher Fitz-Simon, the partners' joint biographer, credits them with having offered "a kaleidoscopic cross-section of modern European and American drama, at a time when Ireland floated in cultural isolation in mid-Atlantic."[7] Such assessments illustrate how Edwards and mac

Liammóir defied the artistic insularity that marked Ireland's anxious first postindependence decades and threatened to curb creative initiatives through censorship and the promotion of state-approved literature.

Yet conventional perceptions of the Gate as a "director's theatre" with an imported repertoire—or even as a "cosmopolitan cuckoo in the national nest"—only partially acknowledge the Gate's attempt at remedying the insularity of the Irish stage during the Free State years.[8] No less importantly, Edwards and mac Liammóir also produced the works of new Irish playwrights, such as Denis Johnston, Mary Manning, David Sears, Robert Collis, and their patrons Edward and Christine Longford.[9] Having grown up in the heyday of the Celtic Twilight, and, more vitally, during an era of political turmoil and bloodshed that saw the creation of an independent yet in many ways bitterly divided Ireland, these playwrights chose to align themselves with an avant-garde theater that explicitly sought to establish Dublin as a modern European capital.

Perhaps the most vocal of these Gate upstarts, Mary Manning wrote a retrospective manifesto for her generation soon after she left Dublin for Boston in 1935. Her reflections on Irish modernity and nationhood invites a contrast with Hilton Edwards's oft-quoted assertion that the Gate is "not a national theatre" but "simply a theatre" whose "policy is the exploitation of all forms of theatrical expression regardless of nationality."[10] Edwards's technical reflections on artistic direction have conventionally been conflated with the Gate's theatrical poetics, but Manning's account of the Gate's early years is one of many texts that belie the idea that the Gate was an austere sanctuary for connoisseurs of elitist drama, instead presenting an interesting mishmash of cosmopolitanism and patriotism:

> We are going through the difficult and hazardous process of becoming a nation once again. Everything goes to prove it—Mr. De Valera's Eden of "Wheat, Beet and Free Meat," General O'Duffy's Blueshirted Fascists, Dr. Drumm's electric trains, the Shannon Scheme pylons, so disturbing to Paul Henry's skyline, the movie palaces dominating every city, town and suburb, the bone-shaking bus services, and the miles and miles of red-brick ideal homes springing up in all directions—this is the real Ireland. We can never again be described as an Abbey kitchen

interior, entirely surrounded by the bog! And with all this rebuilding and re-organisation, a new generation has arisen, a little smothered perhaps by the Giants of the Renaissance—the Old Guard dies but never surrenders—a new generation of young writers, dramatists and actors who have found their inspiration and life's work in the Dublin Gate Theater.

Noting that Edwards and mac Liammóir were "clever enough to see that folk drama did not altogether satisfy the ever-growing intelligentsia," Manning went on to stress the Gate's importance to Irish identity formation:

> If we have done nothing else we have emerged from the Celtic twilight and dragged into the light of day young writers and actors who might otherwise have withered away in obscurity. Ireland is passing through a transition period at the moment and the drama, which naturally reflects the minds of the people, is confused and mainly experimental; but it is taking shape out of the chaos and developing a character, a form of its own, national and international, collective and yet intensely individualistic.[11]

Although the Gate's poetics were, indeed, self-consciously diverse (if not, at times, diffuse), Manning's mordant declaration did articulate a new generation's native understanding and espousal of urban modernity and its denigration of pseudo-organic traditionalism. Clearly taking pleasure in what she construed as shocking the establishment out of its narrow-minded cultivation of the past, Manning claimed that Ireland's cultural insularity had become untenable by exposing the Abbey's ineluctable Irish cottage for what it was: an ideological mise en abyme. The present was to be interpreted as a tentative construct, a time of radical change that required the past and the future to be reimagined in a way that would allow Ireland to modernize its identity by partaking of international culture.

Even though this new generation of playwrights professed their desire to break the strictures of conventional playwriting and explore alternatives to what they perceived to be the conservatism of their Abbey rivals (as well as the equally contestable and censorious notions of Irishness that successive governments promoted), their attempts to modernize Irish drama have mostly been overlooked by theater historiographers.[12] There-fore, this book explores how Gate directors and playwrights engaged with the tension between avant-gardist poetics and traditionalist politics that overshadowed the cultural vanguard of postrevolutionary Ireland and that so strongly inflected dramatic attempts to present innovative visions of the Irish nation.

In disclosing a largely unpublished and generally uncharted corpus of plays and manifestos, it becomes clear that Edwards, mac Liammóir, and many other Gate affiliates were, in a sense, *avant-garde nationalists*: they sought to further Ireland's cultural development not only by exposing Dublin to foreign drama and novel staging techniques (as has generally been acknowledged), but also by writing and producing original Irish plays. While the Gate's playwrights might then have been inspired by the cosmopolitan sensibilities that Edwards and mac Liammóir's eclectic fare provided, this also encouraged them to confront their own nation's problematic history and envisage a new future for Ireland. Their radical-ism thus exemplifies Declan Kiberd's observation that, in an Irish context, "the very meaning of the word *tradition* changes" as artists come to real-ize that it is their "task to show the interdependence of past and future in attempting to restore history's openness."[13]

The Gate Theatre would do so in myriad ways, and, in looking back on his theater company's first two decades on the Dublin stage and its many tours abroad in his 1950 booklet *Theatre in Ireland*, mac Liammóir indeed celebrated the Gate's penchant for diversity. Unlike their Abbey counterparts, he claimed, Gate actors were not recognizable as such; they spurned stylistic uniformity. For all the possibilities that this eclecticism offered, in turn, to the Gate's choice of repertoire, mac Liammóir could not be wholly satisfied with the assortment of talents of the Gate's leading actors that Hilton Edwards, in his role as producer, was fostering. He still craved some sort of defining principle, a hidden unity that would truly fulfill the Gate's ambitions, and so he wondered whether

> it may be that the writer, rather than the producer, shapes the manner of
> the stage and of its people. But as the Abbey failed, by the very strength
> of its popular appeal, to realise the dream of its creator for a poet's

theatre where the players, robed dimly and chanting in many voices, should recreate the arts of minstrelsy, of dancing, and of a symbolic celebration of the mysteries, so have we failed in the main to discover those authors who shall write for us our masterpiece.[14]

Rather than savoring the achievements that are conventionally ascribed to the Gate—its innovations in artistic design and lighting techniques, its success in challenging the conventions of naturalism and opening up Dublin to experimental plays from abroad—mac Liammóir remained unsatisfied. While Yeats had changed the face of Irish drama by producing his own plays and promoting a score of new playwrights, including Lady Gregory, J. M. Synge, and Sean O'Casey, mac Liammóir felt that he had discovered little more than the singular genius of Denis Johnston, and half of his plays had premiered at the Abbey.

Even so, it is more important that mac Liammóir brought up this issue in the first place. By presenting the Gate's lack of resident playwrights as its critical flaw, he underlined his company's continued dedication to the development not only of Irish theater but also of Irish *drama*. The ultimate realization of the Gate's cultural project should, in fact, be interpreted as depending on its success in nurturing new playwrights:

> We secretly hoped, and indeed are still hoping, through our experiments in the field of ancient and modern plays from all sorts of places, and from the varied methods that the handling of the plays demanded, we would at last discover a way, more evocative than literal, more suggestive than photographic, that might serve as the mould for the Irish dramatist of the future, as the Elizabethan way served as the mould for Shakespeare, Marlowe and Ben Johnson, or the modern picture-frame stage's way has served for Wilde, Capek, and Noël Coward.[15]

According to mac Liammóir, then, the Gate's rampant eclecticism, which would become something of a dismissive stereotype of its poetics, actually served the purpose of finding and encouraging writers who could articulate new notions of Irishness.

Furthermore, it is doubtful whether the Gate directorate's attempts to find new playwrights actually failed as badly as mac Liammóir suggested.

Between the establishment of the Gate Theatre in 1928 and the publication of the *Theatre in Ireland* booklet in 1950, "the Boys," as Edwards and mac Liammóir became affectionately known, produced some forty new Irish plays. While few of these have attained a prominent stature in the history of Irish theater, their contemporary popularity, as well as their multifaceted engagement with postcolonial Irish identities, warrant a thorough investigation. Therefore, this book charts some of the ways in which the Gate Theatre contributed to the Free State's cultural identity formation by analyzing an understudied corpus of theatrical poetics and original plays that reveal how the Gate's founders and associates reflected on their theater's role in facilitating Ireland's postcolonial cultural development, and how its playwrights engaged with contested collective identities in their mythological, historical, and contemporary plays, many of which have never been published.

In exploring these topics, this study presents the Dublin Gate Theatre as a site of avant-garde nationalism, a productive confluence of the international and the national, thereby demonstrating that John Gassner did not overstate the Gate's importance to the Free State when he asserted, in his 1954 book *The Theatre in Our Times*, that "what the Abbey Theatre was to the Irish renaissance or Celtic revival of the beginning of the century, the Gate . . . aimed to be to liberated Eire."[16] Gassner's juxtaposition implies contrasts as well as continuities, and the subsequent chapters of this book clarify the wide range of disputed issues that are implied by his evaluation.

An initial step in proving this point will be taken in chapter 1 by embedding the Gate's establishment in Ireland's theatrical history and reconstructing its problematic historiography, thereby focusing on the Gate's immediate sociocultural context and its academic reception. However, a thorough assessment of the Gate as an avant-garde nationalist playhouse also requires reflection on the discourses concerning the perceived conflict between tradition and modernity, as well as on the infrastructures of postindependence Irish theater. Accordingly, chapter 2 draws on various discussions of the paradoxical nature of Irish modernity and the enforced revival of Irish tradition, as well as on recent developments in cultural memory theory, to illustrate how Micheál mac Liammóir sought to exorcise the collective traumas of his adopted nation through the deliberate construction of his Irish persona. Chapter 3 focuses on the Irish stage of the 1930s to discuss the exigencies of drama as a vehicle of national identity formation in relation to a corpus of manifestos, editorials, and articles that were written by the Gate's directors and leading associates to address the meaning of theatrical nationalism—indeed, some of them explicitly label the Gate itself a national theater. Together, these three chapters will demonstrate how tradition, modernity, and (inter)nationalism were conceptualized by the Gate's leadership, who sought to position the Gate in the existing theatrical tradition to effect a dramatic reconfiguration of the Free State's cultural identities.

The subsequent chapters offer analyses of a corpus of original Gate plays that have been selected to illustrate various modes of engaging with issues of collective identity formation. These case studies have been divided into three chapters that deal with mythological, historical, and contemporary themes respectively. Chapter 4 outlines the memory strategies that attend the construction of a postrevolutionary mythology through various emblematic marriages in the Gate's repertoire of mythohistorical plays, which feature legendary characters such as Diarmuid and Gráinne. Chapter 5 addresses engagements with several important episodes of religious strife and armed rebellion in modern Irish history, ranging from a dramatization of the publication of Jonathan Swift's Drapier's Letters (1724–25) to a play that focuses on middle-class loyalties during the Anglo-Irish War (1919–21). Chapter 6 explores various depictions of urban and rural life in the contemporary Free State, reflecting on the problematic fulfillment of nationalist teleologies and discussing various issues of class and social geography that continued to divide the newly independent nation.

Finally, these concerns will come full circle, for, as entities in mac Liammóir's mind, his theater company and his adopted country were not all that distinct: in his autobiography *All for Hecuba* (1946), he joked that, to him, the Gate Theatre was an insatiable mistress and, as such, "another Ireland, in fact."[17] Therefore, it seems appropriate to conclude this evaluation of the Gate's poetics and original drama with a discussion of mac

Liammóir's 1940 play *Where Stars Walk*, which likewise blurs the lines between the stage and the nation and addresses many of the issues that are central to this book.

Of course, the role that Edwards and mac Liammóir's company played in questioning and developing Irish identities was hardly straightforward, since their endeavors were subject to the complex infrastructure of Irish theater during the Free State years and its attendant power relations (political, financial, and otherwise). Yet it is precisely for this reason that evaluating the Gate's avant-garde nationalism and its contribution to Irish identity formation can facilitate a reassessment of this relatively marginalized period in Ireland's cultural history. Accordingly, this book shows how the Gate's directors and playwrights confronted the dominant cultural politics of selective repression and articulation of important collective memories, as well as presented new possibilities of realigning past, present, and future perspectives. In doing so, the discussion and representation of national identities—and the cultural memories that underlie them—will be interpreted as deliberate interventions that sought to redefine Ireland's teleology after independence. Whether they were executed offstage in manifestos and articles or onstage as plays that revisited and performed Irish history time and again in an attempt to bring some kind of resolution to the present and shape the nation's future, such engagements underline Nicholas Andrew Miller's observation that "what always has been at stake in the telling of Ireland's 'story' is nothing less than the country's modernity": the desire to consign the past to its proper place.[18]

# I

# Cosmopolitan Dublin

*The Gate Theatre's Cultural Project*

As the Gate Theatre emerged in the Free State as a site of avant-garde nationalism, it necessarily intervened in a theatrical tradition that had been molded by other dramatic companies, which had accorded varying degrees of importance to espousing an (inter)nationalist agenda. For historiographers, the nature—if not the very existence—of that tradition has been a contested question, especially with regard to the colonial era, which was marked by the influx of English troupes and the exodus of native playwrights. In 1950, Micheál mac Liammóir himself claimed that, prior to the Abbey's establishment, Ireland could boast "no theatre of its own and no voice to tell its story," and, as late as the 1970s, important figures like Micheál Ó hAodha, the chairman of the National Theatre Society, would state that Ireland lacked a "tradition of theatre in the historic sense."[1] Although more nuanced assessments of Irish theater during the eighteenth and nineteenth centuries have since gained traction, the first decades of the twentieth century have invariably been understood to herald a new era for the Irish stage as much as they did in politics. The subtitle of Christopher Murray's seminal *Twentieth-Century Irish Drama: Mirror up to Nation* (1997) expresses this confluence, and indeed Murray contends that "in the Irish historical experience drama (the creation of texts for performance) and the theater (the formation of the means of production and conditions of reception of drama) were both instrumental in defining and sustaining national consciousness."[2]

These attempts at collective identity formation were also themselves historically inflected, and, as Chris Morash has shown, it was precisely by ignoring existing dramatic traditions and presenting itself as an immaculate conception that the Irish Literary Theatre (and its successive incarnations as the Irish National Theatre Society and the Abbey Theatre) could "imagine afresh its relationship to Irish history."[3] At the same time, the plethora of paradoxes that constituted its directors' dramatic poetics—ranging from notions of reviving Celtic folklore, establishing Irish modernity, reveling in a united audience, and scorning the general public—facilitated a creative dynamic that allowed the Abbey to change the face of Irish culture by embodying "divergent and even antagonistic attitudes to politics and class," as Lauren Arrington notes.[4]

The tenacity of this vision, however, was a double-edged sword. On the one hand, the Abbey's artistic idealism did not lead its directorate to avoid breaking political taboos, to which the public protests and occasional riots against controversial plays such as *The Playboy of the Western World* (1907) and *The Plough and the Stars* (1926) testify. On the other hand, the aspirations of the Abbey's directorate could also result in autocratic obstinacy, which incurred negative reactions from aspiring playwrights and producers who sought to pursue their art while thinking outside the National Theatre's parameters. Bulmer Hobson and Lewis Purcell, for example, found themselves rebuffed by Yeats in their desire to establish an Irish Literary Theatre annex in Belfast. Such conflicts also arose within the Abbey itself: in 1906, Máire Nic Shiubhlaigh and several other players left the Abbey to found the Theatre of Ireland after Yeats, Gregory, and Synge effectively established a triumvirate that demoted the Abbey's actors from equal partners to subordinate workers. Likewise, around 1908, Frank W. Fay came to feel that the Abbey management progressively limited his artistic influence. Unable to put his belief that Irish plays should be performed in Irish rather than English into practice, Frank and his brother William decided to seek their fortunes outside the Abbey as well.[5]

As the first resident playwright of the Irish-language Taibhdhearc na Gaillimhe, which he helped set up with Professor Líam O Bríain in 1928, Micheál mac Liammóir could have sympathized with the Fays to some extent. Two other Abbey dissenters, however, proved more decisive in paving the way for the Gate Theatre. The first of these was Edward Martyn, who had already parted ways with the Irish Literary Theatre in

1901 and joined forces with Joseph Plunkett, Thomas MacDonagh, and Patrick Pearse at the Theatre of Ireland a few years later. In 1914, Martyn, claiming that "a theatre which only treats peasant life can never be considered . . . more than a folk theatre," launched the Irish Theatre Company, and, despite the execution of several of its leaders in the aftermath of the 1916 Easter Rising, the ITC lasted until 1920, during which time it successfully produced various novel European plays by such writers as Anton Chekhov and Henrik Ibsen.[6] The ITC also maintained ties with Count Markievicz's Independent Dramatic Company, whose aims partially overlapped.[7]

For the second preliminary internationalist venture, Yeats himself was actively responsible: in 1918, he founded the Dublin Drama League with his fellow playwright and Abbey manager Lennox Robinson, and their company would make its debut with Srgjan Tucić's *The Liberators* (translated by Fanny S. Copeland) in February 1919. Yeats's disenchantment with the Abbey Theatre—which, despite its many triumphs in exalting Irish cultural life, had failed to create truly new forms of theater—led him to underwrite Robinson's ambitious venture to import innovative drama.[8] His protégé recognized that "here in Ireland we are isolated, cut off from the thought of the world" and therefore decided to take on "the production of plays, which, in the ordinary course of events, would not likely be seen in Dublin"—but Robinson was quick to assure his potential audience that "seeing foreign plays will not divorce our minds from Ireland."[9]

The Drama League thus stimulated the stagnant Dublin theatrical scene with an internationalist impulse, and, as Morash describes, "in effect became a sort of phantom image of what the Abbey might have been—a democratically run, flexible organisation presenting the best of European modernist theater to a select audience."[10] Accordingly, Katz Clarke and Ferrar claim that the Dublin Drama League challenged the strictures of national theater by "fulfil[ling] an obligation basic to the imaginative life of the theatre: it would not play safe."[11] The same applies to the Gate Theatre, whose first major playwright, Denis Johnston, expressed his artistic indebtedness to the Dublin Drama League's (DDL) introduction of avant-garde drama to Dublin, while Mary Manning, another young Gate playwright, starred in DDL productions of *The Dear Departing* by

Leonid Andreyev (1926) and *Caesar and Cleopatra* by George Bernard Shaw (1927).[12] In many ways, then, Yeats and Robinson's attempt to remedy the Abbey's reluctance to look beyond Ireland's shores paved the way for the Gate Theatre's internationalist poetics.[13]

## Enter Hilton Edwards and Micheál mac Liammóir

If by the late 1920s the Abbey Theatre had firmly established itself as the national playhouse, its prominent position also sparked accusations of "insularity and chauvinism" that challenged its ambassadorial station.[14] When Hilton Edwards and Micheál mac Liammóir met during the Intimate Theatre Company's 1927 tour of Ireland, the depreciated status of Irish drama quickly became apparent to the Gate founders-to-be: as mac Liammóir would write in his autobiography *All for Hecuba* (1946), he saw that "while it was true that O'Casey could fill the Abbey, Synge had ceased to excite people, and Yeats thinned the stalls down to a few estatic [*sic*] readers of poetry, most of whom came in on their cards."[15] Faced with this lethargy, Hilton Edwards, who also commented on this period in *The Mantle of Harlequin* (1958), believed that nothing less than "theatrical revolution was in the air"—and the two young actors would soon prove to be its agents.[16]

In a way, the man who drove them to the barricades was mac Liammóir's brother-in-law Anew McMaster, the flamboyant actor/manager who led the Intimate Theatre Company.[17] Mac Liammóir had just penned his first play, *Diarmuid agus Gráinne*, and although McMaster had promised him to stage his play (albeit in English) toward the end of their tour, he opted out at the last moment, citing vague logistical reasons. Mac Liammóir was acquainted with McMaster's erratic temperament, but his disappointment was obvious, and Hilton Edwards could easily capitalize on his friend's frustration to further his budding plan of founding a theater of their own, which would then ensure an English-language production of *Diarmuid agus Gráinne*. Edwards's chief desire, however, was not the performance of this mythological piece but, rather, the chance to experiment with various revolutionary lighting and staging techniques that he had discovered on the Continent, envisaging, as the Boys' biographer Christopher Fitz-Simon put it, "a new kind of theatre, where effects of sound and music and massed movement would have as much importance as words, where electric lighting would come into its own."[18]

The two young actors were forced to end the McMaster tour with a protracted stay in Cobh, where mac Liammóir went to great lengths to care for Edwards while the latter was bedridden with pneumonia. By then the similarity of their radical theatrical ideas had become obvious, resulting in a shared desire to establish an avant-garde theater in Dublin. Mac Liammóir's penchant for experimental costume and décor design provided a welcome complement to Edwards's technical knowledge, and the duo thus sought to revolutionize the rather insular Dublin drama scene. In *All for Hecuba*, mac Liammóir would recall how time and again Edwards "would discuss the possibilities of interesting people in Dublin in a subscription theatre, or in the possibilities of a season of European plays, the accepted masterpieces as well as the later unknown experimental works, shoving in Evreinov with Ibsen and Sholem Asche, and Kaiser with Tchehov and Goethe and Jacinto Benavente," while Fitz-Simon, too, notes how "all the time he and Micheál were talking of the German expressionists, of Copeau and the Pitoëffs, of O'Neill and the new American drama, which seemed to be so greatly influenced by J. M. Synge and T. C. Murray."[19] In those final years of the 1920s, "the expressionist movement that was creeping in from Russia and Germany" fueled Edwards to "[talk] theatre for hours on end, laying a stress on production that the rest of us had neglected, and fixing a ferocious eye on [mac Liammóir] whenever stage designs and the great names that Diaghileff had gathered about him were mentioned."[20]

The same applied to Edwards's British and Continental colleagues, among whom he particularly valued Peter Godfrey, the founder of the London Gate Theatre. Aiming to emulate this British fusion of internationalist eclecticism and avant-garde stage design in a different setting, Edwards asked mac Liammóir whether he, too, would not want to create "something like Pete Godfrey's Gate in London. . . . There are lots of exciting things from Russia and all over the place. How do you think Dublin would react?"[21] This supposedly nonchalant question reflects both Edwards's artistic inspiration as well as mac Liammóir's adopted patriotism—and this confluence of international aesthetics and modern dramatics with the partners' choice for Dublin as a cultural base prefigures the role that the Gate Theatre would play in engaging with the nation's postcolonial identities.

The name of the Gate, then, derives from Godfrey's theater in Covent Garden, which, as mac Liammóir recounted, "gave to London its first taste of genuine Continental delicacies, or *Delikatessen* if you will, for most of them came from Germany," such as the Kaiser and Toller productions that had, incidentally, found their way to Dublin as well through the efforts of the Dublin Drama League.[22] Although Edwards traveled to London to discuss his plans with Godfrey and was allowed to borrow the name, the partnership never materialized in the way they had originally envisaged, largely due to practical reasons. The Dublin Gate did copy the style of the London production of Eugene O'Neill's *The Hairy Ape* (1922), which the Irish company produced during its first season, but Godfrey mainly provided a spiritual example: his productions had "a certain quality as of caviar, and filled a real gap in the English theatrical menu."[23] Despite Edwards's eagerness, mac Liammóir initially remained doubtful regarding the viability of their endeavor, considering Dublin "unlikely to crave for exotic foods" since it was used to "honest and supremely well-cooked bacon and cabbage at the Abbey" and only got the smallest taste of foreign flavors during performances by the Dublin Drama League and the New Players.[24] Highly skeptical of their new enterprise, mac Liammóir was convinced that "Dublin cares a great deal for matter, and very little indeed for manner," thereby implicitly confirming the stereotype of Ireland as a plain and rustic country that would fail to appreciate the refined subtleties of cosmopolitan culture.[25]

The possibility of serving his adopted country, however ungrateful it might prove, nevertheless appealed strongly to mac Liammóir, who came to reflect on how postcolonial Dublin was to relate to imperial London, and, by extension, how he himself, in deciding to refashion himself as a Gaelic-speaking Irishman even though he was born an Englishman, should contribute to the development of his nation's modern identity. Looking back on his younger years in *All for Hecuba*, mac Liammóir remembered how he had felt that the "Irish people had contributed enough to London to make it the indispensable monster it had become," even if he had to concede that most of Ireland's greatest talents had left their native soil voluntarily.[26]

For mac Liammóir, then, the main issue boiled down to a question of artistic autonomy:

> Had the artist a duty towards a country? Or was this national-aesthetic movement all a dream, a fantastic and lovely motif in the mind of the besotted individual, a species of dangerous and seductive opium with which he drugged his senses and stepped through gates of green jasper into a land of glowing and visionary heroisms, of sacrifices that burned him like fire and yet were all unreal?

Even at the time, mac Liammóir admitted the possibility that the Celtic Revival was no more than a hallucinatory construct, a simulacrum that would only enslave the postcolonial subject to a new falsehood. In comparing Ireland to its former oppressor and the cultural powerhouses of Continental Europe, mac Liammóir admitted that, for them, "there is no question of sacrifice, of a self-imposed provincialism in serving at the altars of his own land" such as he himself had (or chose) to cope with by lingering in the cultural periphery. This led him to wonder whether he was not actually indulging in "the sentimental heroics of a weakling who wishes to stay with a crippled mother, and who, while longing to join the race, murmurs a grudging refusal to the athlete all muscles and impatience by his side"—receding, that is, into a debilitating mode of postcolonial self-victimization.[27]

No less importantly, mac Liammóir realized in retrospect that his idol W. B. Yeats had perhaps been a collaborator who "stood with Sligo at his back and London at his feet, whereas the actor who would work for Ireland must needs turn his face to his audience for inspiration." In those days, however, nothing could shake his faith in promoting Irish culture, and he fully embraced Yeats's somewhat opportunistic call to arms, believing that it was the Revival's goal "not only to shape a literature and a theatre, but to re-create a capital out of a provincial town, to set a faintly fluttering heart a-beat once more in Ireland's body, surely of all tasks the most enthralling." The Gate, then, should be established in an attempt to bolster Ireland's courage in regaining its proper place and bringing life to Yeats's dream, even if this project was "dangerous, too, it may be, for who can tell what new steps the dancing feet may take when once the heart begins to beat again, the body and limbs to stir?"[28] Fully complicit with Revivalist idealism, then, mac Liammóir implicitly spoke of a *re*establishment of a tradition in which Ireland's beauty was still unsullied by colonial subjugation.

Unexpectedly, mac Liammóir was given the opportunity to indulge his sentiments when, in the spring of 1928, Professor Líam O Bríain requested his help in establishing the Taibhdhearc na Gaillimhe, and so "the mingled excitement of aesthetics and patriotism, like a newly discovered cocktail, was going to our heads" in "this maelstrom of passionate revivalism."[29] Meanwhile, Edwards was hunting for subscribers to the new theater that they were to establish in Dublin, and, capitalizing on the Dublin Drama League's existence as an innocuous fifth column in the highest echelons of the Abbey's direction, his efforts were received with much more enthusiasm than either of them had expected.[30] Even as Irish writers such as James Joyce and Samuel Beckett were choosing exile to find inspiration abroad, Edwards and mac Liammóir started to change Irish culture from within.

In getting ready to do so, they got a running start in Dublin society through the generosity of Madame "Toto" Bannard Cogley, who had established her Studio Art Cabaret Club (also known simply as the Cabaret) in late 1924 and who would become one of the Gate's founding directors. As Elaine Sisson observes, Bannard Cogley's "clientele of artists, students, actors, writers, activists, and dissidents attest to the need for a connection to European cultures, to make something new in Irish form," and she allowed Edwards and mac Liammóir to use her subscription lists to circulate their first manifesto in order to raise funds for their new company.[31] In this manifesto, Edwards and mac Liammóir solemnly declared their intentions:

> It is proposed to open the Dublin Gate Theatre Studio in October, 1928, for the production of modern and progressive plays, unfettered by theatrical convention. The London Gate Theatre has been extraordinarily successful, and the directors of the Dublin Gate Theatre are in a

position to avail themselves of this organization for procuring plays that would not otherwise be within the reach of Dublin theatrical circles.

It would be unfair to suggest that this proclamation hints at a neocolonial collaboration with a London playhouse, for, in the same manifesto, Edwards and mac Liammóir also expressed their dedication to promoting new Irish playwrights, belying the conventional depiction of the Gate as a purely internationalist theater. Indeed, the Boys did not even await the outcome of their first season to announce that "in addition to its Continental repertoire the Dublin Gate Theatre is prepared to consider with a view to production all plays of a suitable nature submitted," and that, in doing so, "the Studio will utilize as much Dublin talent as possible."[32]

While this dual approach of importing experimental foreign plays and fostering indigenous playwrights already infers a particular mode of avant-garde nationalism, Edwards and mac Liammóir did run the risk of estranging themselves from the Abbey, whose directors had loaned them the Peacock Theatre annex for their first season. The newcomers were therefore quick to assuage such fears by claiming that "it is not the intention of the Studio to encroach upon the activities of any existing Dublin theatrical organization; rather it is the desire of the Gate to introduce a new element, both in the play and its production." The list of Continental and American playwrights that follows this preemptive appeasement served to demonstrate that the duo's artistic vision would not overlap with the Abbey's repertoire.[33]

W. B. Yeats and Lennox Robinson did not fail to acknowledge mac Liammóir and Edwards's radical potential in generating a steady influx of avant-garde drama and staging techniques, and the Dublin Drama League accordingly disbanded after the Gate's highly successful first season.[34] Yet this ostensibly easy transfer belies the fact that the establishment of the Gate Theatre as an independent playhouse rather than an itinerant company enabled it to provide Ireland with a professional and well-connected catalyst for artistic innovation. In the Gate, then, the Free State found a forum in which issues of Irish identity formation could be addressed in a cosmopolitan context, thereby creating a buoyant site of avant-garde nationalism.

The conflicted nature of Irish modernity, however, negates any attempt to interpret the Gate's engagement with Irish (inter)nationalism as a straightforward implementation of some imported revolutionary doctrine. This is perhaps most apparent in the paradox of Micheál mac Liammóir's fascination with Celtic mythology and the Irish language alongside his cosmopolitan sensibility, which he shared with Edwards, in terms of combining experimental design and stagecraft with an international repertoire. The Gate's production techniques were thoroughly innovative, if not positively outlandish at times: the first-season performance of Oscar Wilde's *Salomé* (1891), for instance, featured "a lovely set in black and silver and viperish green with the entire caste [*sic*] stripped almost naked."[35] The sensuality of a symbolist play that had been banned by the British authorities was likely to shock Dublin audiences even without such costumes (or, more precisely, such a lack of costumes). Of course, mac Liammóir's and Edwards's homosexuality fueled further debate, especially, as Fitz-Simon notes, "during that reactionary period of intensely inward-looking nationalism and puritanical Catholicism" when some people might "have felt that the 'Bohemian' atmosphere of the Gate was out of line with proper moral thinking"—if not worse.[36] Performing risqué plays in an often impudent fashion consequently meant running the risk of infringing on the censorship regulations of a government that, as Morash observes, suspected that "the dark shadows of global modernity plotted to disorient the fixed certainties of national identity."[37] Religious authorities likewise criticized the Gate's extravagant and sensual productions, with Archbishop John Charles McQuaid describing Edwards and mac Liammóir's enterprise, still with some goodwill, as "brilliant—but dangerous."[38]

Such criticism did not drown out the rave reviews hailing the early Dublin Gate Theatre Studio's "magnificent work," which supposedly consisted of "an unbroken sequence of brilliant artistic successes."[39] Edwards and mac Liammóir's venture at the Peacock had begun thriving soon after its opening on October 14, 1928, with a thoroughly ambitious first Irish production of Ibsen's *Peer Gynt*. Joseph Holloway, who attended the opening night of the Gate's very first production, recorded being part of "a crowded and distinguished audience who followed the strange often weird play with rapt attention." Holloway was lavish in his praise, observing that, "considering the limited space of the stage, wonders were worked thereon, and the settings by Micheál Mac Liammóir and the lighting designed by Hilton Edwards were very beautiful at times and always effective." All in all, he felt that "the opening night of The Dublin Gate Theatre was one to remember with pleasure."[40]

*Peer Gynt* was followed by an English translation of mac Liammóir's mythological piece *Diarmuid agus Gráinne*, which had been produced in Irish at the Taibhdhearc just before. Highly stylized productions of plays by foreign writers such as Eugene O'Neill, Nikolai Evreinov, and Elmer Rice soon followed, while the Gate's most prominent home-grown dramatist, Denis Johnston, made his debut during Edwards and mac Liammóir's second season with *The Old Lady Says "No!"* (1929). Elaine Sisson's reflections on the techniques that Edwards and mac Liammóir employed in staging this play illustrate their revolutionary stylistics, elements of which were borrowed and adapted from Continental expressionism:

> Drawing on the visual influence of German films such as *The Cabinet of Dr Caligari* (1919) and F. W. Mumeau's symphonic *Nosferatu* (1922), Edwards created a new set of critical and aesthetic standards for theatre design. Dispensing with the fixed set, he used lighting as a character, diffusing light from side stage through gauze and working with spotlights to depict time and space as well as characterising interior consciousness. Painted backdrops, by Mac Liammóir[,] were an efficient and inexpensive way of depicting location and, like *Caligari*, the physical instability of the backdrop also suggests lack of mental and social fixity.[41]

In this way, as Christopher Fitz-Simon observes, "the theatre which they created became a part of the *avant-garde*, at a time when that term had meaning," while the newspapers, too, were virtually unanimous in declaring that Edwards and mac Liammóir certainly offered "no mere effusion of high-minded artistic intentions unbraced by technical skill": the Gate offered something truly new to the Dublin theatrical scene.[42] However, the financial losses that the Gate Theatre Studio was incurring despite this glowing reception made Edwards and mac Liammóir's next step inevitable. They needed to procure a larger playhouse of their own.

Publishing another manifesto to raise the funds that would allow them to do so, the duo decided to strike a much more patriotic note, claiming that, "during the five years previous to this year 1929, Ireland may be said to have progressed with greater rapidity than in her whole history." Naturally, Edwards and mac Liammóir suggested that the Gate had lately provided an important impetus to this cultural development, and they felt that it was not in the least due to their contribution that that "Dublin is re-establishing herself upon a much sounder basis than before, as one of the capitals of Europa—a capital which, like other capitals, should represent not only the culture and development of its country" (a declaration that, of course, was in danger of treading on the Abbey directors' toes), "but should be the point of contact between that country and other countries, the medium of international understanding." Dublin's cultural growth, then, obliged her to live up to the indisputable fact of Eurocentric modernity that, "in every great city in Europe, the theatre is of immense importance, not merely as a place of amusement, but as the living medium through which the dramatist, the actor, the producer, the designer and the musician, all of whom are representatives, consciously or unconsciously, of the life of their nation, may find expression."[43]

This final phrase provides a clear echo of Lady Gregory's 1897 Irish Literary Theatre manifesto; much like the Abbey directors-to-be sought to redress the ethnographical wrongs that British rule had wrought, the Gate should be concerned with the Free State's international standing, for "if Dublin is to live and flourish, her theatre must be taken seriously, not only in Ireland but abroad as well." In other words, Irish cultural identities were to be reconfigured in an explicitly international context. Once again, however, Edwards and mac Liammóir avoided trespassing on Abbey territory, pointing out that "Ireland indeed is already ahead of England in as much as she has," which was primarily the case because Ireland "has long had a state-subsidized national literary theatre for the production of plays by Irish authors, and this theatre has already produced a school of memorable writers and actors whose work has brought fame to them and given something of glamour to the name of this city in all parts of the world."[44] Nonetheless, there was still much work to be done.

After lulling the Abbey into the complacency of having satisfactorily uplifted Ireland's reputation, Edwards and mac Liammóir offered some indication of how the Gate should "supplement" the Abbey's endeavors, as their previous manifesto had claimed. Their international repertoire would break this stalemate, for "it is essential . . . that Dublin should see the work of other writers and other countries if only in order to further her understanding and appreciation of her own." The Gate Theatre's approach should therefore be interpreted as a mode of avant-garde nationalism: an attempt to provide an indirect catalyst to national identity formation through a form of self-reflexive "othering," juxtaposing international drama with its own native cultural products to highlight Irish unicity. Contrasts and comparisons could offer the possibility of cultural incorporation, and the Gate founders promoted this strategy by warning against further provincialism. Indeed, they considered it "unthinkable that [Dublin's] citizens should be forced to travel to Paris, or Berlin, or Petersburg or Moscow or Vienna or Buda-Pesth merely in order to see plays performed in a language they may not understand, or else remain ignorant of all drama except their own, with occasional belated variations from London and Manchester" that would only mark the neocolonial continuation of Ireland's peripheral condition. To achieve true parity and rid the Irish nation of its inferiority complex, "an international theatre should be created within her own walls to establish her claim to aesthetic equality with other nations."[45]

After claiming that "the experiment has now served its purpose of bringing home to the people of Dublin the necessity for the existence of the Dublin Gate Theatre or a like institution in the life of the city," Edwards and mac Liammóir appealed to Dubliners' purses to permanently establish a playhouse that would combat Ireland's international subsidiarity, and their request did not fall on deaf ears.[46] After a sufficient sum had been raised, the duo's friend Herbert Buckley pointed out that Rotunda Hospital concert wing was vacant, and soon afterward this large hall was refurbished by the architect Michael Scott and redecorated per mac Liammóir's instructions.[47] The new Dublin playhouse opened on February 17, 1930, with Goethe's *Faust*, featuring mac Liammóir as Mephistopheles and Edwards in the title role.[48]

Within the year, however, the Gate was facing bankruptcy. During a board meeting in December 1930, Edward Pakenham, Sixth Earl of Longford, suddenly stepped up and offered to settle the Gate's debt as well as buy all its remaining shares to ensure its survival. Both Edward and his wife Christine were theater aficionados and aspiring playwrights, and although their relationship with mac Liammóir and Edwards was (understandably) rather amicable at first, the latter duo soon grew weary of the Longfords' attempts at influencing artistic direction. Over the years, ever more quarrels arose, leading to a decisive split in 1936, which occurred while mac Liammóir and Edwards were on a tour of Egypt that had only reluctantly been sanctioned by the Longfords, who duly took charge of the remaining company to play in London. With two troupes performing simultaneously under the same name, a battle soon raged between the camps, in which the financial and logistical problems caused by mac Liammóir and Edwards's irresponsible excursion to Cairo and Alexandria were squared off against the Longfords' subversive hijacking of intellectual property and inhibitive meddling with affairs that should have been decided at the discretion of the artistic directors. Attempts by Denis Johnston and Norman Reddin to adjudicate were of little avail, and the resulting rift led to the establishment of Longford Productions and Edwards–mac Liammóir Productions respectively, both of which would perform at the Gate Theatre for six months each year.

## Historiographical Twists and Turns

For all its success at stimulating Dublin playgoers over the years, the story of Edwards and mac Liammóir's venture, like that of many independent Irish theater companies that operated during the first half of the twentieth century, remains only partially told. While there has been intermittent interest in mac Liammóir's self-fashioned biography as well as relatively sustained academic attention for Denis Johnston's provocative *The Old Lady Says "No!"* (1929), many of the Gate's accomplishments during Edwards and mac Liammóir's directorate have received relatively little scholarly consideration. Most general overviews of Irish dramatic history dedicate no more than a few pages to discussions of the Gate's establishment, and these tend to focus mostly on the duo's stylistic innovations and imported repertoire. It is also telling that the first edited volume of academic essays on the Gate was only published in 2018. In their introduction to this book, David Clare, Des Lally, and Patrick Lonergan identify various causes for this dearth, such as the dispersal of the Gate's archives, but they also address a salient interpretive issue: "The Gate has often been misunderstood."[49]

An evaluation of the Gate's early historiography underlines this observation, for many critics writing between the 1920s and the 1950s actually expressed high hopes for Edwards and mac Liammóir's iconoclastic project, including its potential to foster the careers of new Irish playwrights. Especially during the Gate's first decade, the duo's original productions were generally well received by newspaper reviewers; some of their appraisals will be featured in chapters 4, 5, and 6, which discuss various original Gate plays. However, the Gate's later reputation as a director's theater can be explained more readily by charting the development of its standing in more general reflections on the Irish stage. In gauging the changing historiographical climate in Irish theater studies in this way, it becomes clear that earlier evaluations were surprisingly comprehensive in their appreciation of Edwards and mac Liammóir's efforts to establish what can retroactively be described as an avant-garde nationalist playhouse.

Anne Irene Miller, for example, already mentioned the young duo in *The Independent Theatre in Europe*, which was published only three years after the Gate's establishment, and did not hesitate to call the Gate a "new and daring" venture that presented "unusual plays," nor even to label *The Old Lady Says "No!"* an instant classic.[50] A decade later, George Freedley and John A. Reeves published *A History of the Theatre* (1941); their section on the Gate gives equal attention to its imported and original playwrights, with special praise for Johnston and Lord Longford.[51] Contemporary anthologists likewise recognized the Gate's intrepid support of new playwrights who problematized Irish nationalism: in 1936, four original Gate plays made up half of the *Plays of Changing Ireland* compilation. Its editor, Curtis Canfield, pointed out the Abbey "directorate's reluctance to give new writers a fair hearing on the stage of the State-endowed theatre, . . . [so that] many promising dramatists have turned to the Dublin Gate Theatre," which he labeled "the strongest single influence fostering the experimental drama."[52] In addition to Denis Johnston's *The Old Lady Says "No!"* (1929), Canfield selected Mary Manning's *Youth's the Season—?* (1931), Christine Longford's *Mr. Jiggins of Jigginstown* (1933) and Edward Longford's *Yahoo* (1933) for inclusion.

No less revealingly, the drama critic (and former actor) Gabriel Fallon reserved considerable praise for the duo when he commented on "Some Aspects of Irish Theatre" in 1947. Looking back on the Gate's first two decades, Fallon claimed that their internationalist creations not only "far surpassed the [Dublin Drama] League's best effort" but evinced such stylistic sophistication that the Gate's directors might be said to have "brought vision and design to a peak never attained before in the English-speaking theatre"—a feat for which they received due praise during tours abroad.[53] Despite being an Abbey alumnus, Fallon conceded that the Gate had outstripped Ireland's national theater on all fronts: Edwards and mac Liammóir's international experience and technical proficiency had made them better suited "to further a still closer co-operation between Author, Actor and Audience" than the Abbey had ever been able to achieve, although he felt that recent Gate playwrights lacked "the startling promise of Johnston or the possibilities that fluttered around the *Juggernaut* of Sears."[54] Otherwise, Fallon's praise was unequivocal: notwithstanding the Abbey's many triumphs, the Gate was "an institution which might have far exceeded in reputation the theatre founded by Lady Gregory and W. B. Yeats."[55] With the Abbey and the Gate buildings both slated for demolition, Fallon nevertheless felt that the high hopes that Edwards and mac Liammóir had inspired would have to be abandoned altogether.

Even if some of the duo's greatest personal successes (e.g., mac Liammóir's one-man show *The Importance of Being Oscar* [1960], Edwards's tenure as head of drama at RTÉ) were yet to come, Fallon's premature verdict has, in a sense, proven right. More importantly, however, the sheer potential that he accorded to the Gate stands in stark contrast to much of its later reception. The fact that critics like Alan Cole and John Gassner came to similar verdicts in the 1940s and 1950s confirms the hypothesis that Fallon's judgment was representative of a historiographical appreciation of the Gate that only started to dwindle in the 1960s, when, partly for financial reasons, Edwards and mac Liammóir started to pursue different agendas. As a result, their theater became less visible as an institution and lost some of the attraction that Alan Cole had described in almost hyperbolic terms as "The Gate Influence on Dublin Theatre." In this 1953 contribution to the *Dublin Magazine*, Cole asserted that, even with their very first production, Edwards and mac Liammóir "were setting a new standard for the Dublin theatre, and the Dublin theatre needed it."[56] The Gate, Cole averred, swept through Irish theater with youthful audacity, offering "a reply not only to quietism and behaviourism, but also to the Nationalism, Naturalism and Representationalism that held sway," and, in doing so, "proved that there had been an audience in Dublin . . . waiting for the theatre of style, the theatre of imagination and astonishment."[57] Despite this implied contrast with the Abbey, Cole pronounced a speculative judgment on par with Fallon's conciliatory appreciation of both theaters, as the Gate was, in Cole's opinion, "the kind of theatre which Yeats had sought and, seeking by himself, had never achieved." Again, the whims of history were to blame, for "the conjectures that arise, the splendid towers, had Yeats been young in 1928, bring pointless regrets. Yeats never realized this dramatic visions [*sic*] in the Abbey; he might have done at The Gate."[58]

Written in 1953, Cole's reflection on twenty-five years of Gate productions is remarkably assertive in proclaiming the Gate—like Fallon had done before him—to have been the potential embodiment of Yeats's theatrical dreams. Over the years, such assessments of the interconnectedness of the Abbey and the Gate's artistic principles would be replaced by more polarized critical reflections on the Irish stage, yet for some time the Gate would come out on top more often than not. In *The Theatre in Our Times* (1954), for example, the American theater scholar John Gassner posited an almost binary juxtaposition of the Abbey and the Gate in favor of the latter, stating that "the stimulus provided by exhibiting continental and American drama in Dublin may usher in a new springtime for Irish dramatist, who will no longer play the role of epigones and walk the treadmill of peasant humor and nationalistic romanticism laid down by the Abbey's founders"—a characterization of Ireland's national theater that is a far cry away from Cole's depiction of Yeats as a potential Gate director.[59]

In Gassner's assessment, the Gate's domination of Irish theatrical life might still have served as an inspiration to budding Irish playwrights, its establishment having "imparted a new dispensation in the theatre arts." While "the avowed purpose of breaking down Irish insularity has understandably produced fewer discoveries of indigenous playwriting talent than revivals of European and American drama," Gassner believed (in the mid-1950s, no less) that the future of the Irish stage, which Fallon and Cole could only describe in bleak terms, held much in store, since "the playwrights sponsored by the Gate may introduce a new and healthy cosmopolitanism in native playwriting" once the initial difficulties had been surmounted.[60] Such positivism echoed Mary Manning's fiery 1935 manifesto, and Gassner reserved high praise for several plays that he considered to bear out the Gate's "valiant effort to resist the temptation to conform to professional patriotism in the new republic which is extravagantly averse to criticism of anything Irish."[61]

Although Gassner was writing from a transatlantic perspective, his acute denunciation of the stifled cultural climate in the Free State is pertinent to a reconstruction of how the critical poetics of the Gate's associates and playwrights—as explicitly addressed by Gassner—were to recede into the background over the coming decades. Edwards and mac Liammóir would still receive lavish praise for their stylistic innovations, but their support of new playwrights came to be disregarded as critics started focusing solely on the Gate's imported repertoire. In most theatrical historiographies from the 1960s onward, sober dismissals of the Gate's aspiration to produce innovative works by young Irish playwrights mark the inception of what was to become the received notion that the Gate's sole virtue lay in its introduction of foreign masterpieces and staging techniques to Irish audiences. More and more, the original productions of its early years would only be mentioned in passing, and, even as Edwards and mac Liammóir facilitated the breakthroughs of Maura Laverty and Brian Friel, many historiographers of the Irish stage defaulted to the Abbey's repertoire in chronicling Irish drama, treating debuts at the Gate as anomalies.[62]

The 1970s brought formal recognition both to the Gate as a cultural institution (in the form of a much-needed state subsidy) as well as to its founders, who were presented with honorary doctorates and made Free-men of the City of Dublin; Micheál mac Liammóir was even granted the title of Chevalier in the Légion d'honneur by the French government. Although these years were considered something of a "Gate renaissance" by David Byrne, who starred in the Gate's 1976 and 1977 productions of Desmond Forristal's *The Seventh Sin* (1976) and Peter Shaffer's *Equus* (1973), the company's seasons became ever shorter as its directors (and original lead actors) grew older.[63] Despite sundry tokens of appreciation for the Gate's achievements, most publications on Irish theater only fur-ther consolidated the Abbey's sovereignty by juxtaposing the two play-houses in by now familiar terms: Micheál Ó hAodha, for example, stated that the Abbey should be interpreted as "primarily a playwright's theatre," while the Gate had a much "greater influence on décor and production technique" than what was supposedly the resident theater of Irish dra-matists.[64] Almost a decade later, Christopher Fitz-Simon went one step further by stating that the Gate directors "did not have a particular policy towards the encouragement of Irish playwrights."[65]

The Gate's reception, then, was subject to a radical reorientation over the course of the company's existence. Whereas Edwards and mac Liam-móir's earliest critics generally conceived the Abbey and the Gate to be largely analogous institutions (and, consequently, tried to appraise their respective ventures on similar grounds), later historiographers imposed a dichotomy on the myriad complexities of mid-twentieth-century Irish theater.[66] This polarization of Dublin's leading theater companies into a rather stringent binary opposition between nationalism and interna-tionalism, and—more problematically—between real matter and mere artistry, has been detrimental to a broader understanding of the devel-opment of Irish drama. With most commentators focusing principally on Edwards and mac Liammóir's choice of foreign masterpieces or their pioneering efforts in the fields of artistic direction and staging techniques, the partners have gone down in Irish theatrical history as consummate professionals, passionate connoisseurs, and proverbial men of the stage, but not, in any meaningful way, as advocates of the exigencies of home-grown Irish drama.

Although subsequent chapters will illustrate the Gate's commitment to engaging with national identities through the production of original Irish plays, it is important, as Richard Pine has argued, to differentiate the Gate directors and associates' idiosyncrasies rather than attempt to assess their playhouse as some "monolithic structure, answering a solitary call."[67] In a 124-page book that complemented a box containing fifty slides depicting Gate productions and designs, copublished with Richard Allen Cave in 1984, Pine contrasts explicitly nationalist sentiments concerning the Gate's project with more reserved attitudes among its board members, but his main argument is that Edwards and mac Liammóir's promotion of new playwrights constituted a "policy [that] inevitably made it a national institution" worthy of the label of a "second national theatre."[68] If a plethora of practical constraints, mostly of a financial and infrastructural nature, generally left them "without the opportunity to develop a conscious policy beyond the bare foundation stones with which they began," the Gate's achievements were all the more impressive.[69] According to Pine, "the Gate fully lived up to the claims of its famous 'logo,' bursting confidently through into startlingly new territory, shocking by the very assurance with which it compelled its audiences to share its uncompromising vision."[70]

In this respect, Pine has been one of few scholars, until very recently, to make an attempt at revising conventional historiographical tropes concerning the Gate's internationalism, while also emphasizing the Gate's indebtedness to Yeats's poetics to debunk the perceived rivalry between the Abbey and the Gate as a "largely imaginary controversy."[71] Most importantly, Pine extends this assertion of continuity and similarity to the Gate's playwrights, stating that "the 'new' dramatists in the early years of the Gate fall into no distinct category" from their Abbey colleagues.[72] By squarely placing Gate playwrights in what is conventionally considered to be the Abbey's court, Pine contends that questions of Irishness were addressed at the Gate as well, with Edwards and mac Liammóir's playwrights no less "trying to find a personal way of expressing Irish ambitions, expectations and frustrations." Even if their methods in doing so might have seemed unorthodox to Dublin audiences of the 1930s, Pine still asserts that, "rather than a refuge for 'Abbey rejects,' the Gate should be regarded as an over-flow or a safety valve, with a distinct relationship to the Abbey, producing, as Hilton Edwards said, work 'outside the scope of their policy.'"[73]

While the 1990s saw the publication of two major biographies of the Gate's founders by Micheál Ó hAodha and Christopher Fitz-Simon, Pine's efforts to rectify the Gate's one-dimensional reception initially went largely unnoticed by scholars of the Irish stage.[74] Most historiographers have persisted in commenting on how the Gate imported overseas plays and staging techniques, or discussing individual pieces that premiered there, rather than considering the ways in which Edwards and mac Liammóir's productions contributed to a performative renegotiation of Irish identities or how their onstage and offstage engagement with such issues can be related more generally to Ireland's postcolonial modernity. In *The Literature of Ireland: Culture and Criticism* (2010), for example, Terence Brown even claims that the Gate faced "constant disapproval" and that their eclecticism embodied a "style for style's sake" attitude that was indicative of a "lack of a ruling engagement with ideas."[75] This leads Brown to dismiss the Gate as a cultural institution: "For all its brilliance, its bravura cosmopolitanism, one detects in the Gate Theatre of the 1930s the subversive energies of both the Decadence and the modern becoming somewhat unthreatening in the provincial Irish air."[76]

During the past decade, however, various scholars have begun to offer correctives to such views.[77] In *Mapping Irish Theatre: Theories of Space and Place* (2013), Chris Morash and Shaun Richards accord the Gate the status of "a parallel modernist theatre of space" that has only been partially acknowledged in conventional historiographies of the Irish stage.[78] Their innovative theoretical reflections on the spatiality of Irish theater have offered new insights in how the Gate experimented with various staging techniques to create "a condensational space that made manifest the latent critique of realism in the Abbey's cottage kitchens, which in turn had become metonymic of an equally constrained society."[79] Morash and Richards claim that, consequently, the Gate "was producing a conceptual space that refused to be constrained by geography or politics" during the contentious Free State years.[80]

Nevertheless, these are belated reassessments that are preceded by many decades of historiographical neglect. In light of the process that has been charted above, this earlier perception of the Gate's noncommittal attitude is not indicative of its founders' half-hearted intentions but of their limited visibility as a cultural front. While Yeats, Lady Gregory, Lennox Robinson, and the rest of the Abbey directorate did not always see eye to eye, they were nevertheless considered to be united in their purpose and could be targeted as such. The Gate's eclecticism, however, was not only reflected by its seemingly random repertoire but also by the jocular anarchy of its upper echelons. As chapters 2 and 3 will outline, Micheál mac Liammóir, Hilton Edwards, Lord and Lady Longford, Norman Reddin, Denis Johnston, and Mary Manning all espoused different opinions concerning the Gate's dedication to advancing Ireland's cause— whatever each of them might have considered that to be. This makes it difficult to judge whether scholars and historiographers are wholly responsible for what are, on the whole, rather dismissive sentiments as regards the Gate's relevance to Irish identity formation in a period when, as Lauren Arrington has observed, "the question of what Ireland was, and who the Irish were, was as politically charged as ever."[81]

No less important in this respect, Arrington also points out that, during the 1920s and 1930s, "the Dublin Drama League, the Peacock Theatre, and the Gate Theatre offer counter-histories to a narrative of Irish drama that focuses on the Abbey, and taken together they provide a dynamic picture of Irish Modernist theater that is in dialogue with the Continental avant-garde and the experimental theaters of the United States."[82] Nevertheless, few scholars have looked beyond the usual suspects of Johnston, mac Liammóir, and Manning in addressing this issue, and such a counter-narrative remains to be told. This study, then, will seek to reestablish the Gate Theatre's credentials as a national institution. Since the underlying reasons for this distortion (and consequent neglect) have been shown to be explainable, a reassessment of the Gate's engagement with Irish identities does not so much entail a volte-face as a broadening of perspective. In bringing the Gate Theatre's playwrights back into the picture and highlighting the conflicting poetics of the institution that sought to offer them a platform, it is futile to simply invert the conventional reception of what is actually a strongly heterogeneous cultural project. To the extent that the Gate's historiography has reflected its object's multiplicity, its contradictions, or even its constituent disarray, such acknowledgments have generally been partial and uneasy—yet these characteristics are interpreted more fruitfully as the hallmarks of native modernity.

# 2

## Mac Liammóir's Exorcism

### *Memory, Modernity, Identity*

In *All for Hecuba* (1946), Micheál mac Liammóir sketches his itinerant life wandering from London to Monaco and from the small Irish villages that he visited while playing with Anew McMaster's company in 1927 to Egypt and the Balkans on his tours with the Gate Theatre during the late 1930s. In doing so, mac Liammóir not only presents a multifaceted history of the playhouse that he founded, but also reflects extensively on his own (invented) roots, which he entwines with Ireland's traumatic past and its uncertain postcolonial future. For modern readers, who are aware of mac Liammóir's English ancestry, this makes *All for Hecuba* a strongly emblematic autobiography, as the *personal* identity that mac Liammóir secretly crafts and adopts becomes inextricable from the contested constructions of *national* identities that he overtly discusses—especially in relation to Ireland's tumultuous history.

Even so, mac Liammóir's construction of his own identity presents some interpretative quandaries, since the young artist and actor's transformation from Alfred to Micheál has been attributed to different causes, and the evaluations of this development vary accordingly. In *The Boys* (1994), for example, Christopher Fitz-Simon asserts that "the almost besotted way in which [mac Liammóir] embraced the literature and visual art of the Celtic Revival was the admiration of the discoverer from another bourne."[1] He goes on to describe mac Liammóir as having been changed utterly by his passion for Irish culture, so that, after his death, he "was laid to rest . . . not upon a foreign shore, for he had become part of the land which he had seen in a vision."[2] Éibhear Walshe, on the other hand, delves deeper into mac Liammóir's reasons for adopting a "neo-Celtic thespian" persona and argues that, from a queer perspective, "the Yeatsian mask would enable Willmore to dissent and separate from British masculinist heterosexuality," just as mac Liammóir would appropriate Oscar Wilde's more explicit homosexuality later in life.[3]

In their respective biographies of mac Liammóir, Micheál Ó hAodha and Tom Madden focus more closely on the artistic genesis of this adoptive patriotism. Ó hAodha explains the Gate founder's passion for Irish culture as a creative outlet: his friendship with the Irish actor and director Anew McMaster and his half-Irish companion Máire O'Keefe led him "to identify Ireland and Irishness with all the positive elements of imagination and creativity which he yearned to explore."[4] As a result, Ó hAodha argues, "Ireland and an Irish identity had become his obsession, an obsession which conflicted with the reality of his evidently English background" that necessitated a complete "re-creation" of himself.[5] In a similar vein, Tom Madden describes mac Liammóir's transformation as "a deliberately creative process, which of necessity involved not just casting off his real name, Alfred Willmore, but also the exorcism physically, mentally and emotionally of all traces of his geographical and cultural origins."[6] Like Ó hAodha, Madden directly relates the origins of mac Liammóir's fascination with Irish culture to Máire O'Keefe. In becoming part of her family, he embraced "the promise of a new identity of his own making" in a cultural context that provided a markedly different opportunity of self-fashioning: "The otherness of Celtic mythology . . . and its capacity for shape-changing and, ultimately, for rebirth, was both provocative and seductive to Willmore."[7] Richard Pine also relates mac Liammóir's new identity to artistic inspiration, but attributes this to a different source: he contends that it was seeing the famous Ballets Russes dancer Vaclav Nijinksi perform that led him "towards the catalysis of the indefinite, amorphous, multi-character chameleon . . . who continually reshapes and re-presents himself so as never to be identified, defined, pinned down."[8]

As all three commentators observe, mac Liammóir's adolescent transformation did not yield an unequivocal persona, for, in Ó hAodha's words, "MacLiammóir's double nature bridged both categories"—that of the stateless universal artist and that of the all-too-convincing chameleon—so that "his claim to have given 'All for Hecuba' was not braggadacio [*sic*] but the motto of a man who with the zeal of the convert showed Ireland what a living theatre could be."[9] Accordingly, Hilton Edwards once described his partner as a *seanchaí*, a traditional Celtic bard who is a "spellbinder with words," and, as the actor Simon Callow recounts, mac Liammóir was keen to claim this honorific title.[10] Nevertheless, Ó hAodha is adamant that mac Liammóir could boast "a performance of . . . originality" that "transcends the story the *seanchaí* told," and, in discussing mac Liammóir's engagement with Ireland's history and his attempts to envisage its future, this constructed identity will indeed prove essential to the memory strategies that mac Liammóir employs in *All for Hecuba* to first summon and then dispel the ghosts of the past.[11]

In analyzing the tensions between the interlocking forces of Ireland's violent experience of colonialism and the uncertain place of the Free State in a world that was going to war, the persona that mac Liammóir presents in his autobiography serves to reflect precisely such a confluence of the local and global. On the one hand, mac Liammóir goes to great lengths to romanticize the Irish countryside and the Irish language, while, on the other, he declaims his passion for the cosmopolitanism of avant-garde theater, cubist painting, and the Ballets Russes. This amalgamation can likewise be illustrated by mac Liammóir's reluctant admission that the Celtic Twilight was bound to stagnate, as evinced by his retrospective assessment of *Diarmuid agus Gráinne* (1928). Indeed, mac Liammóir would come to call his first play "this monotonous and dopey elaboration of an old tragic tale, this tasteful compromise between Maeterlinck and the Love Songs of Connacht"—a qualification that serves equally well as a label for the idiosyncratic union of European avant-garde stylistics and Revivalist idealism that he himself embodied.[12] Mac Liammóir formulated this despondent assessment during a later London revival in which he played no part; it was only then that he realized that "my Celtic twilight had died where it had been born, in a reactionary exile among the buses and clattering paving-stones between Soho and the Marble Arch, a worn-out battered garment from the last generation but one."[13] In what was both the capital of

Ireland's colonial oppressor and (secretly) his city of birth, mac Liammóir described himself as being caught between cultures, if not stretched thin in his attempt to keep a grip on the tradition that he had tried to revive even as he sought to jolt his adoptive nation into postcolonial autonomy.

## Tradition and Modernity

The tensions and paradoxes that mac Liammóir describes in revisiting his debut as a playwright are symptomatic of much larger concerns relating to the construction and experience of modernity, which is particularly problematic in an Irish context. Oscar Wilde, mac Liammóir's lifelong idol, had already paved the way for such insights in "The Critic as Artist" (1890), stressing the importance of "[realizing] not merely our own lives, but the collective life of the race, and so to make ourselves absolutely modern, in the true meaning of the word modernity." Wilde specified the cumulative historicism that underlies this conceptualization of modernity by stating that "he to whom the present is the only thing that is present, knows nothing of the age in which he lives. To realise the nineteenth century, one must realise every century that has preceded it and that has contributed to its making. To know anything about oneself one must know all about others."[14] This assertion by the disparaged Irish playwright—for whose literary rehabilitation the Gate Theatre's daring production in the Atlantic Isles of his banned *Salomé* (1891) in 1928 is partly to thank—captures not only the necessity of reliving the nation's past in the present, but also the explicitly communal character of that experience.

As such, Wilde's statement underlines the notion that collective engagements with a nation's history are integral to understanding its processes of identity formation. As later chapters will show, various original Gate playwrights tried to offer productive interventions in these processes, exemplifying that "to reinvent the past as a living transmission of meaning rather than revere it as a deposit of unchangeable truth" is a key element of the "transitional crisis" of Irish modernity, as Richard Kearney has claimed.[15] Both with respect to mac Liammóir's autobiographical reflections and in the larger context of Irish theater during the tumultuous Free State years, the imbrication of past and present serves to frame the audiences that attended performances of Ireland's mythology, history, and contemporaneity as being shaped by their participation in the nation's struggle with the much-maligned concept of modernity.

Of course, the perceived tensions between modernity and tradition—a no less elusive yet discursively potent a posteriori conceptualization—are rooted in the nation's history. Yet to describe Ireland's annals and, with that, the reservoir from which expressions of Irish cultural memories could draw, simply as conflicted would be an understatement: as Joep Leerssen has stated in his study of Irish national identity formation in the nineteenth century, "Irish history seemed to be all incident and no permanence." In this way, Leerssen acknowledges the uniqueness of Ireland, observing that "many European nationalities in the wake of Romanticism are preoccupied with identity construction; in the case of Ireland, that project is grafted onto a long-standing confrontation with the neighbouring isle, takes place in a climate of barely contained hostile divisions, carries a burdensome political heritage and is invested with great, contentious political urgency."[16] In a broader sociological perspective, similarly fraught developments can be charted, leading Joe Cleary to state that, in an Irish context, "modernity meant dispossession, subordination and the loss of sovereignty, the collapse of its indigenous social order, the gradual disintegration of its Gaelic cultural system, and successive waves of politically or economically enforced emigration."[17] With the partition of Ireland and its relationship to the United Kingdom remaining hotly contested topics in the Free State years, which were also marked by massive sociocultural inequities between urban and rural communities, it is clear that, as Terry Eagleton has succinctly phrased it, "the country as a whole [has] not leapt at a bound from tradition to modernity."[18]

However, this prominent dichotomy has been labeled as "crude" and even "sclerotic" by Cleary in his discussion of Ireland's contested status as a postcolonial nation, since, as an empty container that divorces cultural manifestations from larger geopolitical contexts, it is readily adaptable to a wide range of political stances that are mutually exclusive.[19] Rather, Cleary posits his acknowledgment of Irish's postcolonial status on its imbrication in international economic systems, arguing that "Irish nationalism can only be understood contextually, as the complex outcome of local interactions with an aggressively expanding imperialist world economy."[20] Nevertheless, the tradition/modernity dichotomy was discursively prevalent in the Free State years, as Chris Morash and Shaun Richards show in their discussion of John Dowling's attacks on surrealism; they also relate this opposition productively to the globalizing economic forces stressed by Cleary when they argue that the development of mass media infrastructures shows how, "as the culture of the new state became more permeable, with radio, cinema and cheap newspapers, there was a heightened awareness of what was seen as a corrosive materialism of a modernity against which there seemed to be no bulwark."[21]

Cleary's analysis goes a long way toward refuting the arguments that have been levied against identifying Ireland as a (post)colonial nation, such as its proximity to—and later incorporation in—the United Kingdom or Irish complicity with imperialism in other parts of the world, even if this focus on economics is, by his own admission, somewhat alien to what is generally construed as a sociological or cultural debate.[22] One explicit confluence of economics and the discourse of modernity is found, however, in reflections on the nineteenth-century Famine, which serves as the crucial event that irrevocably shaped later reflections on Ireland's contentious modernity and also features in mac Liammóir's autobiography. Even so, this significance has only been properly acknowledged since the government-supported sesquicentennial Famine commemorations of the mid-1990s, which helped break revisionist taboos on the matter.[23]

This development has served to expose the paradoxical role that the Famine has played in Irish history, for, while its devastation led to the swift decline of many Gaeltacht communities, its implications for the advent of Irish modernity have been ambiguous.[24] While the Famine signaled the end of preindustrial rural life and ushered in an era of political self-awareness in a globalizing world, the event itself has also been understood as a monstrous, retrograde failure of modernity.[25] Succumbing to widespread illness and starvation, almost a million people perished in primitive scenes of horror, leading David Lloyd to claim that this dehumanization was indicative of a regressive calamity in an age of progress.[26] Even on the threshold of modernity, Ireland "remains haunted by other possibilities of being-in-the-world," according to Stuart McLean, while Terry

Eagleton describes these prospects as being manifestly "pre-modern."[27] In aesthetic terms, however, scholars such as Luke Gibbons have argued that these spectacles of starvation paradoxically induced a "'proto-modernist' outlook" that made Irish literature prematurely sensitive to existential turmoil and the sheer inadequacy of mimetic and historical self-assertion, raising the question whether Ireland truly "need[ed] to await the importation of modernism to blast open the continuum of history."[28]

When innovative aesthetic techniques (rather than the modernist mindset that had been established avant la lettre) did arrive in Ireland over half a century later, they had to be cultivated in a nation that had seen the violence of the late nineteenth-century Land War as well as the more recent Easter Rising, the War of Independence, and the Civil War. The outcome of these latter conflicts was not simply freedom from direct British rule, but also the tenuous establishment of two separate Irelands that were no less fragmented internally. Although the conflicts themselves had nominally ended, the War of Independence and the Civil War had only partially resolved—if not further exacerbated—the tensions resulting from pervasive divisions between various social, political, religious, and geographical denominations that overlapped in ways that further problematized their often mutually exclusive notions of Irishness.[29]

More specifically, the successive Free State governments struggled to replace the binary politics of insurrection against a common enemy with attempts at integrating disparate sociocultural strata into a monolithic concept of Irish nationhood: as Morash and Richards state, "limitation was adopted as a defining characteristic of national identity."[30] No less importantly, the lingering animosity over the issues that had led to the Civil War proved hard to assuage: during the transfer of power after the 1932 elections that saw Fianna Fáil defeating Cumann na nGaedheal, W. T. Cosgrave, the incumbent president of the Executive Council of the Irish Free State, had to alleviate the danger of revolt among senior government and military officials—such as General O'Duffy, who would go on to lead the fascist Army Comrades Association (ACA), also known as the "Blueshirts," in opposition to the Irish Republican Army (IRA)—as former Sinn Féin leader Éamon de Valera took office.[31]

At the same time, what was left of the Anglo-Irish Ascendancy went into decline without further bloodshed, making it clear, as Luke Gibbons has observed, that "the 'old' order was already shattered, and convulsed by social upheavals to the point of being in a state of anarchy."[32] It is understandable, then, that many attempts at consolidating an overarching Irish cultural identity both before and after the watershed of the Easter Rising were fostered by Anglo-Irish writers who, in Gregory Castle's words, sought to "[monopolize] modernism by translating political dispossession into cultural production."[33] Castle argues that the Celtic Revival, with its programmatic celebration of Celtic mythology and Irish traditions, was the prime manifestation of the fact that "Irish modernism emerged in the estranging contact of modernity with a tradition or archaic culture."[34] Wielding "discursive power over the Catholic-Irish whose lives and folkways are the subject of a redemptive anthropological discourse over which they have little or no control," Ascendancy writers attempted to redress the deterioration of their class supremacy by artificially providing Ireland with a "modernist aesthetic of cultural redemption," a return to the historical womb that repudiated the advent of modernity by asserting a timeless natural harmony.[35] Such deliverance by artistic grace was, of course, highly amenable to a government tasked with fomenting a sense of national unity in the face of the societal fragmentation that characterized the post–Civil War aftermath, and this explains the widespread adoption of unobjectionable Celtic Twilight imagery as a deliberate application of restorative politics through art.

However, if the surreptitiously conservative agenda of Irish modernism necessarily precluded the existence of a truly revolutionary avant-garde movement and the implementation of more subversive poetics, as Castle claims, a spectrum of reactionary collusion also imposes itself in discussing the poetics of the Gate Theatre as a modernist and/or avant-garde theater, especially in light of the concomitant terminological confusion. Although such definitional conflicts are intrinsic not only to both terms but also to the various contrasts between them, Andreas Huyssen offers a valuable means of differentiation in positing that modernism, for all its stylistic innovation, tends to be complicit with some strain of conservativism, while avant-garde movements such as Dada and surrealism rather thrive on all-out destabilization of fixed identities and on the revolutionary potential of societal upheaval.[36]

Of course, various incongruities that prevent a clear differentiation between both concepts do remain, but these actually illustrate the underlying quandary. W. B. Yeats's literary career, for example, veers across both axes, for his early work exhibits the neoconservative idealization of the Gaeltacht even as it recasts Celtic mythology into a new poetical mold. By contrast, his later disenchantment with the Abbey Theatre's ossified poetics led him to establish the Dublin Drama League (as discussed above), which drew on a thoroughly international rather than Irish repertoire, and Yeats's dark and melancholy late plays can hardly be called exultations of Irish life and culture. Despite this ostensible volte-face in promoting the national cause through literature, Yeats remained a lifelong director of the Abbey Theatre, which only further illustrates the difficulty of sketching the conflicted literary articulation of Irish modernity and (inter)nationality. Indeed, Richard Kearney concludes his discussion of Yeats's poetics by observing that he "came to realize that the myths of the Irish Literary Revival which promised to reconcile the rival impulses of vision and desire—and by implication the opposing claims of tradition and modernity—were themselves imaginary constructs."[37]

In light of the problematic nature of Irish modernity, any attempt at conclusively outlining the Gate Theatre's cultural parameters or pigeonholing its poetics is bound to fail. While the Gate's directors certainly strove to end Ireland's self-imposed insularity and introduce revolutionary forms of stage production to a country stifled by conservative realism, Edwards and mac Liammóir absorbed as well as stimulated the Irish dramatic tradition, producing many plays that deal directly with Ireland's history and engage in collective identity formation. While Kearney has introduced several terms to navigate the literary manifestations of the tradition/modernity spectrum, including "revivalist modernism," the Gate's poetics can more effectively be labeled a mode of *avant-garde nationalism*.[38] This term acknowledges and incorporates Andreas Huyssen's key distinctions, as well as Richard Murphy's reflections on how "modernism and the avant-garde often seem to be locked in a dialectical relationship in

which the avant-garde questions the blind spots and unreflected presup-
positions of modernism, while modernism itself reacts to this critique, at
least in later stages, by taking into account its own poetics [and] some of
the spectacular failures and successes of the historical avant-garde."[39] If the
Celtic Twilight and the Abbey Theatre are, for all their internal contradictions, subsumed under the mainstream of Irish modernism, and the Gate
Theatre is considered to be a partially subversive expression of avant-gard-
ism, the term is apt enough, especially since the Gate's manifestos express
a commitment to fostering Ireland's cultural development.[40] In that case,
one important "blind spot" that the Gate revealed—and mac Liammóir
articulated—is that of contested yet constitutive memories, illustrating
Nicholas Andrew Miller's claim that "Ireland's struggle to become modern expresses what is, at its root, a crisis of historical imagination."[41]

## Memory and Teleology

The contested collective memories that inflect Ireland's modernity serve
to further illustrate the conflicts inherent to the nation's fraught engagement with traditional cultural structures, of which the Revivalist attempt
to (re)create a politically salient simulacrum of Ireland's imagined past
is a prime example. In *All for Hecuba*, mac Liammóir demonstrates that
such collective memories function in manifestly personal contexts as well,
likewise confirming Miller's observation that the "continuous renegotiation of selfhood in relation to [the] past" is essential to the functioning
of memory.[42] Reflecting on his desire to contribute to the cause of Irish
independence, mac Liammóir represents the 1916 Easter Rising not only
as a pivotal moment in the nation's history, but also as a key episode in his
adoption of an Irish identity during his London childhood—even though
he, of course, describes the impact of the Rising as a confirmation rather
than an assumption of his nationality. Waxing lyrical, mac Liammóir
recounts that, whenever he felt

> driven insane by some atavistic fever in the blood, tortured by the events
> of Easter 1916, one stole away from the Slade School and ransacked the
> shops for second-hand editions of Douglas Hyde and Pádraic Pearse,
> fumbling one's way in a dream from life-class to Gaelic League, from

theatre to Sinn Féin rooms, searching for memories of old ballads and songs from morning till night, hating the houses, hating the people, ferocious and solitary and impotent, mouthing Ireland's name to oneself in the war-darkened streets.[43]

The ferocity of mac Liammóir's emotions regarding the Rising are manifestations of what Alison Landsberg has termed *prosthetic memories,* which are "neither purely individual nor entirely collective but emerge at the interface of individual and collective experience." Holding this ambiguous middle ground, prosthetic memories, too, are strongly empathic, being "privately felt public memories that develop after an encounter with a mass cultural representation of the past."[44] Landsberg's claim that "prosthetic memory opens the door for a new relation to the past, a strategic form of remembering that has ramifications for the politics of the present" holds true in this case, since the history that mac Liammóir assimilated was a simulacrum of a supposedly lost yet retrievable sense of Irishness rather than a plausibly coherent account of a specific historical event.[45] Therefore, it was the combination of his passion for the Celtic Revival and his indignation at the violent repression of the Easter Rising that transformed the English adolescent Alfred Willmore into the Irishman Micheál mac Liammóir. At the same time, this new identity was mostly based on his personal integration of newspaper accounts about the Rising and Revivalist publications on Irish folklore that he read in London.

In mac Liammóir's assessment, however, the relationship between the retrospection of the Celtic Revival and the prospection of the European avant-garde is not described as a straightforward progression from tradition to modernity. Looking back on the early years of the Gate, for example, mac Liammóir declares that "never had a period sense been more conscious, and never, since the 'nineties, had a decade been more marked than in those frontier days of 1929 and 1930" with its "whole-hearted gay and desperate" air.[46] Contrary to Anthony Giddens's seminal generalization that "the modes of life brought into being by modernity have swept us away from *all* traditional types of social order, in quite unprecedented fashion," mac Liammóir states that "an exaggerated sense of the past was the hall-mark of modernity in the later 'twenties."[47]

Even so, that historical obsession was about to dwindle, for "on the threshold of this more discreet decade with its tired tranquil dawn and the mad melodrama of its nightfall, the immediate past found itself in the position of becoming suddenly outmoded." The Celtic Revival had gone into decline, and, with some self-deprecation, mac Liammóir observed that

> very bitter to their most ardent exponents must have been that slow light dawning in the eye of these more poised and mellow 'thirties that, like a group of newly arrived elder sisters, saw with amusement the emphatic sprawling, the abandoned over-statement, the patchy, excitable make-up of the débutante whose day was done, and decided that on the whole she had been a bizarre little creature, brittle, undisciplined, yes, and rather quaint.[48]

However, since mac Liammóir's understanding of the role that the Gate Theatre was to play in the development of Irish culture had always been more complicit with Twilight idealism than that of his fellow directors, the Gate, too, could be counted among the dallying debutantes that he depicts. Although its innovations in stage design, acting techniques, and dramatic repertoire differed from those that Yeats, Robinson, and Lady Gregory were employing at the Abbey, the Gate also underwent a process of maturation as its directors began to reflect more critically on the eclecticism of its experiments in such publications as *Motley* and the 1934 *Dublin Gate Theatre* book edited by Bulmer Hobson (which will be discussed in the next chapter).

Despite his rejection of Ireland's "exaggerated sense of the past," mac Liammóir's subsequent assessment of the nation's prospects offers an attempt at exorcising Ireland's historical traumas and constructing a viable future. In light of his own prosthetic identity, which facilitated the assimilation of strongly divergent cultural poetics, it is revealing that mac Liammóir recognized that the overpowering intensity of his convert's zeal to improve his adopted nation's standing might prove self-defeating. In fact, this was his greatest "fear for the rebirth of Ireland: that having at last blown back life into the gentle dying woman we loved, we may be confronted one day with the spectacle of a Frankenstein."[49] On the brink of World War II, mac Liammóir articulated such reservations about the feasibility of nationalist ideals in even stronger terms. Roaming around Howth Head in the autumn of 1938, mac Liammóir tried to envisage Ireland's future, wondering, "Would we be hurled into the maelstrom? Or would we find ourselves in Ireland still, smug and virginal on our raft at the world's edge, securely girt by our lashing waves and incidentally the battleships of our old enemies?," thereby prefiguring the blinkered insularity of the Emergency that would be proclaimed by Taoiseach Éamon de Valera in 1939.[50]

Yet mac Liammóir understood that this impending seclusion from world affairs might also offer opportunities for fruitful introspection into the heart of the nation, which sought to achieve redemption from the postcolonial neurosis that Luke Gibbons considers fundamental to Ireland's national identity. Indeed, Gibbons argues that it is not only Ireland's proximity to Britain or the absence of racial disparities that distinctively inflect its postcolonial status: rather, the absolute pervasion of Irish society and culture by alien influences after centuries of imperialist domination ensures that Ireland must forego any clearly demarcated "historical closure." Because this sociocultural hybridization is irreversible and has been completely internalized as such, it is, ironically, "precisely the *absence* of a sense of an ending which has characterized the national narratives of Irish history."[51] As Declan Kiberd also observes, "It was less easy to decolonize the mind than the territory," and this teleological impasse also features in mac Liammóir's musings: he initially believed that World War II might foster meditations that would come as "an apronful of dreams, an armful of intransigent writers, and one single undefeated purpose vague and grandiose as the air we breathed from our birth, a purpose grown stubborn with time and meaningless as a word mouthed over and over by a child; to be rid of the conqueror."[52]

Of course, the hollow repetition of this performance of rebellion against a long-gone oppressor was no longer intrinsically meaningful, which underlines how memory formations are warped by colonial deprivation. Indeed, in a postcolonial context, the need to relate to the accumulated experience of oppression is all the more apparent. In order to re-create a collective historical orientation after imperialist structures of meaning have collapsed, a postcolonial mode of memory must be invoked, since, as Barbara A. Misztal has argued, "collective memory not only reflects the past but also shapes present reality by providing people with understandings and symbolic frameworks that enable them to make sense of the world" that has been shattered by colonial oppression, famine, diaspora, and civil war.[53] Postcolonial memory, therefore, "is essential for self-representation and for readdressing the impact of imperialism" upon Irish national identities, especially in the light of Oona Frawley's contention that sovereign states develop different memory cultures than colonized nations, so that "in a space like Ireland that was deprived of nationhood for many years, memory must be a different phenomenon."[54] This long-suffered absence of a viable national identity can still undermine reconstructive attempts even after independence has been won, so that while "postcolonial memory tends to be indirect, delayed or secondary—that is, received from a previous generation, with the colonial time/space not necessarily personally experienced except in the major fallout effects of decolonization," it is still a vital element in fashioning a newly autonomous nation.[55]

The memory structures that James V. Wertsch describes as "mnemonic templates"—of rebellion against the oppressor, in mac Liammóir's case—can thus endure beyond their initial relevance, but his reflections simultaneously demonstrate that they can be reconfigured to allow for new, hybrid developments.[56] Indeed, mac Liammóir acknowledged that "the conqueror had stayed too long, he had given almost as much as he had plundered, and those who were least to be reconciled had his blood in their veins." This is an especially salient observation, considering mac Liammóir's true roots, indicating that, in postrevolutionary Ireland, the nation's past could no longer serve as the repository for the reenactment of historical rebellions, even if conservative politicians tried to hold on to that spirit of artificial unison. The heroes of the past had simply lost their relevance: "Emmett [sic] and Tone and Pearse passed lowly in the gloom. They were dead; their blood had flowed to make more monstrous yet that monstrous chain of passion linking the two traditions in the embrace of death."[57]

In this sense, mac Liammóir employed what Marianne Hirsch describes as *postmemory*, a term that she has coined to underline the importance of

the temporal gaps between the social groups which lived through the
original traumatic events and the next generations that must mediate
their predecessors' experiences to indirectly relive (and thereby revitalize)
them. This temporal discrepancy necessitates the performance of memory
as a conscious activity rather than the passive experience of something that
has been involuntarily embedded in an individual or group, since, due to
this gap, memory is "not actually mediated by recall but by imaginative
investment, projection, and creation."[58] This awareness of the construct-
edness of memory, coupled with the need to re-create the original emotional impact as a confirmation thereof, brands postmemory as an attempt
at repairing the "intergenerational memorial fabric that has been severed
by catastrophe" by bridging the chasm emotionally.[59] As later chapters
will show, the stage, with its dependence on the empathic and emotive
power of drama, offers a highly suitable platform for postmnemonic performance, allowing audiences to relive traumas and strengthen their transgenerational ties to their ancestors, illustrating Nicholas Grene's argument
that "a large part of the anxious obsession with self-representation in the
Irish dramatic tradition originates with the colonial and postcolonial condition of the country."[60]

Mac Liammóir, too, acknowledged a hybrid complicity with foreign memory structures, which might enable the creation of a future that
would not try to cling to the untenable notion of authenticity that Anglo-
Irish patriots like Tone and Emmet had already problematized.[61] As war
and isolation loomed, this ambiguous insularity was quickly becoming
reality, and so, mac Liammóir observed, "Ireland, her dim and endless
enchantments withdrawing far into the recesses of her earth like the
Tuatha Dé Danann of ancient times, had shrunk distressingly as far as
we were concerned, and become, as George Moore so continually discovered, no broader than a pig's back." In the following passage, mac
Liammóir scrutinizes the remains of this sociocultural recession, as he
identifies and addresses some of the most problematic postmemories that
he had been bequeathed by personifying Ireland in markedly unsettling
terms as a revolting Sean-Bhean Bhocht: "There were moments of despair
when one could see nothing of her but poverty and ignorance and cant,
the famished mouth and stubbly chin, the mackintosh limp with rain,

the greasy comb and broken rosary among the litter in the pocket, the blue eye sodden with drink, dribbling with laughter."[62] In this way, mac Liammóir dispelled this ghostly presence of the past, rendered most distressingly in the form of the Famine, by what Hirsch describes as the postmnemonic strategy of "striv[ing] to *reactivate* and *reembody* more distant social/national and archival/cultural memorial structures by reinvesting them with resonant individual and familial forms of mediation and aesthetic expression."[63] Mac Liammóir thus gave shape to Ireland's historical demons, endowing them with retrospective life so that he could confront and ultimately dismiss them, but first he elaborated on his purpose in summoning these specters in the first place, arguing that "if Ireland had buried her enchantments we must dig for them. There was gold hidden in heart of her mountains. . . . Some day when war came to Europe and we were shut in alone with ourselves, confronted by the penury and the magnificence of our souls, we might discover it all."[64]

The death of Yeats, in January 1939, allowed mac Liammóir to set the scene for this exorcism: considering his idol's death to mark the end of an era, he sought to imagine a different future for the nation by waking up Ireland as she was "turning restlessly from side to side in her long dream-haunted sleep."[65] In this sense, mac Liammóir's subsequent satire of Ireland, personified as a decrepit Cathleen ni Houlihan, constitutes a postmnemonic invocation of the ghosts of Irish history:

> Now look here, my dear, what is the matter with you? Haven't you washed or what is it? Your hair's all over the place, you talk of nothing but trivialities, you slouch about half-dressed. . . . Oh, I know you've had a bad time, but good God, that's all over years ago. Can't you forget it? Can't you stop wearing that old grey shawl? Can't you stop crying? Can't you stop telling nasty stories about your children? Can't you have your teeth seen to?[66]

While mac Liammóir's invective is humorous, this rejection of Ireland's morbid introspection underscores the need to resolve rather than obsess over historical traumas, and thus offers a potent illustration of Nicholas Andrew Miller's claim that "in acts of memory, forgetting must be acknowledged as an instrumental aspect of remembering rather than its

opposite" even if mac Liammóir was clearly aware that this mere statement will not provide immediate closure.[67] As Emilie Pine has argued,
however, historical resolution lies in the performative repetition of memory, and so this initial attempt provides a strategy that might be adopted
and reiterated—for, however repulsive Ireland's postcolonial condition
may seem, mac Liammóir states that "one is still in love, still hopelessly
at her mercy."[68]

While mac Liammóir, by his own admission, then, considered Yeats
to be "the seer, the visionary, the father of a whole nation's reawakening"
and always felt drawn to the receding Celtic Twilight, "which in those
days of self-conscious virility and neurasthenic fact-facing was at its low-
est ebb," he also tried to facilitate Ireland's international advancement by
engaging with the question of Ireland's traumatic history.[69] In doing so,
he recalibrated the common postcolonial misalignment of past and future,
deciding in favor of the latter:

> We Irish are accused eternally of brooding over the images of the past,
> but in reality it is by the future, more it may be than other people in the
> world, that we are driven. . . . We have created a past for ourselves that
> we may the more clearly see the future of our hearts' desire, and in the
> continual striving and sacrifice offered up for that future lies perhaps the
> only Irish virtue.[70]

Mac Liammóir thus carefully avoided the mistake of simply invert-
ing Ireland's supposedly pathological obsession with its history by instead
reinterpreting the nation's past as a deliberate construct that might be confronted directly and reinfused, through repetition, with a new teleological
function. This acknowledgement of the malleable nature of Irish history,
which is empowered by mac Liammóir's transnational construction of a
patriotic persona that adopts a wide range of perspectives, facilitates a much
more fruitful interplay of the past and the future in the present. More generally, such inventive historicism will also be shown to be integral to the
Gate's contribution to cultural identity formation on the Irish stage.

# 3

# Playing Their Part for Ireland
*Avant-Garde Patriotism and (Inter)nationalist Poetics*

If mac Liammóir's attempt to dispel the ghosts of Irish history in *All for Hecuba* seems almost comically idiosyncratic, this is mainly because he explicitly foregrounded his strategy by personifying transgenerational traumas. In recent years, however, Irish theater scholars have begun to emphasize some of the more implicit parallels between dramaturgy and exorcism as well. In referring to the designated space for the performance of traumatic memories and conflicted identities of Irish modernity, Emilie Pine, for example, claims that twentieth-century Irish drama was enacted on what she, borrowing Marvin Carlson's phrase, brands a "haunted stage." This conceptualization of Irish theater precludes any straightforward rendition of a national teleology, for in this space the eerie embodiments of collective traumas loom large to "[represent] the unbiddable, irrepressible, and uncontainable nature of memory, which disrupts linear progress and thus haunts not only the present, but the future also."[1]

Despite the danger of stagnation that they seem to embody, such confrontations on the Irish stage also offer a chance at historical redemption. As Oona Frawley has argued, these troubled ghosts may be invoked precisely with the intention of laying them to rest and thereby ending Stephen Dedalus's notorious nightmare.[2] Pine, too, subscribes to such progressive historicism, arguing that it is necessary to address and eventually resolve historical traumas so that a viable future can be imagined and constructed "in order to become an ethical form of memory."[3] Pine's optimism in believing that such redemptive altercations with the demons of the past may create a better future mainly stems from the explicitly cathartic confrontations with Irish history that abound in late twentieth-century plays by, for example, Brian Friel, Tom Murphy, Frank McGuinness, and Christina Reid, implying that mnemonic purgation is a fairly recent phenomenon.[4] However, Pine's thesis that the performance of memory is "an ongoing process, being re-shaped constantly, so that it is iterated and reiterated, a process of repetition that creates a ritual of the performance," must, by definition, acknowledge the existence of initial engagements from which each reprise takes its cue.[5] It is precisely this kind of preliminary encounter with historical traumas in earlier twentieth-century plays that will come under review in the chapters that follow.

When such tentative invocations of cultural memories pertaining to collective traumas do not occur in print but are performed and witnessed in a temporally distinctive space, the specific character of this public setting must be acknowledged. In *Mapping Irish Theatre* (2013), Chris Morash and Shaun Richards evaluate these temporal and spatial imbrications, arguing that "place on stage is not something that *has been* produced; it *is* produced, moment by moment, layering past memory and future anticipation in the active present (and presence) of the audience."[6] This is especially relevant if, in the absence of the architectural monumentality that generally characterizes processes of national identity formation, the twentieth-century Irish stage was invested with particular collective significance, so that "theatre itself fulfilled at least some of the monumentality function in the production of Irish space."[7] More specifically, Irish theater during the Free State years can be construed, as Nicholas Allen has observed, as a "public platform on which ideas of Ireland were tested in correspondence with turmoil in the state."[8] Before it becomes possible to analyze how original Gate plays from the 1920s and 1930s engaged with such issues, it is necessary, then, to reflect on what the defining characteristics of a "national theater" (both in its historical and its current sense) might be, and to relate these qualities to the diffuse yet pronounced modes of avant-garde nationalism that the Gate's leading affiliates espoused.

Indeed, the politically constitutive power of theater in the context of national identity formation has been a topic of intensive scrutiny in comparative theater scholarship. While Nadine Holdsworth, for instance, concedes that "it is a grandiose claim to suggest that theater has the power to bring the nation into being literally or metaphorically," she does construe theater as generally "taking place in a communal public arena" and describes it as a means for "members of a nation [to] contribute to public discourse."[9] As subsequent chapters will show, Holdsworth's classification of theater as "a cultural form that is capable of provoking a complex interrogation of national histories, politics, icons and the affective power of national affiliation" is particularly applicable to the Gate's cultural poetics as well.[10] The conflicted political context in which the Gate was established further underlines its productive potential, as Holdsworth contends that for "those in the aftermath of colonial or quasi-colonial rule, theatre has played a vital role in asserting a remembered or emergent cultural identity as a form of empowerment and confidence building."[11]

If this sounds overly buoyant, Loren Kruger's Marxist reflections on the ways in which the position of the theater is contested in such conflicted societies offer a pertinent complement, since she argues that "the simulacrum of a united nation in the image of an assembled audience" can be challenged by groups that engage with "persistent contradictions between apparent audience and underrepresented counterpublics." In this way, Kruger reveals the concept of national theater to be dichotomous: on the one hand, it refers to "a cultural monument to the legitimate but nonetheless exclusionary hegemony (the moment of autonomy's functional duplicity)," while on the other, it is "a site on which the excavation and perhaps toppling of that monument may be enacted (the moment of liminality as the site of social critique and insurrection)."[12] Indeed, the Gate's cosmopolitan outlook led it to face such exclusionary sentiments, exemplifying Kruger's observation that "certain practices are treated as legitimate theatre with national aspirations, while others are illegitimated as foreign, or even more potently, as untheatrical (propaganda or entertainment)."[13]

Christopher Murray's *Twentieth-Century Irish Drama: Mirror up to Nation* (1997) serves to illustrate Kruger's point about the issues that attend legitimization. In his discussion of the premiere of *The Old Lady Says "No!"* at the Gate in 1929, Murray argues that the Abbey Theatre's rejection of Johnston's first play did not simply stem from misgivings about its expressionist novelties. While Murray admits that Johnston's stylistic extravaganza did not agree with the Abbey directors' mostly realist tastes, he also contends that the playwright's evident desire to "rub noses in the muck of facile mythologising" would not have helped to make his play palatable to the Abbey's patrons. This point can be conceded, but the fact that Edwards and mac Liammóir did jump at the opportunity of producing Johnston's startling play is explained away rather abruptly by Murray, who maintains that Johnston was "in the wrong shop" at the Gate. Murray observes that the budding playwright "needed a forum where questions of identity and Irish politics could be forcibly put"—and, in that capacity, the Gate supposedly could not hold a candle to Ireland's official national theater.[14]

In support of his dismissal of the Gate's nationalist credentials, Murray refers to an open letter, ostensibly addressed to Yeats but targeted at the entire Abbey directorate, which Seán O'Faoláin, the future founder of the *Bell* magazine, published in the *Irish Times* in 1935. This epistle not only shows that the Gate had to contend with a form of patriotic prejudice that would eventually resolve itself into a fallacious historiographical opposition between the Abbey and the Gate (as discussed in chapter 1), but also provides a valuable insight into contemporaneous notions about what constituted a national theater. O'Faoláin addressed this issue with strong rhetoric, interspersing his unfavorable assessment of the Abbey's policies with mildly positive remarks about Edwards and mac Liammóir's company, only to take several jabs at their actors' skills and then write off whatever virtues they might boast by proclaiming that the Gate

> is not a national theatre. It has no constant atmosphere. One week, expressionism; another, realism, melodrama to-day, fantasy to-morrow; China is followed by Yorkshire; Dublin by Scotland; antiquity by the present-day. And as a result the one precious thing missing is that intimacy with life which is natural to a national theatre. There is no criterion of goodness but what will be effective or amusing.

O'Faoláin hammered his point home by stating that "where there is no sense of tradition in a theatre the dramatist who writes for it will never found a school." Accordingly, he implored Yeats to revive plays that were "intimate and earnest searchings of the national consciousness" and to have the Abbey company produce those pieces in theaters across the country, so that aspiring playwrights would be properly instructed in their craft. The Gate's dramatists, meanwhile, were summarily dismissed: O'Faoláin quipped that a playwright who submitted a text to Edwards and mac Liammóir's company was simply trying to get a taste of Gate's boisterous camaraderie, since "to be produced there is in itself an incentive to write"—but that was also the only conceivable reason.[15]

It may be tempting to follow Murray in accepting O'Faoláin's demarcations of what a playhouse aspiring to national significance should (or, rather, should not) do and thereby arrive at a representative historical definition of a national theater—or even, as Murray's lack of criticism implies, at a universal description. However, O'Faoláin's proclamation and Murray's acquiescence are unsatisfactory in two respects. Firstly, and more generally, O'Faoláin chisels away every trace of diversity and multiplicity in construing a monolithic—and thereby highly restrictive—delineation of nationhood and its dramatic expression. This results in a mode of introspection that precludes all the exigencies of Irish modernity (and their manifestations as cultural memories) that have been outlined in the previous chapter. A meaningful characterization of how a playhouse might contribute to national identity formation would, conversely, need to acknowledge the various conflicting elements at play and incorporate, rather than curb, such diversity. That multiplicity is related to the second (and more specific) point of criticism: O'Faoláin, Murray, and many later historiographers have ignored a considerable body of publications by Gate affiliates on the topic of theatrical nationalism, and some of these, in fact, explicitly label the Gate itself a national theater.

To properly gauge those credentials and interpret the Gate's poetics as a mode of avant-garde nationalism, Lionel Pilkington's reflections on what constitutes a modern national theater are more helpful. In his discussion of the Abbey Theatre's engagement with Irish politics, Pilkington initially states that a national theater is a playhouse whose "primary purpose is to operate as a prestige site for the performance of a society's representative dramatic narratives," but he offsets this traditional characterization by arguing that such a theater, "through its enactment of familiar conventions of action and of representation" can "[help to] outline the parameters of political action itself."[16] This acknowledgment of the interactivity of theater and the public sphere opens up the possibility that other playhouses succeeded in becoming more than the isolated bulwarks to societal anarchy or the truthful mirrors of Irish home and hearth that O'Faoláin envisaged.

Moreover, Pilkington's explicit attempt to contextualize the Abbey's political dealings as an index of Irish modernity and Dublin's standing as a European capital correlates with the internationalist sentiments that feature prominently in Edwards and mac Liammóir's earliest proposals for the establishment of a new Dublin playhouse.[17] If mainstream Irish theater embodied "the reassurance that national identity can be realised through forms of behaviour that seem normal and that show action itself as constrained by known and familiar conventions," as Pilkington contends with respect to the Abbey's naturalist tenets, the Gate's innovative poetics engaged with such issues by *questioning* the parameters of cultural politics.[18] Indeed, Patrick Lonergan's examination of the recent globalization of Irish theater concludes by observing how "national theatres are uniquely positioned to address audiences that can be conceived of in civic rather than essentially national terms," precisely because such playhouses "may present plays that are not about an abstract conception of a nation, but which instead address the concerns—or challenge the assumptions— of people who happen to be living in the same place at the same time."[19] Lonergan stresses that importing foreign drama and touring abroad are important ways of achieving this goal, which further underlines such an interpretation of the Gate as an alternative national theater.

In this sense, the Gate's project can be understood in terms of a deviant yet no less legitimate attempt to contribute to the nation's identity formation during a period when the Irish stage functioned as a politicized platform for collective reimagining. Elaine Sisson has observed that, during the 1920s, "the stage becomes a defined space which emerges in the aftermath of a fractured post-revolutionary Ireland, and experimental drama and theatre design allows us to see, as well as to hear, what dissent looks like."[20] Likewise, Mary Trotter has shown how the establishment of more experimental playhouses in the 1930s, of which the Gate Theatre was the most prominent, provided a cultural counterbalance to the conservative mainstream and thereby demonstrated how "the stage [might be] employed as a site to present experiences of dissent against the growing homogeneity of Irish life being promoted by the Fianna Fáil government."[21] This positive assessment of Irish theater in the 1930s as subversive and recalcitrant ties in with attempts to revise the conventional depiction of the Free State decades as years of isolation and regression. For example, in *An Age of Innocence* (1998) Brian Fallon argues that this era in Irish history has always been depicted in "a kind of levelling monochrome," featuring a society "dominated by insularity, defensive-minded nationalism, the Church, censorship, a retreat from the outer world."[22] Alternatively, Nicholas Allen refers to the chaos that ensued after the conclusion of the Anglo-Irish Treaty negotiations to illustrate that "Ireland was already modern and so already fragmented" in ways that many Irish writers of the time did recognize and could articulate.[23] Consequently, he reveals how Ireland in the 1930s was home to "a culture [that was] centrally engaged with the problems of global modernity post–world war."[24]

Fallon and Allen have (independently) developed this less restricted line of thinking, with Allen aiming to draw attention to how "now forgotten cultures flared and disappeared, little magazines, cabaret clubs, riots and theatres erupting in a fluctuating public sphere" as "a smouldering city found form in art and literature."[25] Fallon shares this optimism about the Gate's effectiveness in reviving Irish culture in the 1930s, claiming that Edwards and mac Liammóir's venture "gave new impetus to writers, actors and producers at a time when the Abbey appeared to have lost its original spirit of adventure and was becoming an institution rather than a creative force."[26] Likewise, Allen accords the Gate an important task "in [the] negotiation of the new Ireland's cultural boundaries," stating that "if the Abbey Theatre was, as some critics have argued, the state incarnate, then the Gate Theatre was the still active flying column, its actors agents of a guerrilla modernism that brought the provisional conditions of post-independence to stage."[27] Most importantly, however, Allen also stresses the role of cultural memory in this process by recognizing that "remembrance is the necessary (and perhaps only) mechanism that allows failure its active place in the dissident imagination."[28]

In the context of Irish theater, then, "performance" is not to be taken to equal historical or cultural escapism. Instead, it enables new forms of engaging history by stimulating, in Nicholas Andrew Miller's phrase, "the expression of every present culture's material experience of the past's insistence" through what Fredric Jameson and James Longenbach have termed an "existential historicism" that characterizes—in its ostensibly negative form—the Irish cultural condition of being haunted by memories of the past that block the road to native modernity.[29] Chris Morash, however, has contended that drama might equally be understood as the creation of alternative routes, for it embodies "an awareness of the ghosts of Ireland's theatre history, continually challenging performers in the present to do something so remarkable that the past will have to be reimagined yet again."[30]

Yet, even if this more differentiated line of thinking about Irish culture in the 1930s is accepted and the constituent elements of a national theater are freed from essentialist restrictions, the problem remains that Irish theater *audiences* have more often than not been thought to make up a league of their own. In *Modernism, Drama, and the Audience for Irish Spectacle* (2007), Paige Reynolds provides an example of the relevance of understanding how early twentieth-century Irish audiences stood out from their Continental counterparts, which she attributes not in the least to the fact that "unlike international modernism, which defined itself in part through skepticism towards its audiences, Irish revivalism from its inception espoused great confidence in its publics."[31] Reynolds interprets Irish modernism as a fruitful overlap between avant-garde aesthetics and revivalist cultural politics, which enables her to observe that "even though the audience represents a reconstitution of traditional communities, its form bears the distinctive characteristics of modernity" like constitutive ephemerality, individualism, or even breaking the fourth wall.[32] This conceptualization will offer an important frame of reference in discussing the Gate Theatre's strategies in performing Ireland's conflicted modernity and the reconfiguration of national identities in a contested postcolonial setting, even though it must be acknowledged, as Kathleen Heinige does, that postcolonial audiences can (unwittingly) facilitate the proliferation of negative stereotypes if they "[misread] the identifications on the stage because of a conviction that authorship is inherently hegemonic."[33]

More specifically, the role of the audience will feature strongly in this chapter's final section, which deals with Hilton Edwards's reaction against the encroachment of the cinema by promoting a paradoxically traditional notion of what avant-garde theater should be. Before placing Edwards's idiosyncratic imbrication of tradition and modernity under scrutiny, however, a collation of a wider range of publications on the Gate's poetics (in various magazines, books, and interviews) will serve to establish to what extent the Gate Theatre's directors and its most important associates considered their playhouse to be an alternative national theater. As these documents will show, the Gate's management espoused a variety of avant-garde nationalist poetics: they sought to improve Ireland's international standing by importing innovative modes of staging and dramaturgy to question the traditional forms that had dominated the Irish stage, while simultaneously soliciting native dramatists, who might be inspired by these foreign plays, to envisage a different future for Ireland. Such reflections on Ireland's need for a new theater—and, no less importantly, for new playwrights—bear out the notion that the stage is a virtual yet vigorous space in which the forces of past and future coalesce in front of a participating audience and where postcolonial identities can be imagined, contested, and reconfigured. In this sense, the Gate, too, underlines Christopher Murray's adage that "the theatre that matters, the theatre likely to produce new voices, is the theatre that breaks with the past, or, at the very least, the theatre that operates with such an awareness of the past that audiences will recognize and react to difference."[34]

### An Alternative National Theater?

As discussed above, Edwards and mac Liammóir's founding manifestos—as well as the latter's declaration that their "experiments in the field of ancient and modern plays from all sorts of places" aimed to shape "the mould for the Irish dramatist of the future"—already suggest that the conventional characterization of the Gate as an international playhouse is too limited.[35] After the Gate had properly established itself as an independent playhouse and could depend on Lord Longford's financial support, this preoccupation with cultural identity formation did not disappear in favor of the casual experimentalism stereotypically attributed to the Gate. In numerous publications, various Gate directors, playwrights, and affiliates explicitly accorded their playhouse the standing of a "national theater"; they sought to address Ireland's cultural development by attempting to break the theatrical status quo and declaring Ireland's national identity and international reputation to be of vital concern. Indeed, the Gate's associates reflected extensively on questions of national identity and cultural progress and made several remarkably patriotic avowals of the Gate's importance in furthering Ireland's development.

One of the most valuable sources in reconstructing the Gate's attempts at fashioning its (inter)nationalist stance is its house journal, *Motley*, which was edited by Mary Manning and appeared from March 1932 until May 1934 in nineteen roughly bimonthly issues. The magazine's title refers to Jaques's request in *As You Like It* to "invest me in my motley. Give me leave / To speak my mind," suggesting the creation of an open forum for candid cultural discussion.[36] Indeed, Nicholas Allen considers *Motley* to have been part of "a counter-cultural collage of polemical extravaganza" that "offered public space for fugitive thought" in postindependence Ireland.[37] While Allen stresses the existence of several such magazines in Ireland at the time and considers *Motley* to have cultivated a stance that was thoroughly internationalist, he does acknowledge that, paradoxically, a certain degree of introspection underlay *Motley*'s radical alignment, observing that, "for all its desire to understand the *avant-garde* as an escape from the past, the longer *Motley* ran the more history intruded."[38] However, this persistence of the past is not necessarily ominous or traumatic; it functions primarily as a focal point in calibrating postcolonial identities, as Allen also notes: "*Motley* had set itself to look to a future in which the intellect might be monitor of sentiment's excesses, parody and play two modes by which to negotiate the stress of history that might split the Gate Theatre's audience" over the sectarian divides that persisted after the problematic resolution of the recent Civil War.[39]

An explicit attempt to avoid that danger and ground the Gate in Irish history is found in Lord Edward Longford's articulation of the Gate's importance as a public project. Indeed, the company's bulk shareholder dedicated the opening words of *Motley*'s first issue to assert that the Gate "claims sympathy not merely as a place of entertainment but as a national asset." According to Longford, any allegation that the Gate's international orientation belied such a status should be forcefully rebutted, even as he sarcastically admitted that their playhouse "has not fettered itself by pseudo-national Shibboleths: it has not tied itself to the letter of Nationality, which is death only too often to the spirit. It has not confined itself to plays written by men with faultless Gaelic pedigrees, acted by Gaelic footballers and produced by professional politicians." Not unlike Edwards and mac Liammóir's earlier manifestos, Longford implicitly referred to Yeats's belief in the full artistic license of playwrights, even suggesting that the Gate could boast a better appreciation of truly original Irish talent than the Abbey Theatre, for they had "discovered several new Irish dramatists, who would never have otherwise had a chance to show their abilities, and [who have] present[ed] on the stage hitherto untouched aspects of Irish life and thought." To this, he averred, Denis Johnston's, Mary Manning's, and David Sears's plays testified.[40]

Longford was adamant that these new theatrical productions offered a major contribution to the advancement of Ireland's standing, since "without these and other Irish plays produced by this Theatre, the dramatic standards of Ireland would be lower, her intellectual life poorer." Boasting that Irish plays comprise sixty per cent of the Gate's 1932 seasons, he accorded his own playhouse the title of national theater, for "few national theatres in the world could show as much work done for national drama and the national life."[41] In an essay on the Greek Ethnikon Theatron published the next year, Longford would stake this claim for the Gate's supremacy in even stronger terms, declaring that "the Gate is the true National Theatre of Ireland, and when Ireland and her rulers realise this, and do as the Greeks have done [i.e., provide the Gate with a subsidy], we shall be able to hold up our heads in the theatre before any nation in the world."[42] Therefore, it is clear that the vital relationship between cultural politics and the dramatic stage was experienced as such in no uncertain terms by one of the Gate's leading directors, illustrating Feargal Whelan's claim that Longford was "a crucial figure in what was a conscious effort by those involved in the Gate to develop a coherent national narrative in the nascent Free State."[43]

Indeed, Longford contended that the Gate's overt internationalism should not be contrasted with its contribution to Ireland's cultural development, but must rather be construed as a constitutive element thereof: the Gate "presented not the offscourings of alien culture, but world masterpieces, without a knowledge of which our own culture would be starved and poor indeed." According to Longford, then, the Gate sought to make the terms *national* and *international* mutually inclusive. In thus combining an inward gaze with an outward look, the Gate was to offer grand new perspectives to Ireland—and, in so doing, Longford believed, it would remain "the central point in the Irish dramatic movements of the future."[44]

The past, however, was not so easily dispelled, and Longford acknowledged its spectral presence as a potential disturbance of the national prospects that this fusion of national and international drama sought to create: "Firm of purpose, unencumbered in action, the 'Gate' declares war upon the ghosts and demons that have haunted the Irish drama and sets out confidently to conquer the future."[45] It is precisely Longford's professed self-assurance, veiled in a jab at the Abbey's powerlessness to dispel the phantoms of the past from Carlson and Pine's "haunted stage," that suggests the need for a strong resolve against sentimentalizing the past, lest these contested memories undermine the Free State's prospects. As Nicholas Allen argues in his discussion of Longford's article, "The modern here suggests a break from a past whose difficulty can no longer be considered, the future impulse unwilling to wait for history's resolution."[46]

In his celebratory preface to *The Gate Theatre* (1934), a photographical record of the Gate's first six years of existence that was edited by the Ulster dramatist and former Irish Republican Brotherhood (IRB) leader Bulmer Hobson, Longford repeated his assertion that the Gate was "a national asset" almost verbatim, yet the rest of his contribution focused much more closely on Ireland's international reputation, stating that the Gate was "advertis[ing] to the outside world the fact that this country is not theatrically inactive or intellectually dead" despite its fairly recent emergence from colonial subjugation. Longford placed great stress on Ireland's cosmopolitan standing and the role that the Gate could play in establishing an independent Irish culture, and the same applies for his description of the contrast between the immediate past and the present. By 1934, Longford claimed, the conservative politics of the 1920s, which had repressed Ireland's natural growth, had been somewhat allayed, for "ten years ago the man who suggested that Dublin could or would support a new, intellectual, non-commercial theatre run on modern lines would have been derided or pitied as an unpractical dreamer or an idiot." This change could, of course, be directly attributed to the Gate's own success in proving the opposite, yet Longford also acknowledged that a more profound shift in Dublin's cultural climate had taken place, contending that "both the theatre and the city can take some credit" for this improvement.[47] Longford thereby implied that the avant-garde had taken root despite the pervasive revivalism that many considered to be Ireland's only effective method of cultural fertilization.

Accordingly, Longford went on to offset the score of translated foreign playwrights who constituted the larger share of the Gate's repertoire with "the authors who have kept the theatre supplied with the living Irish drama of to-day to leaven our output of plays of other nations and other times." Longford even accorded these writers, as well as the Gate's shareholders, the distinction of "serving the cultural welfare of the Irish nation"—incidentally, the majority of the Gate's shares belonged to none other than himself.[48] Notwithstanding such implicit self-congratulation, it is clear that six years after the Gate's establishment—and while operating in relative financial security—Longford considered it important to stress its commitment to promoting new Irish dramatists, no less than its ambition to produce innovative foreign plays.

In the many editorials that were published in *Motley* during its three-year run—a single issue would often feature several rather general reflections on the Gate's affairs scattered throughout its pages—we find a remarkably similar concern: in the November 1932 issue, Mary Manning jocularly labeled Dublin "the playwritingest city in Europe" and requested her readers to submit plays with a view to production, for while "the Gate has given Ireland E.W. Tocher [Denis Johnston], Mary Manning, David Sears, and some other young people of great promise," there was only a "stream of genius if you like, but hardly a flood as yet."[49] Manning elaborated on the promotion of new playwrights in various editorials: in the April/May 1933 issue, she expressed the "continued devotion of the theatre to all that is best in national drama" and averred that it "fostered the cause of drama in general and of Irish drama in particular." Manning felt that the Gate could pride itself on its many early discoveries, asserting that "if we have not produced as many new plays by Irish authors as in some previous seasons, we only regret that material of sufficient merit was temporarily lacking."[50]

Accordingly, in the subsequent issue of *Motley*, Manning claimed that "the Gate never forgets its ambition to be in the truest sense a national as well as an international theatre, and to give a chance to native writers whose works show merit, if they are suited to our Company, our methods of production and our audience." At the same time, Manning felt she needed to clarify the practical difficulties that attended the promotion of new playwrights even as she stressed that the Gate's directors

> invite, as in the past, the dramatists of Ireland to send us their plays, and promise a sympathetic reading, and we will endeavour to produce the best and most suitable, when an opportunity occurs. We cannot, however run the risk of severe financial loss and of alienating our audience by putting on works, which, though showing some promise, are yet more or less unsatisfactory as plays.[51]

No less importantly, Manning employed her editorials to reflect on Ireland's postcolonial condition with a remarkably multifaceted perspective, observing that "Ireland is in transition; the nation is finding its soul. New forces are at work; new ideas are crowding in upon us. At the same time, many ancient things that are a vital part of our nationality are coming once again to be honoured." Manning not only believed that this confluence of past and present was highly productive, but also that the Gate was to become a conduit for progress, so that "greatness may return to our drama sooner than we think. The Gate awaits its coming, and will do its share in giving that greatness to the people of Ireland."[52]

Manning's inclusivity was, of course, suspiciously even-handed and nonpartisan, carefully avoiding the contentious topic of Irish politics. In his preface to *The Gate Theatre* (1934), Longford also treaded lightly in this regard: initially, he repeated his argument of how the Gate was to be a perfect amalgamation of nationalism and internationalism—though a playhouse "conscious in all its activities of doing a service to the nation"— and then obliged his acquaintances in government by vaguely stating that "our political leaders of every party have been among the Gate's staunchest supporters; successive Irish governments have facilitated our work in various ways." It is unclear, however, what that assistance might have been, since Longford declared at the same time that the theater's directors "have no politics, and have never received a penny of public money. The theatre is in fact a grand example of united constructive effort, relying as it does entirely upon its own resources."[53]

Manning's and Longford's depictions of the Gate as a nonpartisan vehicle of cultural progress in the face of Ireland's insularity are reinforced by Norman Reddin's pronouncements on the Gate's nationalist credentials. But before Reddin broached this topic in "A National Theatre" (1932), the Gate's solicitor first invoked the ghostly presence of one of the darker pages of Irish history by lamenting the decline of the Irish Theatre Company due to the deaths of its directors Thomas MacDonagh, Joseph Plunkett, and Edward Martyn, two of whom were executed in the aftermath of the 1916 Easter Rising. That bereavement, however, had been assuaged to a significant extent, for Reddin went on to praise "the Gate Theatre, which, in my view, so closely conforms in ideals and objects with the late Irish Theatre, as to be almost indistinguishable."[54] In this way, Reddin, like Lord Longford, labeled the Gate a national theater, thereby also implicitly equating its goals with those of the Abbey.

Pondering, subsequently, "whether a National Theatre should be political or non-political," Reddin decided that it was unavoidable to have a national theater drawing its matter from politics, since "Irish political life is, and always has been, fraught with drama—both tragedy and broad farce" that could not simply be glossed over.[55] Nonetheless, Reddin argued, politics, like religion, should not be seized upon to simply draw lines to divide an audience over a propagandistic message; rather, the larger realm of politics should function as an equitable source of dramatic inspiration and transcendent commitment to national progress, regardless of one's denomination. Reddin, then, envisaged the Gate as little different from what the Abbey should have been: an impartial, nonaligned, yet passionately national theater.

If the Gate thus served a national purpose in providing a dramatic forum that facilitated the formation of Irish identities after independence, Reddin believed that it should also receive financial support from the state, if only to avoid having to perform mediocre plays that appealed to the "buffoon section of the Theatre-going public" in an attempt to ward off insolvency. Reddin believed that granting a permanent subsidy to the Gate could ensure that "attention would be more directed to the excellence of the play being produced than to the receipts at the Booking-office."[56] When such dependence on mainstream hits was eliminated, the Gate would be able to live up to its true purpose, for "a National Theatre should primarily be the source of intellectual education and refinement, and a patron would expect to be the recipient of these benefits when he pays for his seat." Reddin thus envisaged a one-on-one exchange of money—both the state's and the playgoer's—for cultural and intellectual improvement, since a spectator was "in the position of a pupil listening to his teacher."[57]

Finally, Reddin declared his avowed "ambition to see the 'Gate' not merely conforming with that definition of being a National Theatre, but one day of meriting it," so that "not merely Dublin only, but Ireland as well, will then have a possession of which they may be justly proud."[58] While Reddin did not conflate nationalism and internationalism in the way that Longford's manifestos propounded, he did join his fellow director in conceptualizing the Gate as a national theater that sought to advance both Irish cultural life and the nation's international standing, albeit in a much more politically charged context than either Longford or Manning advocated.

Although several of the topics that have been discussed above—the Gate's incorporation of nationalism and internationalism, its efforts to promote original playwrights, its standing as a (non)political playhouse, and its attempts to engage with Irish history—return time and again in *Motley* and related Gate publications, several of its associates also highlighted various dangers that threatened to subvert the Gate's cultural project. Most of these pertain to the strictures of facilities and finances, but Longford also lashed out against the "ignorance and indifference of sections of the public," as well as "the competition of other forms of entertainment," such as the cinema.[59] Hilton Edwards, too, expressed his apprehension about the increasing popularity of the cinema in the 1930s, but before analyzing his plea for a revaluation of the theater *as theater* in opposition to the motion picture in the concluding section to this chapter, it is revealing to contrast the overtly nationalist pronouncements that have been discussed above with Edwards's contribution to the first issue of *Motley*, titled "Why the Dublin Gate Theatre?" (1932). This short essay features much less explicit concerns with the intellectual development of the Free State and therefore provides an important counterpoint to the patriotic sentiments that characterize the cultural poetics of Edwards's fellow directors.

Edwards's answer to the question that the title of his article put forward expresses a purely artistic drive: his reason for establishing the Gate was simply that "ideas were piling up within me that demanded expression."[60] After discussing the aesthetic inspiration that Peter Godfrey's London Gate Theatre provided, Edwards offered a fairly mundane explanation for choosing Dublin as the home of his ambitious venture: it happened to be "a capital well supplied with National drama, but only spasmodically with the type of play that we desired to produce."[61] Edwards did acknowledge, however, that his partner Micheál mac Liammóir, like Edward Longford, was much more concerned with questions of national edification from the start, Dublin "being the capital city of his own country, which, of all countries, he most desired to serve artistically," as the excerpts from mac Liammóir's autobiographies that were discussed in earlier chapters also illustrate.[62]

For Edwards, by contrast, Ireland's relative isolation from Continental drama provided the perfect receptacle for an infusion of avant-garde aesthetics, for "here was virgin soil into which we prepared energetically to delve, although the spade had already been dug into the earth by the Drama League, and by Mr. Denis Johnston . . . [, who] was the first to produce expressionistic plays in the country."[63] As Edwards recounted several decades later in his only book, *The Mantle of Harlequin* (1958), the Gate likewise thrived on overseas stimuli: "Just as the Abbey had been swept along on the tide of naturalism, not in itself a native product of the soil, so the Gate bore a more obvious evidence of foreign influences." However, Edwards did not subscribe to Longford's conflation of internationalism with nationalism, adopting a more reserved stance that contradicted Longford's belief in the Gate as a "national asset" by declaring that "the Gate, although it has presented many plays by Irish authors and on Irish themes, is not a national theatre. It is simply a theatre. Its policy is the exploitation of all forms of theatrical expression regardless of nationality. It embraces upon occasion, the naturalistic play, but its concern has always been with the whole gamut of the stage."[64] For Edwards, Ireland merely provided an opportunity to experiment with avant-garde stage production in relative freedom, with no nationalist strings attached to him personally, which only reinforces Richard Pine's observation that the Gate's poetics should not be construed in monolithic terms.[65]

Indeed, in his preface to *The Mantle of Harlequin*, Micheál mac Liammóir stated that Edwards did not "lay stress on any form of personal kinship, factual, or sentimental, with Irish passions and traditions," and, a few pages later, Edwards himself admitted in more general terms that "by a curious incident the Gate approached, I think, nearer to the vision of Yeats than did his own theatre, but it lacked his intensity of national purpose."[66] Edwards also professed his wariness where "plays of national significance" were concerned, for "all plays must, I suppose, bear some marks of their origins, but the intense national consciousness of Ireland makes Irish characteristics . . . appeal in themselves, divorced from their dramatic qualities"—which means that the latter might not hold up to close scrutiny.[67]

Nevertheless, Edwards occasionally made concessions to this disinterested outlook. In an interview with the *Irish Times* in 1936, he admitted that his opinions on the interaction between drama and nationalism had altered: "I believed that theatre work was purely international, but I have learned that it must have its origins in nationality . . . , not necessarily conscious[ly], but with some character which is unique because it is national. That is a change of mind I have come to since I have been here."[68] Although Edwards clearly did not share Longford's patriotic zeal in founding a new Irish theater, his dismissal was not categorical, and it is precisely this kind of (inter)nationalist paradox that illustrates the Gate's importance in engaging with contested Irish identities.

All of the contributions to *Motley* and the 1934 book discussed above were attempts by the Gate's directorate to address interlocking issues of nationalism and internationalism, tradition and modernity, Ireland's past and the Free State's future. As such, these manifestos show that the Gate Theatre's enduring engagement with national identity formation produced a substantial corpus of texts that contest the conventional historiography of Irish theater, which, until fairly recently, tended to depict the Gate as a politically uncommitted company. These commentaries thus prompt a revision of the Gate's standing as an (inter)national theater, for many of its leading affiliates considered the introduction of experimental foreign plays and the promotion of innovative Irish drama to be mutually inclusive endeavors that retroactively labels the Gate as a site of avant-garde nationalism. Quite appropriately, the Italian philosopher Camillo Pellizzi, in an article on the poet Æ (George Russell) that he contributed to one of *Motley*'s final issues, described the construction of Irish identities to be problematically diffuse in precisely such a paradoxical manner: "This Irish literary efflorescence is so bound up with a spiritual interchange with other countries that even to-day many are unable to recognize an autonomous national profile."[69]

## The Dangers of Cinema and the Essence of Drama

Especially during its early years, then, the Gate Theatre was vitally concerned with redefining the Irish stage, rallying against the debilitating strictures of traditional drama but also warning its audience against the subversive effects of modern consumerism that the early cinema embodied. These perceived threats to the very existence of the theater provide a final case study of the importance of the stage in engaging audiences and facilitating collective identity formation before the Gate's corpus of mythological, historical, and contemporary plays come under review in subsequent chapters.

In "A National Morality Play" (1932), which appeared in the first issue of *Motley*, Denis Johnston attempted to illuminate not only the "blind alley" that Irish theater had supposedly plunged into, but also a general despondency in the face of commercial modernity, claiming that "everywhere there is the same decay of invention and dearth of material. It is only in those countries where the problem has been tackled experimentally that the Theatre has managed to hold its own with the Cinema." However, Johnston did not attribute these shortcomings solely to the rise of the motion picture, for he also contended that dramatists had simply "forgotten the fundamentals, thanks to a long period of picture stages and the reign of a set of artificial conventions misnamed Realism," whereas "the Theatre should be theatrical. It should be a practical expression of the experiences and emotions of the people" through a communal encounter that by definition transcended the constraints of the cinema.[70]

For this reason, Johnston stressed the importance not only of fostering direct interactions between players and playgoers, but also of facilitating an individual experience of drama, since he believed in "that strange personal value for the spectator that is the real function of the Theatre as an institution."[71] In Johnston's conceptualization, theater should draw its matter from collective experiences, yet simultaneously refashion such events into tangible incidents that directly involve the individual playgoer. In this way, Johnston illustrates Paige Reynolds's argument that analyses of early twentieth-century Irish audiences should acknowledge a dynamic "investment in participatory social experience" as well as Elaine Sisson's observation that "as cinema increased in popularity throughout the 1930s theatre had to renegotiate its relationship with its audience."[72] Johnston's discussion of the role of the playgoer in modern theater was followed in subsequent issues of *Motley* by various editorial reflections on the Gate's audience, including the claim that they were "lead[ing] a public, very willing to be led, to new and untrammelled experiments and adventures."[73] As Nicholas Allen remarks, such engagements illustrate the journal's importance as "a central co-ordinate in the formation of Dublin's bourgeois aesthetic," which is further borne out by Johnston's differentiations between theater and cinema in a manifesto titled "Towards a Dynamic Theatre," in which he presented such axioms as "the play does not take place upon the stage, but in the reflexes of the audience" and advocated "full three-dimensional contact with the audience."[74]

For the purpose of analyzing how dramatic techniques were historicized at the Gate, however, Hilton Edwards's contribution to Hobson's *The Gate Theatre* (1934), simply titled "Production," is more pertinent. Edwards commenced his account by arguing that "it is necessary to state what we desired to achieve and the nature of the limitations from which we desired to be free." This ostensible escapism is belied, nonetheless, by Edwards's aspiration to salvage ancient stage traditions: through his collaboration with mac Liammóir, he sought to employ "first-hand knowledge of the new methods of presentation discovered by the Continental experimental theatre. We wanted ourselves to discover new forms. We wanted to revive, or at least take advantage of, and learn from the best of discarded old traditions." Accordingly, the Gate founders espoused the all-encompassing goal of "putting at the disposal of our audiences all the riches of the theatre, past, present and future, culled from the theatres of all the world and irrespective of their nationality. A theatre limited only by the limits of the imagination."[75] For Edwards, modernity did not constitute Anthony Giddens's negation of tradition, nor, conversely, the reinstatement of ancient cultural codes, as the Celtic Revivalists envisaged. Instead, a truly modern production should activate the audience by confronting them with an mixture of styles that required active, critical engagement.

Following the example of "certain *avant-garde* experimental theaters of the Continent"—presumably such as those run by Vera Kommisarzhevskaya, Vsevolod Meyerhold, and Erwin Piscator—Edwards aimed to deliver Ireland from "the thraldom of naturalism," which was associated with the Abbey's production techniques. While Edwards did not consider naturalism to be an intrinsically misguided form of art, he argued that this mode must be considered "limiting, misleading and even degrading when applied to works that have no intrinsic relation to actuality," such as plays that seek to create a "world of imagination" rather than present an authentic picture of reality. It is at this crucial juncture that "realism becomes no longer a valuable asset to the theater, but a menace," because imagination is sacrificed to a preconceived notion of experience: "The misconcept of the advice to the players to hold the mirror up to nature has resulted in the confusion of nature with its image," resulting in the false supremacy of the simulacrum over a multiplicity of realities.[76] The fragmented nature of modernity, then, could not be captured in these one-dimensional forms, even if they claimed to avail themselves of the same tradition that Edwards repeatedly invoked.

To counter this debilitating trend, Edwards wondered "how the 'Theatre Theatrical' was to be re-established" in a more even-handed way, which would know "when to use realism and when to leave it alone." To achieve this, he tried to envisage a partial yet decisive break from realism, "some means that would defy the diminutive appearance of the stage; and spacial [sic] limitations once conquered there would in theory, at least, be no limit to what we could produce."[77] Most importantly, however, Edwards acknowledged that stage realism could not be surmounted by simply inverting or fully discarding one mode in favor of unbridled expressionism or any other single avant-garde technique, since this would only start the process of self-limitation over again. Instead, he recognized that realism should be refined through a "process of elimination whereby only essentials were used."[78]

Edwards went to great lengths to describe the new stylistics and production methods that he adapted from innovators such as Adolphe Appia and Edward Gordon Craig, which involved creating new lighting techniques, employing mac Liammóir's evocative decors, and conceiving various inflected manners of speaking. Such innovations are highly interesting in their defiance (or, more precisely, reworking) of theatrical conventions: as Morash and Richards attest in their discussion of space and place, which builds on Yi-Fu Tuan's work, "a large stage that is constantly being transformed by light or stage machinery never becomes familiar, and so it is a form of space that is constantly in a state of becoming; as such, it is a zone of danger (but also of freedom)."[79] Edwards and mac Liammóir's choice of plays was deliberately provocative in this regard: Edwards recalled how Evreinov's *A Merry Death* (1908), for example, "combines modernity with the traditions of the earliest theater, consciously admitting the presence of the audience." The same argument applies for the original play that is generally considered to be their greatest success: Denis Johnston's *The Old Lady Says "No!"* (1929), which likewise breaks the fourth wall by having the main character suffer a blow to the head that requires the attention of a doctor from the audience. The greater part of the play is, in fact, a hallucination by this actor, and this experience is externalized on the stage, revealing how "expressionism [is] closely allied to orchestral scoring to create an impression as abstract as music."[80]

This explicit aspiration to break the fourth wall—one of the key constituents of the realist stage—and thereby subvert the conventional role of the audience underlines Paige Reynolds's observation that "even though the audience represents a reconstitution of traditional communities, its form bears the distinctive characteristics of modernity."[81] This innovative reconfiguration of the modern audience on markedly traditional lines, which are more reminiscent of the early modern commedia dell'arte, was prompted by the cinema's encroachment on the theater, for Edwards embedded his discussion of interactive dramatics in a direct response to the popularity of the "talking pictures." He recalls that, if "instinctively we had felt the need of examining the full resources of theatrical art and the danger of the limitations that were being imposed upon it," the cinema provided the main impetus for this reappraisal of the theater, for "the stage, as a mirror reflecting merely the images of nature, stood no chance" against the seemingly perfect reproduction of reality that cinema-goers were promised to experience.[82] Reappropriating, however, the traditional Aristotelian values of "unity and speed" as "necessary to the very existence of the theatre as a whole," Edwards sought to salvage drama from being belittled as the outmoded predecessor of the truly modern cinema. Tradition, he argued, could survive and even enrich modernity if producers would once again exploit the roots of drama as an interactive, communal experience, because "when the theatre once again makes its audiences conscious of the presence of its art, people will go to the theatre to see and hear a theatrical performance, and to the cinema to see and hear a cinematic one."[83] Indeed, the validity of Edwards's assertion is underlined by Morash and Richards's statement that the "sharing of a real space is one of the defining characteristics of theatre, and as such is a crucial element that distinguishes theatre from the cinema."[84]

Edwards's faith in an authentic stage that could conflate tradition and modernity led him to declare that "the theatre will be the theatre precisely because it is theatrical," allowing him to admit that "there is no doubt that the cinema affords many advantages as sheer entertainment to the modern mind, and of these advantages the elimination of intervals and the consequent continuity of impression received is perhaps the greatest."[85] However, he considered "talking pictures" to be no more than precisely that: films rely on purely technical ploys, whereas "the theatre at its best has always depended upon brain rather than upon machinery" and could consequently benefit from liberated artistic proliferation that lived up to "our desire to present all manner of plays in all manner of ways, freeing ourselves from the limitations of one over-used and abused method of presentation."[86] Edwards thus subscribed to "the wish, or rather the need, to discover and retain the individuality of the theatre as an art unmixed with matter foreign to its nature," which, of course, paradoxically entails a reaffirmation of tradition through avant-garde experimentation: "The theatre has lost the individuality it once had; therefore we seek, not for something new, but for something once possessed and now mislaid; and that is the conscious realisation of the presence of the audience."[87] In essence, Edwards envisaged the Gate as a modern revival not of a single dramatic strategy, but of the multiplicity of tradition, thereby intensifying the audience's dramatic experience.

Although Edwards did not espouse any underlying nationalist agenda, his attempts to break the fourth wall (as well as other experimental efforts at reinstating various dramatic traditions that acknowledge the artificiality of drama) did seek to foster a particular communal mode, for he argued that "the audience must be acknowledged again and from the unity and awareness of each other will spring the drama that can live only by the active presence and co-operation of the actor and his audience." Ironically, this celebration of the presence of the audience involved a verification of the realism that Edwards set out to defy, for his ideal theater "must live, not by its semblance of reality, but because it is reality—real actors speaking real words to real audiences. There is your realism for you, whatever the method of its presentation."[88] In this way, Edwards could still label himself an avant-gardist rather than a traditionalist, since his conceptualization of theater posits no such contradiction.

If we follow Andreas Huyssen's differentiation between modernism and the avant-garde, Edwards's wish to encompass all tradition to refashion modernity might actually be interpreted as a mode of unacknowledged conservatism rather than societal subversion. Indeed, his desire for a refashioned stage is clearly articulated in his promise of how "our next season will be devoted to experiments, against tradition but with the belief in their necessity and essential rightness. They will constitute an attempt to establish a contact between actor and audience that will make them both parts of a spontaneously created whole which is the art of the living theatre."[89] In another way, however, Edwards's proclamation can claim an archetypal status, as Marvin Carlson's statement regarding the contested status of the theater in the digital age confirms: "The complex and always shifting interplay of reality and illusion, presence and absence, distance and empathy . . . has always been a part of the theatre experience."[90]

Edwards's reflections on the modernization of the Irish stage can be read in conjunction with the numerous affirmations of the Gate's credentials as an alternative national theater that were discussed in the previous section to illustrate how the Gate's directors and associates attempted to contribute to Ireland's postcolonial cultural development. Indeed, as Ian R. Walsh has observed, Edward's direction "offered Irish audiences a space in which to confront and experience affectively the process of modernization that the country was undergoing."[91] In providing the Free State with a cosmopolitan theater that promoted innovative dramatic techniques while acknowledging the historical and contemporary strictures of the context to which they were transposed, the Gate's founders explicitly committed themselves to engaging their audiences in ways that not only challenged conventional modes of collective identity formation, but also paved the way for new Irish playwrights.

# 4

## Mythology Making History

### Prospective/Prescriptive Memory in Irish Legends

In his discussion of the mythologization of revolutionary sacrifice in Irish politics and literature, Richard Kearney observes that "myth often harbours memories which reason ignores at its peril. Myths of motherland are more than antique curiosities; they retain a purchase on the contemporary mind and can play a pivotal role in mobilizing sentiments of national identity."[1] While Kearney mostly focuses on the politics of prose and poetry, his discussion of the potency—as well as the risk—of literal myth-making is implicitly confirmed in a theatrical context by Richard Allen Cave's comprehensive analysis of W. B. Yeats and George Moore's *Diarmuid and Grania* (1901), Æ's *Deirdre* (1902), Yeats's *Deirdre* (1906), J. M. Synge's *Deirdre of the Sorrows* (1910), and Lady Gregory's *Grania* (1912), which notes that, in early twentieth-century Ireland, "dramatising the lives of Deirdre or Grania was fraught with creative and moral dangers."[2] While Cave convincingly argues that Synge's posthumous play, for example, was "skirting close to the winds of outrage and disapproval" in depicting "the *healthy* joys of sensuality" and thereby questioning "the intricate moral climate in Dublin at the time of the play's conception," Irish mythological drama that was staged *after* the watershed of the revolutionary period (1912–23)

Parts of this chapter have previously appeared in Van den Beuken, "A Lament for the Fianna in a Time When Ireland Shall Be Changed: Prospective/Prescriptive Memory and (Post-)Revolutionary Discourse in Mythological Gate Plays," *Études irlandaises* 43, no. 2 (2018): 197–208. Reprinted by permission of the publisher.

engaged with equally contentious matters—albeit in the political rather than the moral realm.[3]

Several new mythological plays that were produced at the Gate Theatre serve to illustrate this point, even if the existence of such a category might seem surprising: the literary and dramatic retelling of mythological tales, in a revolutionary vein or otherwise, has, of course, been strongly associated with Revivalist compendiums such as Gregory's *Gods and Fighting Men* (1905), as well as the Irish Literary Theatre and Abbey productions listed above. In this respect, the Gate, with its cosmopolitan outlook and its largely international repertoire of contemporary plays, would hardly seem to be an appropriate venue for the staging of original pieces featuring legendary heroes and magical potions. Nevertheless, the three plays discussed in the first section of this chapter—Micheál mac Liammóir's *Diarmuid and Gráinne* (1928), An Philibín's *Tristram and Iseult* (1929), and David Sears's *Grania of the Ships* (1933)—draw heavily from the Irish mythological canon.[4] Rather than adhering to the conventional Revivalist mode of recreating something of the grandeur that was Éire, these plays reimagine the function of mythology in the Free State by exploiting the genre's malleability as they infuse these ancient tales with Irish revolutionary discourse of a much later period. Indeed, their politicized representations of undesirable marriages that might be contested through rebellion feature anachronistic cultural memories of the Easter Rising, which serve to vindicate the nation's sovereignty and construct a postcolonial teleology. Such appeals to the Irish people also feature prominently in the subsequent discussion of the first five episodes of mac Liammóir's ambitious pageant *The Ford of the Hurdles* (1929), which likewise imbues Ireland's turbulent history with a hidden telos by dramatizing key moments in the nation's colonial subjugation.

These nuptial and mnemonic elements both require some initial remarks. With regard to the politicization of traditional female gender roles, the colonial connotations of political marriages in Irish literature have been well-documented. In her study of the ways in which the Act of Union was metaphorically represented in literary texts, Mary Jean Corbett observes that "colonial discourses in the nineteenth century were always gendered insofar as they naturalized the subordination of some peoples and races to others by a pervasive rhetoric of feminization."[5] Her subsequent analyses establish the primacy of marriage tropes in representing Anglo-Irish relations by showing how "throughout post-Union fiction, the marriage plot operates as a rhetorical instrument for promoting colonial hegemony in making the private relations of romance and reproduction central to the public and imperial good."[6]

However, dissenting voices employed similar nuptial metaphors to decry the Union as a violation of spousal relations: as Jim Hansen has examined, contemporary pamphlets and caricatures depicted Ireland as a "confined, threatened, terrorized female," while England was portrayed as "her terrorizing, avaricious, and lustful captor-suitor," with more recent literary texts such as Seamus Heaney's "Act of Union" (1975) exemplifying the persistence of this metaphor.[7] Likewise, Richard Kearney has charted how such imagery of "a vulnerable virgin ravished by the aggressive masculine invader from England" developed into allegories in which the nation became "personified as a visionary daughter or *spéirbhean* threatened by the alien marauder, or, inversely, following the same logic, as a shameless hag—*meirdreach*—who lifted her skirts for the invader's pleasure)."[8] As will be shown, this topos was also employed in a postrevolutionary context to articulate a retroactive vindication of rebellion: by representing Ireland's colonial subjugation in terms of an unhappy marriage to a cold-hearted husband, the native bride is shown to be forced to solicit the help of a valiant warrior, who must then choose between romantic love and loyalty to his liege lord.

Scholarship in the fields of cultural memory theory and collective trauma theory has also come to reflect on the inevitable impact of colonial subjugation on collective memory, as Edward Said posits in his afterword to *Ireland and Postcolonial Theory* (2003): "How can we assume that one phase of history does not imprint the next ones with its pressures, and if so, how are they to be discerned, recalled, rebutted, resisted if they are not admitted in the first place?"[9] Postcolonial studies that give affirmative answers to such questions facilitate an understanding of the multifaceted cultural structures that underlie the ways in which an oppressed people may implicitly articulate and explicitly commemorate traumatic periods in its shared history. In this way, they acknowledge such episodes—and, in many cases, the enforced silencing thereof—as enduring formative influences that continue to generate identities, since, as Ian McBride has observed, "in Ireland, perhaps more than in other cultures, collective groups have . . . expressed their values and assumptions through their representations of the past."[10] Such reconfigurations of cultural identities, however, are not straightforward; indeed, McBride contends that "the past has to be reconstructed over and over again, with all the attendant transferences, short-circuits and distortions which that process involves."[11]

This malleability is intrinsic to, if not constitutive of, the praxis of drama. As Chris Morash and Shaun Richards have argued, "Onstage, space becomes place when a specific site is defined by events that occurred there in the past," so that it is precisely "this tension—between the onto-logical presentness of performance and the contradictory need to allow the past to inform the present—[that] is one of the definitional structural qualities of the theatrical."[12] Such interactions are not limited to a con-fluence of past and present; they also endow the stage with an additional prospective dimension, since "place presupposes an understanding of time in which past, present and future can melt into one another, in which the space occupied in the present is also the active site of memories of the past, and anticipations of the future."[13]

Indeed, one of the most prominent dramatic tactics that these original Gate plays will be shown to have in common is their explicit articulation of the function of remembrance. In a break with the Aristotelian unity of time, they do not simply depict a series of dramatic events that are tempo-rally encapsulated; instead, they problematize the concept of memory in an attempt to designate the future relevance of those events as they unfold. As a result, the historical action of these plays is explicitly endowed with the quality of something *that should be remembered*. This temporal confla-tion yields a narrative strategy that is both *prospective* and *prescriptive*: rather than embodying the persistence and continuing relevance of past events, it is orientated toward the future and attempts to enforce very specific manifestations of the memories that it is propagating. Although this con-ceptualization would seem to imply a linear temporality—the narrative present is to be recollected in the narrative future—it is actually circu-lar: the vindication of the imperative occurs precisely through the act of writing the lines that posit its permanence in the first place. In this sense, prospective and prescriptive memory presents a historiographical Möbius strip in which the prophecy occurs both *after* and *through* its fulfillment: it is a mode of memory that is imbued with a retroactive (and, in the plays discussed below, revolutionary) teleology.

## Celtic Femmes Fatales

There are several examples of this complex strategy in *Diarmuid and Gráinne*, the very first original play to be performed at the Gate. After their debut at the Peacock Theatre in October 1928 with Henrik Ibsen's *Peer Gynt* (1876) and Eugene O'Neill's *The Hairy Ape* (1922), Edwards and mac Liammóir produced the latter's *Diarmuid and Gráinne* in English; the original Gaelic version had served as the inaugural play of the Taibhdhearc na Gaillimhe only a few months before. The reviewer for the *Irish Times* commented favorably on the translated production, describing Gráinne as "the 'vamp' of Hollywood" and stating that it was "the first serious attempt in this country to stage Irish mythology, and it deserves to be as great a success in the commercial as it undoubtedly is in the artistic sphere."[14] Joseph Holloway felt that mac Liammóir's drama was "most impressively played, on the whole, by the company," and that "the setting was excellent and the dressing most artistic." Overall, Holloway observed that "most of the speeches shewed careful writing, but many could be shortened with advantage to the dramatic intensity of the tragedy. MacLíammóir has a great gift of descriptive writing, and the text of his play is studded with such."[15] Mac Liammóir's version of the myth condenses Lady Gregory's classic account from *Gods and Fighting Men* (1905) to four major scenes: the wedding of Fionn Mac Cumhaill and Gráinne in the first act, which ends with Diarmuid's reluctant betrayal of his liege lord; Diarmuid and Gráinne's flight to a woodland dwelling (presumably at Doire-da-Bhoth) and their sojourn in a cavern at the shore, where he breaks his promise to Fionn and makes love to Gráinne, in the second act; and the hunt for the Boar of Beann Gulbain in the final act, which results in Diarmuid's death and Gráinne's dejected submission to Fionn.

The play is not only remarkably lavish in its use of the future tense when referring to events that occur within its narrative arc, but it also abounds in instances of prospective mythologizing, especially in its open-ing and closing scenes—and, in several instances, this narrative strategy is imbued with revolutionary discourse. At the beginning of the first act, the process of myth-making itself is made ironically explicit when the Wise Woman explains how Diarmuid received his magic star: Gráinne's nurse comments that "you'd think it was out of an old tale."[16] The trans-formative power of stories being told and retold is likewise accentuated in a more condensed form by Sadhbh, Gráinne's servant, who states that "in Tara every word that is spoken over the fires at twilight has grown to be a fabulous story at the dawn of day" (5). The (post)revolutionary potency of such aggrandizements is revealed when the Nurse is speculat-ing which of the guests who are present at Fionn and Gráinne's wedding are being contemplated by a Wise Woman. Her initial guesses, the High King and Queen, are incorrect: "Ireland will not remember them," the Wise Woman claims, whereas "those that are in my secret thoughts will be remembered in Ireland forever" (2).

This intertextual reference to Yeats and Gregory's *Cathleen ni Houli-han* (1902), in which the Old Woman sings of how the men who die for her "shall be remembered for ever, / they shall be alive for ever," under-scores the political power of mythology: as Kearney states, "Yeats offered the myth of Mother Ireland as symbolic compensation for the colonial calamities of history. The mythological motherland served as a goddess of sovereignty who, at least at imaginary level, might restore a lost national identity by summoning her sons to the sacred rite of renewal through sac-rifice."[17] In this sense, mac Liammóir's enigmatic strategy of embedding the future mythologization of Fionn Mac Cumhaill, Gráinne, and Diar-muid in historically circumscribed revolutionary discourse offers a tem-poral variant of the equally paradoxical spatial multiplicity that Morash and Richards observe with regard to the Old Woman's strongly meta-phoric role in Yeats and Gregory's play, which allows her to "[enter] what is effectively the mimetic onstage place of the stage from an offstage space that is conceptual, not mimetic," even as she embodies an "ambivalent temporality."[18]

Just as the play's opening scenes project themselves beyond the con-fines of the narrative proper, its conclusion, while seemingly bringing an end to Diarmuid's tale in a darkness that is both literal and moral, tries and fails to provide closure in a more distant narrative future. Diarmuid's deathbed scene focuses only partially on his own passing; in a vatic monologue, the fallen hero begins to foretell the deaths of his fellow warriors Osgar, Caoilte, Goll, Cuan, and Oisín. Oisín's fate especially offers a bleak vista of the future, for Diarmuid avows that he "will live after all of them, an old withered man, making a lament for the Fianna in a time when Ireland shall be changed, an old white broken man bending low with the burden of his sorrow beneath the heavy clouds, listening to the voice of bells" (111).

This sudden leap into the future is, in fact, eerily similar to the audience's recent past, for Yeats's famous lines from "Easter, 1916" ("All changed, changed utterly: / A terrible beauty is born") echo in Diarmuid's prophecy.[19] Moreover, in conjunction with Gráinne's earlier observation that "men, when they fight willingly, fight for dreams and for the shadows of dreams," the play thus reaffirms Yeats's resignation in stating that "we know their dream; enough / To know they dreamed and are dead."[20] As such, Diarmuid's temporally projected representation of the decline of Ireland's most famous mythological band of warriors serves as an ex post facto vindication of the Easter Rising: at a time when the Fianna was no more and even Oisín's powers had waned, the only thing that he would still wait for was the tolling of the bells on Easter Monday, 1916.

A final example of this dramatic strategy, which retroactively endows mythological characters with an awareness of Ireland's later revolutionary history, is the contradictory characterization of Gráinne: in the beginning of the play, her servant Sadhbh is berated by the Wise Woman as a "child without knowledge without wisdom [sic]," and her mistress, too, characterizes herself as "a good child! Yes that is . . . what they all want me to be in this place" (6, 12). Gráinne decries this patronizing attitude and her unequal marriage to Fionn, bitterly proclaiming that it is a "strange and wonderful thing to be the Bride of an old man whose fame is ranted and raved over the fire by the companies of bloody and brutish hunters or of the gray-haired lisping women"—a vision that she contrasts with her dreams of "see[ing] the clouds that are free chasing each other on the hillside without" (16). Gráinne's powerlessness is also evoked through a pastoral image of Ireland: Diarmuid describes her as "a young girl more beautiful than a bough of the apple tree under blossom, one lighter and more swift than a golden fawn of the woods, softer and more sweet than the honey of the bees, wilder and more frail than the cold clouds of dawn" (20). Fionn, to whom Diarmuid is speaking, is of a different mind altogether. He experiences a terrible dread at beholding his fiancée and wonders at Diarmuid's choice of words; his friend then explains Gráinne's fragility by referring to "the glance of her eyes that tells of fleeting wishes and of passions lighter than a moment's thought" (20). This image establishes Gráinne as a fatal paradox: she is both vulnerable and powerful, feeble and terrible, and, as such, she functions as a rejuvenated incarnation of the Sean-Bhean Bhocht, which, in a contemporary context, had proven to be an incendiary emblem of Irish republicanism.

In *Diarmuid and Gráinne*, then, the titular characters repeatedly transcend their mythological roles to figure as historicized symbols of revolutionary struggle. Gráinne's marriage constitutes an individuated equivalent to Ireland's colonial subjugation, while Fionn's dread underlines the capriciousness with which she accepts the martyrdom of future generations for her revolutionary cause. Diarmuid serves to embody this sacrifice, but he, too, exceeds the bounds of the narrative proper by prophesying Ireland's future through imagery that is readily associated with the Easter Rising. This innovative rendition of the tale of Diarmuid and Gráinne thus illustrates how mythological tropes could be retroactively imbued with implicit historical markers to provide the newly independent nation with a redemptive teleology.

This (post)revolutionary intersection of marriage and rebellion is also a key plot element in two other early Gate plays, and, in both cases, this problematical combination is likewise reinforced through very specific memory strategies. The first of these is *Tristram and Iseult* by An Philibín, a pseudonym of the pathologist J. H. Pollock, whose "dramatic poem" had originally been published in 1924 by Talbot Press but was only performed for the first time by Edwards and mac Liammóir in conjunction with John Galsworthy's *The Little Man* (1915) and Nikolai Evreinov's *A Merry Death* (1908) during their second season at the Peacock Theatre in 1929. The reviewer for the *Irish Independent* stated that "'An Philibín's' one-act dramatic poem . . . was a gratifying proof that courage to undertake what is ordinarily regarded as a hazardous experiment does not always go unrewarded."[21] Joseph Holloway mentioned that "there were some purple patches of descriptive poetry, but little drama in the episode of the ill-fated pair taking the love potion of 'Brangwaine.' The staging was fantastical and the lighting excellent. MacLiammóir and Coralie Carmichael made an ideal pair of lovers, though the dawning of their love was rather talked away in long speeches."[22]

Pollock depicts only a very concise episode from the famous legend: his one-act play is set on the ship that is taking Iseult, an Irish princess, to Cornwall, where she is to marry King Mark, the uncle and liege lord of Tristram, who is escorting her. During the voyage, Iseult and Tristram have fallen in love with each other, and Iseult has come to regret her betrothal. In an attempt to bolster her spirit and restrain his own feelings, Tristram tries to convince Iseult of King Mark's virtues, but she remains unhappy. Afterward, Brangwaine, her servant, tells her stories about King Arthur's knights to comfort her, but her efforts, too, are to little avail. When Iseult retreats, Brangwaine sings to the audience, revealing that she possesses a love potion that she will give to Iseult and Mark after their wedding so that they will win each other's affections. In the next scene, however, Tristram tells Iseult that he is thirsty; unwittingly, she brings the love potion, and both drink of it to fortify their respective oaths to King Mark. The potion's effect is swift: the lovers swoon, only to wake up in the throes of their impossible love. At the conclusion of the play, Brangwaine returns to contemplate their tragic yet divinely sanctioned fate.

In several ways, *Tristram and Iseult* mirrors *Diarmuid and Gráinne*: in both plays, a young girl is forced into an undesirable marriage that is averted through magical means, with Gráinne feeling herself being dragged "from one prison to another" on her wedding eve, and Iseult realizing that she has lived a sheltered existence that has made her delicate yet passionate, stating that

> all my life
> Lay fenced about with care, like some frail plant

In a walled garden, whose bright flowers burn
Against a constant sun; being plucked from thence,
The roots are bleeding.[23]

Iseult's longing for her native land might likewise be gleaned from her reaction to seeing swallows flying around the ship: she wonders whether they "have looked upon the tumbled roofs / Of Dublin, or have even bred beneath / The shadow of my turret" (12)—indeed, her greatest desire is to turn the ship around and sail back to Ireland (28). Taking these pastoral yearnings into account, Iseult's fear of "a throne / That hath and unknown quality and a king / I have no knowledge of" (9) resembles the sense of oppression that also frustrates Gráinne before she becomes enthralled by Diarmuid's star. This initial subjugation is reinforced by another parallel with mac Liammóir's first play, when Brangwaine describes her mistress Iseult as being "but a child" (20).

While Iseult does not choose to rebel against the marriage that has been imposed upon her, she loses this sense of duty when she drinks of the love potion. In light of her subsequent denial of her betrothal and her elopement with Tristram, both Gráinne and Iseult thus manifest Cathleen ni Houlihan's revolutionary potential: their youth and frailty turn into a powerful magic when they become threatened, which allows them to rally the true heroes of Ireland (Diarmuid, Tristram) against the encroachment of their liege lords (Fionn, Mark), and they must break their feudal bonds in doing so. More specifically, Brangwaine's song combines these ostensibly contradictory elements—a forbidden love that seeks to wed masculine martyrdom with the feminine promise of national rejuvenation—through an intertextual link to Yeats's "The Rose Tree" (1921). Brangwaine describes how "the subtle women, in their wisdom haste, / To pluck out of the sacrificial sod / A blood-red flower"—an image of martyrdom that Yeats had imbued with the legacy of the Rising by using Patrick Pearse's voice to state that it is as "plain as plain can be / There's nothing but our own red blood / Can make a right Rose Tree."[24] In An Philibín's play, this image is adapted to show how, through druidic magic, women have the power to "chant the birth-song of the springing day" (34) as Ireland becomes young again.

In this sense, Iseult's elopement becomes emblematic of much larger concerns. Although the story arc of *Tristram and Iseult* is even more temporally compressed than that of *Diarmuid and Gráinne*, the ending of An Philibín's play is similarly characterized by an attempt to transcend the narrative present. It is Iseult who enables this digression: as she leaves the stage with Tristram in the final scene, she declares that her escape from bondage is not merely a personal victory but rather the fulfillment of a deeper imperative: "Come, let the stars, who, with benignant eyes, / Beheld the first espousals of our race, / Look upon this—the sweetest and the last!"(45). Her departure is followed by Brangwaine's return, who ends the play with a song that endows the lovers' fateful encounter with an almost metafictional quality when she observes how the gods "choose out that hour wherein / We rest, to strike us, who awakening find / Our peace was but the passage of a dream" (46). This radical divergence from narrative constraints is further augmented by Brangwaine's closing lines, which are both prospective and prescriptive: after foretelling how "in sea-washed Brittany, / As vapour, breathéd on a glass, / These, Love's poor pensioners, must die," she declares that "the gods, in divine equality, / Shall touch with immortality / Their names, that these may nowise pass" (47).

In retrospect, then, the entire play might seem to have been little more than a brief excerpt—Tristram and Iseult's subsequent adventures, and even their deaths, are reduced to a few lines of verse—yet it is precisely this act of condensation that endows the preceding scenes with an emblematic status. On the ship that bears them away from their native land, Tristram and Iseult rebel against their liege lord, if not a foreign oppressor, but this defiance also marks their submission to a tragic fate that is rendered in terms that evoke the Easter Rising. Brangwaine's song provides the memory strategy that resolves this paradox: by sketching the future completion of the lovers' narrative arc and their ultimate demise in the present, her vindication of their impossible love through the future consecration of their names becomes imminent. Her *prospective* reflection is simultaneously a *prescriptive* act of memory that is left to the audience, rather than the gods, to perform.

The third and final Gate play to feature a politically and mnemonically problematic marriage is *Grania of the Ships* (1933) by David Sears, who had previously seen his Anglo-Irish War play *Juggernaut* (1929) produced during the Gate's second season. Although *Grania of the Ships* is, strictly speaking, a historical rather than a mythological play, since it focuses on the sixteenth-century queen Gráinne Ní Mháille, the representation of its titular character is strongly derived from her mythological namesake— and, as Christopher Murray has noted, the distinction is rather moot: "In Ireland history tends always towards myth, for what shapes political attitudes are the versions and images of the past standing as symbols rather than as factual records of experience."[25] Sears's play relates Graine's affair with Richard Burke, a Norman soldier who has been washed ashore after a sea battle; despite killing one of her clansmen, he quickly wins the Queen's affections. Their fledgling relationship is undermined by the love triangle that exists between Graine's captain, Morogh; her servant Nuala; and Pilar, the young Spanish girl whose suicide estranges Burke and the Queen.[26] After Burke has been acquitted in the subsequent trial, he decides to leave Ireland, but after a long deliberation on the lives that they will have to live without each other, the couple is reconciled.

This happy ending only allows for a partial resolution of the various tensions that attend Sears's largely fictitious depiction of Gráinne Ní Mháille, whom the reviewer for the *Irish Independent* defined as "partly pirate and wholly patriot."[27] Indeed, the play's attempts to associate the Irish queen with Diarmuid's lover in order to create a historical penchant for a mythological figure, and its concomitant reliance on prospective memory structures, both reflect the political import of such internal conflicts. In terms of the plot's development, the most relevant clash occurs in the play's depiction of sixteenth-century gender roles: although Burke and Morogh are portrayed as valiant soldiers, they remain largely passive characters, while it is the infighting of the three women (Graine, Pilar, and Nuala) that actually propels the narrative. These conflicts might seem to be little more than hackneyed romantic rivalries, but they function in a context that is strongly political: Burke and Pilar are foreigners, and their marriages to Graine and Morogh respectively are problematic precisely because of their status as outsiders.

Moreover, Graine's verdict regarding the prisoners' fate is postponed when she is forced to contend with the imperialistic machinations of yet another woman: she learns that "the Sassenach from Sligo, under Sir Rupert Mowbray, have broken across our marches, and are advancing, and burning and slaying all in their path. They come to demand rent and cess in the name of Elizabeth of England."[28] Although the rival queen remains unseen in the play, Graine's response demonstrates that she perceives her to be a personal adversary: she mocks Elizabeth's demands by confirming that she "will give the red-headed bitch rents. Gaping rents in the bodies of her soldiery" (60), and, after her victorious return, she sends Mowbray's head directly to the English queen.

Even after this military danger has been averted, personal predicaments persist in ways similar to the mythological dramas that were discussed above. Not unlike Iseult's character in An Philibín's play, Pilar faces an undesirable marriage with a foreigner, while Graine resembles mac Liammóir's depiction of her mythological namesake in her fruitless attempts to woo Burke. These issues take their toll on both Pilar's as well as Graine's sense of identity: after Burke rejects Graine because he holds her responsible for Pilar's death, she veils her grief by defining herself in markedly masculine terms, stating that she is "the O'Maille, daughter of a thousand sea kings, a warrior and a queen. If love be not for me, there is life, and power, the joy of battle, and the sea" (69). Pilar, on the other hand, further problematizes her political position by presenting herself as a foreign Cathleen ni Houlihan, whose sorrow is an ambiguous amalgamation of youth and senescence: "What I have lived, and known, of late, has made me older than my years, and womanhood knows where duty may bring her" (39). Like Michael Gillane in Yeats and Gregory's play, however, Burke is initially dismissive of these signs of deterioration: "Come child, you would not have me hold you a grave and solemn woman weighted with cares and duties" (39).

Although Pilar's sense of duty-in-exile does not provide the play's main paradox, she does offer the first articulations of the ways in which the myth of Diarmuid and Gráinne is resituated in a specific historical setting. Of course, the plot of *Grania of the Ships*—pirate queen falls in love with foreign swashbuckler—is relatively fantastical to a modern audience, but its memory strategies are also employed in other Gate plays to provide a mythological justification for national identity formation. In

Sears's play, Pilar repeatedly describes Graine as a "witch" (37, 55, 61) who uses magic means to seduce Burke. While this mostly projects her own romantic frustrations, Nuala provides a more direct link to Irish folklore when she compares Graine to "Maeve of the Red Hair" (68), and the Queen herself refers to the "the old wives tale that I am kin of Mananaan Mac Lir" (94), the god of the sea. Such references to Graine's supposed mythological lineage initially seem flattering jests, but, when the Queen describes her legacy as a burden, as something with which she has been endowed, the connection with the Sean-Bhean Bhocht that Pilar resembles to a limited degree becomes clearer. Indeed, Graine's feeling that "sometimes it seems to me as if my name is always in men's talk. 'Twas so almost from my cradle. At times I would prefer less of such fame" (43) resembles Old Woman's remark in *Cathleen ni Houlihan* (1902) about how "they are wondering that there were songs made for me; there have been many songs made for me."[29] Burke provides the final link in the mythological chain when he explicitly compares the Queen with her legendary namesake in a revealing paradox: "Your lips have the softness and the sweetness of that other Graine who kissed Diarmuid of the Fianna to dishonour and bliss" (64).

The deleted lines that follow this flattering remark are even more telling, for Burke goes on to endow Graine with a dangerous transformative power that is rendered in absolute terms: "Unconquerable one, your body has the beauty that destroys all memory by filling it completely. Invincible one, your spirit is the blazing beacon that lightens the dark shadows of my loneliness, and beckons me to the glorious light of ecstacy [*sic*]" (64). The enigmatic fusion of beauty and annihilation that also characterized mac Liammóir's Gráinne and An Philibín's Iseult inspires men to martyrdom, which marks both their sublimation and their obliteration. If Graine is a paradox, then, she is also emblematic: as Nuala observes during Burke's trial, "There is no riddle . . . compared to the riddle of Graine's mind" (77). Burke's defense during the proceedings amounts to little more than an attempt to probe this mystery: his variously inflected descriptions of the immortality of Graine's enchanting aspects—"in your gracious spirit lie the wisdom and the justice you have learned from the eternal sea"— might only elicit a haughty response from Graine ("This is lover's talk") but Burke answers with the stereotypical zeal of Irish rebels rallying at Cathleen ni Houlihan's side: "So shall I ever talk to you" (86–87).

This absolutism also underwrites the memory structures on which *Grania of the Ships* is built. From the sea battle between the Irish and the Spanish that opens the play and that is prophesied to "make a brave tale for the Seanachies" (5) until the play's very end, Sears employs prospective and prescriptive memory strategies to articulate the construction of his characters' identities. The most revealing examples can be found during Burke's trial and his subsequent reconciliation with Graine. When the Queen rejects the Norman's meager dowry and he asks her whether he will be allowed to leave her court without harm, she is acutely aware of her own mythologization and her power to shape—or even counteract—future memories:

> Surely, I would not slay you, for I am Graine of the Ships, and that name shall not be food for mockery while you lie forgotten in your grave. We both shall live, Norman. Thus will the tale be different. The tale of the queen who obtained what she needed for victory over the Sassenach, and of the beggar walking the roads of Ireland, because in his folly he thought to make a plaything of a queen. (88)

Burke, however, is quick to adopt this strategy as well: in telling her that "you did not merely cheat me, Graine, you cheated my love which is a far greater thing than I" (89), he imposes a death sentence on his own love. This leaves her with a sterile dichotomy, since both alternatives that he posits entail his freedom (through oblivion) and her bondage (through memory): "Shall I go free, or die? In either case I shall forget—but you—you will remember" (89).

Of course, Burke is allowed to leave, only to further problematize the play's memory structures in the very final scene, when the lovers begin wooing each other again; in doing so, however, they refer to themselves in the third person. This deliberate distance is not merely a playful trick, for it is directly related to very specific memory strategies. Talking about herself, Graine asks Burke whether "she [lives] royal in your memory," and his answer serves to double the distance that had already been grammatically established by situating her at yet another remove, "royal and remote, like the Gods and Heroes of old, whom memory holds in incompleteness, forgetful of all save what was great in them" (93). Graine's response reveals her partial acceptance of this strategy: she believes that "those will be kindly, but dull and chilly memories. . . . Men think so of Gods and Heroes, but not of women" (93).

Despite her misgivings, Burke's strategy proves effective, for the lovers' mutual descent into dissociation is completely inverted when Graine embeds a prospective memory in her reflections on the future. Burke now responds affirmatively to her conditional phrasing ("If you remember me at all") and acknowledges the potency of the strategies that she employs: "I said I would remember, and you have taught me how to do it best. Shall you remember, Graine?" (94, 96). The previous series of detachments is subsequently inverted into a mise en abyme—a memory of memories—when Burke asks, "What will you remember? Let me add that to my memories" (96). Finally, in a resolution of whatever distrust may linger between the Queen and her former captive, Graine's simple question—"You can forgive my words to you?"—prompts a definite act on Burke's part. His reaction demonstrates an impossible sense of empowerment as he posits a prescription *to himself*: "I have forgotten them" (97). In the light of this increasingly layered exchange, a stray remark from Fergus, a minor character in the play who states that "nothing is forgotten by a woman so it suits her purpose to remember it" (71) serves to emphasize the play's complicity with programmatic memory structures.

The memory strategies that complicate the various emblematic love triangles in these three original mythohistorical plays show how such novel reimaginations of the tales of Gráinne and Iseult could absorb the political discourse of Irish republicanism even as the artificiality of this process is explored. By infusing these mythological tales with a distinctively modern historical awareness of Irish rebellion, mac Liammóir, An Philibín, and Sears confronted their audiences with a complex mode of memory that is simultaneously prospective and prescriptive: even as narrative confines are either condensed or expanded to a point that almost effects their abolition, mnemonic imperatives proliferate, transforming the dramaturgical conventions of Irish mythology into a politicized realm of futurity. In this sense, they confirm Kearney's contention that, in experimental postcolonial texts such as James Joyce's *Finnegans Wake* (1939), "myth is revealed as history, history as myth" in a way that "shows us that our narrative of self-identity is itself a fiction—an 'epical forged cheque'—and that each one of us has the freedom to re-invent our past."[30] Such plays thus extend Chris Morash and Shaun Richards's argument that the Gate "was producing a conceptual space that refused to be constrained by geography or politics" during the contentious Free State years into the temporal realm.[31] This also signals an important shift from prerevolutionary mythological drama, for if, as Richard Allen Cave has argued, the anguished characters in Lady Gregory's *Grania* (1912) "sense that they have stepped out of time without achieving the transcendence which is their goal," the exact opposite applies to the heroes and heroines who are featured in these Gate plays: firmly embedded in their distant epochs, they nevertheless articulate a cathartic awareness of their potency in shaping Ireland's postcolonial future.[32]

## The Minstrel Sings

If these three plays already destabilized the unity of time by projecting their narratives into the future through a dual act of prospection and prescription, mac Liammóir's *The Ford of the Hurdles* adopts an even more elaborate narrative strategy. During the Dublin Civic Week of 1929, the Mansion House set the stage for this historical masque, which sought to both span and transcend Ireland's history by depicting seven key episodes of colonial subjugation, ranging from the eighth-century Viking raids through Diarmuid MacMurchadha's treachery and Oliver Cromwell's conquest to the Easter Rising. The *Irish Times* described mac Liammóir's pageant as "a well-deserved triumph" that received a standing ovation from its audience, which had "sat enthralled by the beauty of the swift-passing panorama of events that were presented with such exquisite effect."[33] The *Irish Independent* interpreted the play as a mixture of "almost mystical dialogue, a vision, great beauty, historical atmosphere, symbolic characterisation, and very appropriate settings—all vitalised by almost magical lighting effects, with very appropriate music." In this way, the pageant offered "a swift impression of the passions, ambitions and aspirations that have tended to create the beautiful city of to-day as compared with the little hutments standing on the Liffey on the landing of the fair strangers."[34]

In her discussion of this unpublished tour de force, Joan FitzPatrick Dean observes that mac Liammóir took this opportunity to explore such "familiar tropes as the betrayal of the Irish cause from within by a Judas figure and the contrast between the life-affirming Irish and the repressive English."[35] Although *The Ford of the Hurdles* indeed underlines this stereotypical dichotomy, it also offers a postcolonial assessment of a millennium of imperial conquest that employs prospective and prescriptive memories to forge a retroactively redemptive teleology for the Irish people.

In an additional inversion of dramatic convention, the play opens with an epiphany: an Old Woman living in eighth-century Dublin receives a vision of the city's tragic future and prophesizes that "blood will be spilled on the earth, and the Town will rise up and fall down many times, and the sons of the Gael will perish and die like the blades of the grass."[36] Although the stage is crowded with fellow citizens, her distress is only acknowledged by offstage voices, with the Voices of Women repeating her ill omens and One Voice from "very far away" providing the singular confirmation that "we shall remember" (1.2). The incredulous responses from the onstage Dubliners suggest that these voices from the wings represent the worn-out spirits of future generations, and the Old Woman goes on to berate "the blind, the deaf, the unremembering children of the Gael" (1.6) that wander around the stage for their failure to heed her warnings about the imminent sack of Dublin by Danish marauders.

In this respect, the Old Woman's role is comparable to that of the Wise Woman from *Diarmuid and Gráinne,* or even to that of Brangwaine in *Tristram and Iseult,* both of whom provide similar prospective (and implicitly prescriptive) introductory reflections on the future import of their respective narratives. The Old Woman, however, is not a subsidiary character, for she is also endowed with the transformative characteristics of the Sean-Bhean Bhocht. Although she dies at the end of the first episode, she is described in terms that are strongly reminiscent of those that Yeats and Gregory use to portray Cathleen ni Houlihan: a lone Minstrel foresees that "your daughters, and your daughters' daughters will be in rags as beggars and in silks as a queen. You have many changes to see[,] old mother."[37] The Minstrel goes on to articulate this paradoxical nature of the Sean-Bhean Bhocht—who is simultaneously young and old, subjected and sovereign, frail and powerful—in strongly prospective terms when he divines that "from your womb shall come all the stories of this quiet place. Red war, and ruin, and black defeat, and laughing triumph, and all from you, old mother" (1.6). Such phrasing likewise recalls the Old Woman in *Cathleen ni Houlihan*, who talks about the men "that died for love of me" and explains that there were "some that died hundreds of years ago, and there are some that will die to-morrow."[38] In the millennium-spanning prophecy that mac Liammóir construes, the fledgling town of Dublin is granted a prospective eulogy that already prefigures the recurring instances of rebellion, corruption, and even famine that will shape its history: "Ringed round with flame she'll be, gored up with blood and with hunger and gold" (1. 8).

As the city is pillaged and the girls who had previously mocked the Old Woman's prophecies wallow in despair, the Minstrel promises the Old Woman that he will live down the centuries to tell her tale, urging his kinsmen in various ages of colonial subjugation to recognize that their bondage is merely a link in the chain of an ultimately redemptive history (1.9). Unfortunately, he proves to be afflicted with a Cassandra complex as well: in every subsequent episode, the Minstrel's exhortations prove to be in vain. Despite this failure, his various reincarnations are able to articulate a mode of progress that the audience can learn to recognize: even in the very first episode, he explains that the Vikings are "but the shadow of them that will follow, who shall build and destroy, who shall smile and enslave, who shall lay snares and pay bribes, who shall swarm over the land" (1.5). Their arrival, then, is a prefiguration of how the Irish will eventually become native exiles, for "hundreds of years stretch away . . . and you shall be cast from the gates of this place, or be kept within the walls as slaves and serfs. You shall be strangers and outcasts that batter against the stones that shut you from your own land" (1.5). This banishment is identified as a historical condition that will ultimately prove to be transitory, for the Minstrel's final words constitute a prescriptive statement that reveal his detached perspective: "This is the beginning. Wait, wait and remember" (1.9).

The Minstrel's exhortation becomes a passive battle cry that is repeated at the end of every historical episode to underscore the provisional status of historical events even as their emblematic status as images of colonial violence is confirmed. The second episode, which depicts the partially consensual abduction of Dervogilla, the wife of Tiernán O'Ruiare, King of Bréifne, by Diarmuid MacMurchadha, King of Leinster, provides the most potent example of this memory strategy. In an ironic contrast with the myth of Diarmuid and Gráinne, the twelfth-century king proves to be more intrepid than his legendary namesake: when Dervogilla— whom Dean describes as "equal parts of Celtic princess, flapper, and home wrecker"—keeps postponing her promised departure in a half-hearted attempt to remain faithful to Tiernán, Diarmuid decides to set her husband's house on fire.[39] The resulting inferno is not interpreted as a constituent event in the episode's narrative, but rather as a potent image of Ireland's future: "This burning house is but a torch, a portent of all Ireland aflame that will set all Ireland to a fire" (2.9). In this way, the Minstrel becomes able to chart Ireland's progress and to exhort his audience to recognize these historical continuities: "From this deed to-night will spring another deed, and yet another from its loins" (2.9).

At this stage, however, a vindication of Irish suffering is still impossible, for the Minstrel's message is undermined time and again by the forgetfulness of the Dubliners. From the very first episode, where a Piper urges the people to "listen to my pipes, to my pipes that will keep your feet from remembering sorrow. Listen to my pipes and forget" (1.4) until the fifth act, in which the local townsfolk regard the advent of Cromwell's army to be little more than an economic difficulty, this opposition between remembering and forgetting impedes the proliferation of the Minstrel's message.

The exact nature of that exhortation to remember only becomes clear in the course of the third and fourth episodes, which depict Diarmuid's exile by Ruaidhri O Cenchubhair, the High King of Ireland, and his return at the head of an English army in 1169. These two central episodes establish Diarmuid's treachery and the subsequent Norman invasion of

Ireland to have been the nadir of the nation's march through history. It is the faithless exile rather than the Minstrel who delivers the third episode's final monologue, and his voice is markedly different from its precedent: "May the gutters and the ditches of the streets be dark with your blood and the marching feet of your enemies be the music you shall dance to" (3/4.13). These images, however, also serve to underscore the universal nature of colonial destruction: Diarmuid's wish for "rags fluttering in the wind, grey ashes soaking in the rain, red war, and desolation to you now, Dublin of my hatred" (3/4.13) could just as well have been uttered in any of the other episodes. The Minstrel is forced to acknowledge that "it is dark now, and the light shall make the darkness stronger," for the break of day reveals the English army marching across the land, which enables him to repeat (and thereby verify) his earlier prophecy to the Irish people: "Outcasts you shall be in your land" (3/4.15–16).

If Diarmuid's high treason marks the low point of Ireland's development, this means that subsequent episodes should enable an ascent. While the fifth episode, which is set during the Cromwellian campaigns of 1653, initially seems to show an Irish population that has grown materialistic and lethargic, the Minstrel draws the audience's attention to a Ballad Seller. He is introduced as an emblem of mercantile opportunism, but when a group of Roundhead soldiers passes by, he curses the "Sean Buidhe" (5.6)—Gaelic for "Yellow John," signifying John Bull and thereby England—and utters further Gaelic expletives directed at the English troops.[40] Cromwell's soldiers, who fail to comprehend his remarks but know that they are being ridiculed, come to blows with the local population. As the fight continues offstage, the Ballad Seller proposes a minor but potent act of rebellion: "Come let us show them we are free to sing our own songs if we will" (5.9). Rather surprisingly, this remark is taken up by the Minstrel, who temporarily adopts the forgetful stance that the Piper advocated centuries before, when he tells the people to "dance on the wind and forget for a moment" (5.9). This apparent paradox proves productive, for the Ballad Seller's desire to sing Gaelic songs is the first stepping stone toward independence: the teleology of Irish history has been vindicated through his minor act of defiance.

The final two episodes of *The Ford of the Hurdles* (which will be discussed in the subsequent chapter on the Gate's staging of modern Irish history) depict the abortive 1803 and 1916 insurrections. While those military engagements ostensibly constitute much more potent acts of rebellion by any historiographical definition, mac Liammóir thus grounds them in a much smaller feat: the singing of a song, the affirmation of one's cultural roots. While Charlotte McIvor and Siobhán O'Gorman contend that pageants such as *The Ford of the Hurdles* are exemplars of "a politicized practice aiming to (re)construct communities" by promoting "highly selective, romanticized versions of Irish history in the service of postcolonial nation-building," and Paige Reynolds claims that "these large-scale public events were intended to incubate national pride, to soothe political turmoil in recently partitioned Ireland, and to lure tourists," mac Liammóir's engagement with Irish history also has a redemptive dimension.[41] Even if *The Ford of the Hurdles* can be read, in Joan FitzPatrick Dean's words, as "a sentimental, sanitized reading of Irish history that remains popular with militant nationalists, songwriters, and Irish-Americans," and such appraisals are extended to the mythohistorical plays discussed above, these works are simultaneously marked by mnemonic and intertextual density.[42]

If anything, a character such as the Minstrel confirms Helen Gilbert and Jeanne Tompkins's claim that "one of the most significant manipulators of historical narrative in colonized societies is the story-teller."[43] However, the Minstrel's temporally fluid identity transcends the mere validation of the role of "potential political agitator" with his "tenor of resistance" that the storyteller embodies in Gilbert and Tompkins's politicized evaluation of postcolonial dramatic structures.[44] In this sense, mac Liammóir's project also underlines Nadine Holdsworth's claim that "the recycling of traditional national myths, stories, legends and characters by successive dramatists and theatre-makers who draw on an audience's familiarity with the original" functions "as a form of expediency, a prior cultural referent that can help to market a new piece or to highlight an interpretive vision."[45] In *The Ford of the Hurdles*, then, as well as in various mythological Gate plays, mnemonic exhortations function as resolute vindications of national traumas that are both retrospective and retroactive. In engaging with contested collective memories, these original Gate playwrights simultaneously mythologize and personify the sufferings of the Irish people throughout the nation's history as they attempt to transform Ireland's past into a realm of future provenance.

# 5

# From History to Identity

*Religion, Rebellion, and the Resilience of Memory*

In the autumn of 1897, Lady Gregory circulated the Irish Literary Theatre's (ILT) fundraising manifesto, which famously expressed the intention "to have performed in Dublin in the spring of every year certain Celtic and Irish plays, which whatever be their degree of excellence will be written with a high ambition, and so to build up a Celtic and Irish school of dramatic literature."[1] One respondent, whose identity Lady Gregory declined to reveal in *Our Irish Theatre* (1913), sent her a check in a markedly defeatist vein ("more as a proof of regard for *you* than a belief in the drama"), since "any attempt at treating Irish history is a fatal handicap, not to say an absolute *bar*, to anything in the shape of popularity."[2] In an essay published two years after the ILT manifesto, John Eglinton came to a similar conclusion, but on different grounds. His answer to the question that he raised in his title—"What Should Be the Subjects of National Drama?"—was that any excursion into Irish history or mythology would only "form a drag" on the "further evolution" of the Irish

Parts of this chapter have previously appeared in Van den Beuken, "MacLiammóir's Minstrel and Johnston's Morality: Cultural Memories of the Easter Rising at the Dublin Gate Theatre," *Irish Studies Review* 23, no. 1 (2015): 1–14, reprinted by permission of Informa UK Limited, trading as Taylor & Francis Group, and "Remembering the Drapier and King Dan: The Sectarian Legacies of Swift and O'Connell in Edward Longford's *Yahoo* (1933) and *Ascendancy* (1935)," in *Irish Studies and the Dynamics of Memory: Transitions and Transformations*, ed. Marguérite Corporaal, Christopher Cusack, and Ruud van den Beuken (Oxford: Peter Lang, 2017), 19–39, reprinted by permission of the editors.

stage. According to Eglinton, Irish drama must have an acute bearing on contemporary issues to be truly viable, for just as "the Saxon believes in the present, and, indeed, it belongs to him," Irish theater should reinvent itself by adopting a teleological approach: "Ireland must exchange the patriotism which looks back for the patriotism which looks forward."[3]

Of course, this dichotomy is overly reductive. As Declan Kiberd states, "In Ireland the past is never a different country and scarcely even the past: instead it becomes just one more battleground contested by the forces of the present."[4] Indeed, performing the past has provided a particularly salient means of politicizing Irish drama, leading Christopher Murray to observe that "the role of the history play in Ireland, as in England, has always been politico-cultural," complicit as it is with issues of "power, identity, and the national consciousness."[5] This also applies to onstage engagements with several episodes of religious strife and armed rebellion in modern Irish history that were featured in original plays at the Gate Theatre, ranging from a dramatization of the publication of Jonathan Swift's Drapier's Letters (1724–25) to a play that focuses on middle-class loyalties during the War of Independence (1919–21). The various memory structures that Gate playwrights employed to address these traumatic and divisive events are likewise indebted to the prospective and prescriptive modes that were discussed in the previous chapter. However, in these historical plays, the compulsion to actually assimilate such transgenerational memories is rendered problematic in the context of Irish modernity, regardless of whether this impulse is experienced as an intrinsic characteristic of national identities or imposed through external (and often violent) means.

The first section of this chapter will focus on how Irish nationalism is compromised by pervasive tensions between Catholic and Protestant identities in two plays by Edward Longford: *Yahoo* (1933), a historical play about Jonathan Swift that addresses the Dean's attempts to transcend religious divides in his vision of Irish nationhood; and *Ascendancy* (1935), which depicts the sectarian tensions that intensified in the wake of Daniel O'Connell's campaign for Catholic emancipation. The second section will continue the previous chapter's discussion of Micheál mac Liammóir's *The Ford of the Hurdles* (1929) by focusing on its penultimate episode, which depicts the trial of Robert Emmet; this scene will be analyzed in conjunction with Denis Johnston's *The Old Lady Says "No!"* (1929), a revolutionary expressionist play that was the early Gate's greatest success. In both pieces, mac Liammóir played the part of Robert Emmet, whose paradoxical attempt to simultaneously efface and effect his own legacy will be discussed by contextualizing the constructions of Irishness that the 1803 rebellion and its later appropriations sought to promulgate. The third section will further explore the Gate's engagement with nationalist martyrdom by examining two texts that construe the 1916 Easter Rising as a teleological marker in Irish history despite its failure: the final episode of *The Ford of the Hurdles*, which comprises an expressionist rendition of the insurrection that was revived repeatedly as a standalone play; and a proposal to stage a massive reenactment of the Rising on O'Connell Street that Denis Johnston published in the Gate's house magazine, *Motley* (1932). The final section will address various conflicting notions of national identity and mnemonic assimilation in David Sears's *Juggernaut* (1929), a tragedy set during the War of Independence.

## Remembering the Drapier and King Dan

To a certain extent, the historical settings of these plays seem incongruous, since they span a period of almost two centuries, but it is precisely their constructions of a retroactive teleology of Irish nationhood that underline such attempts to bridge history and modernity. In the wake of the French Revolution (1789), the perceived necessity of violence to achieve independence—and even the desirability of blood sacrifices, which Patrick Pearse propagated to his pupils at St. Enda's School in the years leading up to the Easter Rising—would become ubiquitous, but when Jonathan Swift published the Drapier's Letters in 1724 and 1725, he contested British imperialism in a wholly different manner. This polemic series of pamphlets was issued under a pseudonym to decry the patent that King George I had granted to William Wood, an ironmonger, to mint base copper coins that threatened to destabilize the Irish economy.[6] Although Dublin Castle issued a reward to be paid to the man who would reveal the true identity of "M. B. Drapier," Swift's authorship only became publicly known after Wood's patent had been annulled. Despite this danger, Swift not only wrote a personal letter to Lord Carteret, the Lord Lieutenant of Ireland, to apprise the viceroy of his opposition to Wood's patent, but also included a copy of his first Drapier's Letter, cunningly claiming that it "is entitled to a weaver, and suited to the vulgar, but thought to be the work of a better hand."[7]

Hailed by contemporaries as an act of national heroism, Swift's polemic has come to be interpreted as a turning point in Irish history; according to Joseph McMinn, the Dean of St. Patrick's Cathedral had granted "English-speaking Ireland a new sense of a separate identity, one which would enter into the mainstream of later Irish nationalism."[8] Likewise, Carole Fabricant has commented on the remarkable generality of Swift's notion of Irishness in the Drapier's Letters, arguing that "Swift's outlook extends beyond the boundaries of a narrowly defined 'colonial nationalism' to embrace a more expansive vision, one that undoubtedly assumed the continued hegemony of the Anglo-Irish elite but that also makes room for a range of other groups in Irish society."[9]

In 1933, Hilton Edwards portrayed Jonathan Swift in the Earl of Longford's third Gate play, *Yahoo*, which is set in 1724 and depicts the Dean's decision to challenge Wood's patent by writing the Drapier's Letters. In a sense, the performance of Longford's play was not an isolated occurrence, for the immediate postindependence decades saw something of a flurry of plays depicting Swift's tumultuous life: *Yahoo* had been preceded at the Abbey in 1930 by W. B. Yeats's *The Words upon the Window-Pane*, while Edwards and mac Liammóir would go on to produce Denis Johnston's *The Dreaming Dust* during their first season at the Gaiety in 1940.[10] Yeats's play depicts a séance at which Swift's spirit is invoked and suggests that the Dean was unwilling to marry because he did not want to father children: he feared that they would inherit his infirmities (which were interpreted as signs of incipient mental illness) and despaired at the state of the world into which they would be born. In Johnston's metatheatrical play, the characters refer to each other as the seven deadly sins and perform various scenes from the Dean's life in an attempt to understand his motives in spurning his lovers. They come to the conclusion that Swift and Stella were unable to marry because they were related by blood, since both of them were supposedly born out of wedlock. Swift's subsequent attempt to marry Vanessa is thwarted by Stella, who demands that he reveal their shared illegitimacy before she consents to the match.

At the time, Curtis Canfield referred to this "newly-awakened enthusiasm for Swift" in rather overstated terms: although it is understandable that he believed that this departure from the usual fare of mythological dramas was desirable, his observation that "with Yeats as with the new Ireland the break with the past is complete" is more tenuous.[11] Indeed, as Mary Trotter notes, the Protestant background of these playwrights is particularly relevant to their implicit revisionism, since "writing about Swift allowed Anglo-Irish like Yeats and Longford to consider the Irish patriot who sacrifices his position of imperial power for his national patriotism, but who is never completely accepted by his countrymen because of his ancestral position of imperial privilege."[12] Feargal Whelan has likewise observed that the publication of various biographies and plays in the 1930s show that "the promotion of Swift as an icon, albeit a Protestant one, of self-sufficient Irish nationalism defending the community within a nascent state is obviously attractive for the Anglo-Irish."[13] Even as Yeats's and Johnston's plays mostly explore the Dean's romantic affiliations, Lord Longford's *Yahoo* ultimately transcends this relatively mundane topic by also addressing Swift's ambiguous attitude toward Irish nationalism and his contested place in Ireland's history. In thus questioning Swift's legacy, Longford provides a strong critique of the embedded anti-Irish colonial discourse that persisted even after independence had been achieved and employs prospective memory strategies to accuse his postcolonial audience of espousing a narrow conceptualization of Irishness.

David Sears's review in the *Irish Independent* reveals the effectiveness of that strategy. He states that "some of the reminders of our forgetfulness and ingratitude to Swift came like a slap in the face. The final curtain leaves us ashamed of ourselves, which is probably how the author meant us to feel."[14] More generally, Sears considered Longford's characterization of Swift as having been "drawn for us with a faithfulness that carries absolute conviction," while the *Irish Press* commented favorably on how the production of *Yahoo* illustrated the Gate's promotion of original Irish plays: "Was there ever a theatre more bravely adventurous than the Dublin 'Gate'? After the piratical romanticism of *Grania of the Ships* they present another new play, and again it is a play by an Irish author and with, for subject, an Irish personality." Although the reviewer found some of the actors' performances to be uneven, they considered *Yahoo* a success: "Lord Longford has brought to the theme what it needed—an almost impassioned sympathy and insight into Swift's tortured mind." With regard to Longford's conclusion, the critic observed that "the third and last Act is daringly experimental in conception, and will provide nights of controversy in Dublin, both as to its estimate of Swift's position and as to its theatre technique."[15]

However, the play opens in a much more realistic vein, with Swift reading the final passage of his *Gulliver's Travels* (1726) manuscript to his housekeeper, Mrs. Dingley, and Esther Johnson (Stella), whose rivalry with Esther Vanhomrigh (Vanessa) for the Dean's affections remains one of the most debated aspects of Swift's biography.[16] Although the Dean has just completed his masterpiece, he is dejected by his recent political downfall and subsequent exile to Dublin, which he describes in blatantly imperialist terms as "this foul city, this nest of malice and slander, this country of bogs and fogs and savages."[17] Stella tries to rebuke Swift for his slander by referring to his vocal support for local Irish industries, but the Dean is adamant: "I might as well throw my pamphlets into the stinking, black waters of the Liffey and myself after them as expect the people of the place to have the money to buy them, the wit to read them, or the patriotism to obey them."[18]

Moving beyond the stereotypical dichotomy between colonizer and colonized, however, Swift equates both the Irish as well as the English with the despicable Yahoos that feature in *Gulliver's Travels* and consequently refuses to heed Stella's pleas to "cry aloud and wake" the Irish people and incite them to win their freedom: "I will not fight for a tribe of these loathsome vermin against the depredations of another filthy tribe, because the one is weak and slavish, the other strong and rapacious."[19] While Swift's characterizations betray at least a partial complicity with colonial discourse, the roots of his denunciations are universal rather than particular: the Dean's ostensible anti-Irish racism ultimately derives from his general distaste for humankind. As a result, Swift remains uninterested when William Wood's controversial patent is first brought to his attention, and the larger part of the play is dedicated to quarrelling with Stella and Vanessa while George Berkeley (the future Bishop Berkeley) attempts to mediate; like many of Swift's commentators, the Earl of Longford subscribes to the popular theory (which has been debunked by Louise Barnett) that the Dean secretly married Stella to undermine Vanessa's attempts at blackmailing him.[20]

Over the course of the play, however, Swift slowly warms to the idea of becoming "an Irish Leonidas [who] might stand at a new Thermopylæ" and speculates that if Catholics and Protestants "could . . . but be combined into one whole, were human nature not so utterly vile that man and his neighbour will not agree together even in their common misery, could these slaves but understand the horror of servitude and the splendour of freedom, Ireland might yet be the admiration of the world" (158, 162). Longford even construes this remarkably inclusive notion of Irishness as eventually having been Swift's principal concern, for during a heated argument with Vanessa about his perceived faithlessness, he suddenly reveals that his "private griefs, [which are] such as no man hath ever borne," are the conditions in which the Irish people live:

> A whole nation is slave to a tyrant and does not know that it is enslaved. The people of Ireland are miserable and oppressed, they are filthy and ragged, and hungry and diseased, and how am I to rouse them to a sense of their miseries? A king's mistress and a cheating hardware man take a toll on the halfpenny in the pocket of an Irish beggar. Is not that enough to rend my heart with grief and fury? (175)

Although Vanessa refuses to be drawn into colonial politics and expresses her superiority by coldly dismissing his concerns—"I am none of your Irishwomen" (175)—this explication of Swift's nationalism reveals Longford's unequivocal assertion of the Dean's attempts to transcend religious divides and articulate a unified Irish identity. Indeed, in his fourth Drapier's Letter, Swift stated that "people of all ranks, parties and denominations are convinced to a man, that the utter undoing of themselves and their posterity for ever, will be dated from the admission of that execrable coin," and, notwithstanding the Irish people's undying loyalty to King George I, even hinted at the possibility of establishing their autonomy by claiming that "the remedy is wholly in your own hands, . . . [for] by the laws of GOD, of NATURE, of NATIONS, and of your own Country, you ARE and OUGHT to be as FREE a people as your brethren in England."[21]

While Longford's emotionally charged depiction of Swift's Irishness provides an interesting counterpoint to his earlier celebrations of the literary and political triumphs that characterized his London life, the play's most important statement about Irish history occurs in its concluding act, which Canfield described as "a *mélange* of impressions all bearing either seriously or satirically, as the case may be, on Swift's place in the modern consciousness."[22] This final part of the play, which disparages the audience's conceptualization of Irish nationalism, is set a few months after Swift's marriage to Stella and his denunciation of Vanessa, and the Dean has grown increasingly reclusive; some of his associates even believe that he is losing his mind.[23] Stella, who has not seen her husband in months either, gathers her resolve and decides to visit Swift so she can provide him with moral support, since she fears that he has come under scrutiny as the pseudonymous author of the Drapier's Letters.

As Stella reveals that she is succumbing to a fatal illness and pleads with him to finally consummate their marriage, a crowd gathers outside to celebrate the outcome of Swift's polemics, which have achieved the abolishment of the counterfeit currency (183–85). The people even rush in to congratulate Swift, whose identity had been well guarded by the general population in defiance of Dublin Castle. However, while the Dean is giving a speech to assert that "England has no right to rule Ireland" and praise the fact that "you have shown to all that you will not permit your country to be subordinated to English corruption and tyranny" (185), he suddenly collapses. During his stupor, the ghost of Vanessa, who did not survive Swift's rejection, comes to torment him on what might be described as a literal version of Marvin Carlson's "haunted stage," to which Emilie Pine attributes the status of being "representative of the larger haunting of Irish culture by the past." Arguing that "ghosts are a sign of what Ricoeur calls the 'excesses' of memory, a manifestation of the excessive grip of the past on the imagination of culture in the present," Pine observes that this pathological obsession with the past often fails to properly address its "implications for the future."[24]

However, in the subsequent scenes of *Yahoo,* Longford does perform the exorcism that Pine calls for, as the Dean experiences nightmarish visions of expurgated editions of *Gulliver's Travels* being sold as children's books, of people arguing against naming a road after him, of his possessions being sold at an auction, of a psychoanalytic lecture that denounces his works, and of a mental hospital being founded in his name.[25] While Swift is being paraded before a crowd that repeatedly shouts that "he's mad!," a Distant Voice describes him as "the Mad Dean" and states that "Swift expires, a driveller and a show" (190). Before the curtain drops, however, Swift faces God and confesses his sins as an angelic chorus sings him to his rest.

This expressionistic hallucination, which is strongly reminiscent of the innovative techniques that Denis Johnston had used in *The Old Lady Says "No!"* (1929), is imbued with memory strategies that problematize Swift's position in the Irish Free State and implicitly criticize the play's postcolonial audience in a manner that, as Feargal Whelan describes, confronts them "with the parallel debate outside of the theatre in which Irish history was being mined as the basis of the narrative of the still-nascent Free State."[26] Even before he becomes lost in delirium, the Dean expresses his doubts about the longevity of Irish memory: "If ever a time came when the slave had thrown off the last of his fetters, would he remember in his liberty who it was stirred him to strike the first blow?" (181). Swift composes a satirical poem to illustrate his point:

Can we the Drapier then forget?
Is not our nation in his debt?
'Twas he that wrote the Drapier's letters;
He should have left them to his betters.
We had a hundred abler men,
Nor need depend upon his pen.
Say what you will about his reading,
You never can defend his breeding. (182)

Such pessimism is likewise evinced by Swift's conviction that "in the Annals of Ireland you will scarce find a grudging reference to his name" (182), which, by describing a future that is actually the audience's *present,* constitutes a sarcastic application of a prospective memory structure that serves as an unambiguous indictment of the modern Irish nation. Indeed, when Berkeley contends that "the people of this kingdom will ever love and venerate their champion! Will he be forgotten while an Irishman lives? Will his memory fade?," Swift answers that this effacement will occur "as fast as friendship. Time, prejudice, calumny and the jealous pretensions of men less honest in their hate and scorn, yet no more sincere in their love, will thrust into oblivion the greatest benefactor" (182). By prophesying the bleakness of Swift's future, Longford berates his contemporary audience as ungrateful, forgetful, and, more generally, faithless to the cause of Irish nationalism.

Although the crowd that celebrates Swift's victory repeats the first two lines of his scathing poem in a much more assertive manner and goes on to alter its conclusion in a way that emphasizes their loyalty, the degradations of the Dean during his dark night of the soul belie their jubilant devotion.[27] While there are unseen voices that explicitly endow him with a primary position in an enumeration of Irish nationalists to come—"Swift, Flood, Grattan, Tone, Emmet, Davis, Mitchel, Parnell, Griffith, Pearse" (188)—the creation of this teleology is problematized by the continuous effacement of his legacy that occurs throughout his otherworldly ordeal. The Man in a Bowler Hat, for example, speaks against the naming of a "Dean Swift Road": he describes Swift as "a man of anti-Irish outlook and degraded morals, and a writer of dirty reading matter, not in any way suited for use in our schools and colleges" and even urges the inhabitants of the district to "leave the Dean in the obscurity he deserves."[28] Likewise, during the psychoanalytic lecture, which asserts that Swift had a pathological anal fixation, the Dean is described as a "great Englishman" (189), to which the onstage audience applauds, thereby erasing his Irish identity and validating Britain's neoimperialistic hegemony. In foregrounding these processes, *Yahoo* reveals not only the artificiality of both personal as well as national identities, but also the necessity to maintain viable memory strategies to reinforce such identities despite their tenuous nature.

*Ascendancy* (1935), the last play that the Earl of Longford wrote before terminating his partnership with Edwards and mac Liammóir, likewise addresses the construction of national identities through modes of prospective historiography, albeit in a less dramaturgically experimental manner. The play's main theme—the Protestant elite's fear of the Catholic Emancipation movement of the 1820s—might seem to be historically circumscribed, as David Sears's review also suggests: he praised the actors' respective performances and described the play as "a merciless exposé of the weakness of the position of the Irish Protestant ascendancy as early as the first decades of the nineteenth century."[29] However, the political questions that *Ascendancy* raises were no less pertinent to its contemporary audience, as the reviewer for the *Irish Press* did note, observing that it had "so close a political contact with our minds that one was inclined at first to regard it as politics rather than as a play."[30] Indeed, Longford's historical drama problematizes postcolonial attempts at national identity formation by revealing the trenchant nature of sectarian strife and political violence, on the one hand, and articulating a more inclusive (if elusive) notion of Irishness, on the other.

Set roughly a century after the publication of the Drapier's Letters, *Ascendancy* depicts the fictional Earl of Clonave, a somewhat lascivious but generally sympathetic Westmeath landlord. While the Earl is surveying his estate with his two sons, Arthur and Robert, who are overly hedonistic and ascetic, respectively, they discuss the swift rise of Daniel O'Connell, whom the Earl believes to be well on his way to becoming the "ruler of Ireland and of England, too, perhaps."[31] Indeed, O'Connell, who had founded the Catholic Association in 1823, would spend the better part of that decade campaigning for Catholic Emancipation, which aimed to end the Protestant dominion over public life in the United Kingdom of Great Britain and Ireland.[32] O'Connell's efforts succeeded in rallying the disenfranchised Irish population and his plans came to fruition in 1829, when he stood for election in Parliament, even though, as a Catholic, he was constitutionally barred from taking his seat. Fearing widespread revolt if O'Connell's election were overturned, the Duke of Wellington, the British prime minister, decided to sanction a constrained bill in favor of Catholic Emancipation.[33] Although the strictures that Wellington imposed severely limited the act's effectiveness, it marked an important step toward mitigating the sectarian tensions that had been flaring up in Irish society.

In Longford's play, the Earl of Clonave openly acknowledges the deep religious divides of the 1820s: he would rather die than see "this country being handed over to Papists to ruin" (8). In the Earl's mind, this imminent disaster is linked to the dwindled legacy of the Orangemen, who had defended their new Protestant king William III against the deposed Catholic monarch James II at the Battle of the Boyne in 1690, but who had grown complacent "with their glorious, pious and immortal memory, their sashes and their banquets! Eating and drinking damnation to their enemies!" (8). To prevent further degeneration, the Earl has decided to establish a "new virile society for the maintenance of Protestant ascendancy" (8), which will defend their interests by force if necessary. Arthur shows little interest in his father's endeavor, however, stating that he will simply move to England if "O'Connell starts to cut Protestant throats," while Robert claims that the Protestant cause is already lost: "Men of your type have held power in Ireland for a long time, but now you have not the strength and hardly even the will to hold it any longer" (9).

Robert substantiates his assessment of the Ascendancy's terminal decline by referring to recent history, reminding his father that "some twenty years ago you threw away the power to help yourselves" (9) by voting in favor of the Act of Union (1800), which dissolved the Parliament of Ireland and established the United Kingdom of Great Britain and Ireland (1801) in the wake of Theobald Wolfe Tone's failed United Irishmen rebellion (1798). The Earl has begun to doubt the wisdom of that decision, fearing that the British will not rally against O'Connell, but Arthur cynically reminds him that "of course you were not mistaken, sir, your vote won you an Earldom" (10). Robert, who is indifferent to wealth and power, goes one step further and casts this self-inflicted loss of the right to govern into a prospective statement: "The gentry are doomed. . . . There'll be big changes in Ireland in the next hundred years" (12). His father chooses to interpret Robert's pronouncement in fatalistically dichotomous terms, for he believes that "if Protestant ascendancy goes, everything goes. If Catholic Emancipation becomes law it's the end of us" (14). For the Earl, then, societal inequity is a prerequisite for the survival of his class.

Although the aristocracy's political consciousness is entrenched in Irish history, the deeper roots of their imminent decline are revealed at the end of the first act, when the Clonave family leaves the scene and Patrick Moynagh, a disgruntled tenant, takes center stage. Despite his anti-Catholic sentiments, the Earl is generally depicted as a considerate landlord, but Patrick resents his decision to offer a housekeeping job at this mansion to Katie Dwyer, a local girl whom the irate tenant wanted to marry. In Patrick's mind, his personal loss—and the possibility that Katie will fall prey to the Earl's seductions—becomes an emblem of Ireland's colonial subjugation: in a towering rage that reaches back two centuries rather than twenty years, he delivers his "curse upon you and upon your master and upon the race of Cromwell one and all," for they "took away our lands and our goods and our fine houses, our gold and our silver, our abbeys and our churches" (30). In this way, Robert's reference to the Act of Union and Patrick's diatribe against Cromwell's Irish campaign effect a double historicization of the play's events: both remarks not only establish a historical backdrop for sectarian conflict in the 1820s, but also serve to set the stage for a more viable conceptualization of Irishness that might be pursued in the 1930s.

This orientation toward the future becomes more pronounced in the second act, which takes place a week later and begins just before the party at which the Earl will announce the formation of the William Society. In a last-ditch effort, Robert pleads with his father to reconsider this belligerent enterprise and thereby avoid the "bloodshed and war in this country" (34) that will result from the Earl's proposal. In light of Robert's anticipations about Ireland's future, this remark refers not only to his father's military opposition to O'Connell, but also to the Land War of the later nineteenth century and the recent massacres of the Civil War (1922–23). The Earl is adamant, however, even though his other son, Arthur, has grown weary of his father's strident patriotism, complaining that it is "always Irish this and Irish that" (34). His subsequent declaration—Arthur states that he is simply "utterly tired of Ireland" (34)—would also have rung true to contemporary ears, which had become all too used to chauvinistic rhetoric.

Despite his sons' fatalism, the Earl goes on to deliver his speech to the assembled gentry, stating that "it is only through the maintenance of this Ascendancy that this country of ours can prosper" (39)—a sentiment that is met with drunken approval. His elation begins to wane, however, when Lady Maxwell approaches him to prevent her husband, Sir Benjamin Maxwell, who is one of the Earl's most important supporters, from rounding up and executing prominent Catholics in a preemptive strike.[34] While the Earl is willing to moderate his policies to avoid this impending massacre, he is shocked by her subsequent request to deny Maxwell membership of the William Society altogether to ensure the latter's safety from Catholic reprisals. This plea undermines the Earl's staunch nationalism, for he interprets her dread of "men lying in their blood, of little children stabbed to death with pikes, of helpless women perishing in their burning houses" as an absolute rejection of not only his patriotism, but of his historical identity: "You are asking me to betray Ireland, our liberties, our children's future, the hopes of our children's children, even our religion, our God" (50). By thus combining images of violence that would have been familiar to an audience that had lived through the Civil War with allusions to securing Ireland's future, the play also addresses the threat of ever-growing paramilitary organizations such as Maurice Twomey's Anti-Treaty IRA and Eoin O'Duffy's fascist ACA (the "Blueshirts"), and the danger of violence when Fianna Fáil defeated Cumann na nGaedheal in the 1932 election.

In his dejection, the Earl turns to Robert for help, proclaiming his sacred responsibility "never to be an absentee, but to remember that an Irishman's first duty is to his country" (54), yet his younger son remains steadfast in his denial, claiming that the Earl's cause is unjust and that his supporters will abandon him soon enough. By asking a set of rhetorical questions to answer his father's blind zeal, Robert tries to offer an alternative vision of Irishness:

> Can this country you profess to love, ever have peace or happiness whilst some four out of every five of her inhabitants are slaves to the fifth, and if slaves, then enemies, secret, revengeful, implacable enemies, ever at war with their masters? Must this country be bound for ever to fester with this endless internal warfare? Can you not imagine as something finer than your Protestant Ascendancy an Ireland where the heart of Catholic and Protestant, native and planter, lord and peasant, will be

as one? A country where there will be no more factions and parties, but only Irishmen? (55)

Robert's articulation of his sense of societal justice and his desire for communal harmony can hardly be interpreted as a pragmatic attempt to sway his father's sentiments; indeed, the Earl quickly dismisses his son's ideas as irrelevant. To the play's audience, however, Robert's plea would have had a different resonance: the grandiloquence and infighting of the various political groups and paramilitary organizations that still claimed to be struggling for the nation's survival more than a decade after independence had been achieved underline the fact that Robert's dream of "a country where there will be no more factions and parties, but only Irishmen" had not yet been realized in 1935.

Indeed, throughout the play, Longford's characters clash over their different appraisals of true Irishness, and their lack of harmony proves especially debilitating when it manifests itself as the blatant racism that flares up to construe the play's final plot twist. Fanny, an English girl whom Arthur married because of her wealth, is having an affair with Captain Lyndhurst, an English officer who is stationed in Ireland. When she gets into a fight with Louisa, one of her sisters-in-law, Arthur merely laughs at her, and she decides to run off with Lyndhurst. Fanny's distaste for Ireland is expressed time and again. When she first appears on stage, she does not deign to conceal her revulsion at both the Irish weather and its people's manners: "What a climate! What a country! You never have a chance to dress prettily here. And who would appreciate it if you did?" (19). The disparity that she experiences is absolute and even functions as a confirmation of her own identity, for she feels that "every day I stay here I grow more English. I'll never get used to Ireland" (45). Her scathing remarks, which reflect an imperial discourse that depicts the Irish as brutes, are not lost on her husband, who knows that "she thinks us all savages, peer as well as peasant" (6) and his brother even agrees with this statement to some extent. When Louisa lauds "the tradition of the Irish gentleman," Robert confronts her with an enumeration of the failings of the Irish gentry: "Drinking, swearing and blaspheming, bullying, duelling, wenching" (23). Captain Lyndhurst's distaste for the Irish people is even more explicit: he would "like to break the bones of any dirty Paddy that laid a finger on [Fanny's] little white body" (45).

When the couple meet up to run away at the end of the second act, they are confronted by Robert, who questions Lyndhurst's character; in response, Lyndhurst hits Fanny's brother-in-law, calling Robert a "canting hound" (58) and challenges him to a duel. The brief third act takes place at dawn: Robert fires into the air to signify his pacifism, but Lyndhurst fatally wounds him. The English officer is overcome with grief and blames Fanny for his deeds, as does her husband, who demands that his wife leave the Clonave estate. The Earl himself, however, forgives his daughter-in-law for causing the death of his younger son, but, when he goes inside the house to see Robert's corpse, Patrick, the resentful tenant, suddenly appears with a gun and shoots him, laughing like a maniac while the curtain drops.

Ironically, then, the play's killings do not occur as a result of O'Connell's alleged thirst for Protestant blood or the Earl's paramilitary posturing. Rather, they are the result of straightforward personal quarrels: Lyndhurst feels that Robert has offended his honor, and Patrick believes that the Earl has taken away the girl that he wanted to marry. In another sense, however, both deaths are historically emblematic: the most principled and conciliatory Irishman falls victim to British aggression, and the well-meaning Protestant landlord is targeted as the embodiment of collective exploitation. Robert's and his father's death thus prefigure the violent British reprisals that would occur during the War of Independence and the landlord murders that would take place during the Famine (1845–51), of which the shooting of Major Denis Mahon at Strokestown Park in 1847 is the most well-known example.[35]

More important still, Robert's presentiments, Patrick's misgivings, and the rumors that another one of the Earl's tenants has heard—"the people of Ireland will rise up and throw down the great people of the land" (4)—function as prospective memory strategies that would have resonated strongly in the 1930s. Despite their simultaneously prescriptive nature, however, these collective memories belie assimilation: to a contemporary audience, who are aware of the violent historical events that the play foreshadows but whose present is no less fraught with sectarian and paramilitary aggression, Robert's appeals for unanimity must have seemed elusive.

In this respect, plays such as *Yahoo* and *Ascendancy* are much more than mere historical dramas: while rooted in the nation's past, they offer postcolonial critiques, if not indictments, of the Free State and the conflicting notions of Irishness that threatened to tear it apart. By drawing implicit and explicit parallels between various contested episodes of colonial and sectarian strife in Irish history, on the one hand, and the nation's contemporary political climate, on the other, both plays employ complex narrative strategies that reveal the disconcerting nature of such analogies. Accordingly, the nightmarish specters that haunt Jonathan Swift and the bloodcurdling laughter that attends Patrick Moynagh's murder of the Earl of Clonave underline Emilie Pine's observations about how the spectrality of memory is projected into the future and thus refuses easy assimilation.[36]

Moreover, Pine's plea for a pacifying exorcism of traumatic memories is exemplified by Longford's progressive historicist defiance in the face of this struggle.[37] While many characters in *Yahoo* and *Ascendancy* embody the entrenched political and religious divides that also destabilized the contemporary Irish nation, Longford offsets such sectarianism with much more inclusive and conciliatory conceptualizations of Irishness. Even if such sentiments fall on deaf ears in their respective historical settings, they exploit the fact that the establishment of the Free State, by definition, marked the resolution of a teleological endgame: in an independent Irish nation, ancient factions and antipathies should become irrelevant, so that celebrations of unity and social harmony might finally offer the possibility of historical redemption.

### Robert Emmet's Dancing Shadow

While it was the War of Independence that led to the establishment of the Irish Free State in 1922, the innate "right to national freedom and sovereignty" that the signatories of the Proclamation of the Irish Republic had affirmed in 1916 was an aspiration that had spanned centuries: "Six times during the past three hundred years [the Irish people] have asserted it in arms."[38] Of these attempts, Robert Emmet's 1803 rebellion was one of the least successful in military terms—it involved only a few dozen men and was quelled in a matter of hours—but its aftermath would neverthe-less provide a cornerstone of Irish nationalism for more than a century. In 1929, the Gate Theatre prominently featured the 1803 rebellion in the pair of plays that rounded off its second season: the penultimate episode of Micheál mac Liammóir's *The Ford of the Hurdles* and Denis Johnston's *The Old Lady Says "No!"* Both plays explicitly address (and problematize) the importance of collective memories of insurrection to national identity formation. Mac Liammóir presents the paradoxical imperative to future generations to both forget and remember the 1803 rebellion as a teleo-logical marker on the road to Irish nationhood, while Johnston decon-structs the rhetoric of that uprising and the memorialized iconography of its leader to question the means by which independence was ultimately achieved.

In doing so, both plays engage with Emmet's political and cultural legacy, which had become enshrined in Irish nationalism through elegiac poems by contemporary writers such as Robert Southey and Percy Bysshe Shelley as well as scores of late nineteenth-century melodramas.[39] As Mau-reen S. G. Hawkins notes, Dion Boucicault's *Robert Emmet* (1884), while unsuccessful during its initial run in Chicago, would provide the mold for later representations of the young rebel's tragic story, many of which would find their way to the Queen's Royal Theatre in Dublin.[40] While Emmet was less prominent on the Abbey stage, Conal O'Riordan's *An Imaginary Conversation* (1909) and Lennox Robinson's *The Dreamers* (1915) are examples of plays that borrowed heavily from the existing melodra-matic tradition in celebrating Emmet's patriotism.[41] However, no tribute to Emmet has become more renowned than "She Is Far from the Land," the poem that his friend Thomas Moore wrote about Sarah Curran, the woman whom Emmet adored:

> She is far from the land where her young hero sleeps,
> And lovers around her are sighing;
> But coldly she turns from their gaze and weeps,
> For her heart in his grave is lying![42]

Of course, in light of Sarah Curran's later marriage to a British officer, the despairing sentiments with which Moore endows Curran are fairly spurious: she functions as a metonymical figure of Ireland rather than as a historical individual.

Robert Emmet also wrote poetry himself, and the texts that survive show not only his nationalist zeal, but also a strong awareness of the importance of collective memories to advocating insurgency. In "Arbour Hill," for example, Emmet first bewails the lack of physical monuments dedicated to past Irish rebels, but he goes on to stress the intangible yet potent testaments that are "consecrate[d]" by "the patriot's tears": "Their memories are for ever blest— / consigned to endless fame."[43] With each act of remembrance, then, the mystical legacy of previous attempts at attaining Irish nationhood is reinforced, and it is precisely this elusive yet indestructible quality of the memory that cannot be quenched that provides the most potent historical consciousness. Of course, the same applies to Emmet's own legacy: as Patrick M. Geoghegan contends, "The failure to find Emmet's body has contributed to his deification," as illustrated by Yeats's poetic observation that the government's refusal to properly bury Emmet has "unwittingly made all Ireland his tomb."[44] Alan Davies has argued that the possibility of a metaphorical rebirth would be developed into an important trope in later representations of Emmet's death, for his legacy—especially with regard to Patrick Pearse's reflections on the 1803 rebellion—became imbued with Christian iconography.[45]

Emmet's concerns about the way in which he would remembered feature prominently in his famous speech from the dock, and the penultimate episode of *The Ford of the Hurdles* stages this courtroom drama through what Joan FitzPatrick Dean describes as "a sustained typology, more often associated with biblical texts, [that] provides internal unity, reinforces the narrative structure, and advances religious parallels in [mac Liammóir's] rendition of Irish history."[46] The scene is opened once again by the Minstrel, who bewails the fate of "he that has loved you too much, the dull, the blind, the forgetful children of the Gael," thereby highlighting the dysfunctional memory of the Irish people as well as their treacherous passivity: "Woe to you . . . that stood not by him."[47]

Historically, the thematic importance of memory in Emmet's oration had been foreshadowed by Standish O'Grady, the attorney general in Emmet's trial, who reflected on the importance of collective memories to Irish insurgency during his two-and-half hour address to the court. O'Grady dispelled the legitimacy of Emmet's rebellion by claiming that it had no grounds other than "the memory of grievances which, if they ever existed, must have long since passed away." The attorney general underscored his denial of the validity of transgenerational traumatic memories by stating that "the provocations of 600 years have been ransacked, the sufferings of our ancestors have been exaggerated."[48] Such attempts at discrediting the main tenets of Emmet's Proclamation of the Provisional Government, which actually decreed that all enemy combatants "be treated with humanity . . . to the end that all the world may know that the Irish nation is not actuated by a spirit of revenge, but of justice," demonstrate that O'Grady primarily sought to disavow the notion that there could be any differences between British and Irish interests.[49]

In *The Ford of the Hurdles*, however, O'Grady's statements about Emmet's supposedly disingenuous appeals are omitted; rather, his indictments are interspersed with the Minstrel's exhortations to listen and with the exclamations of various Voices of Men and Women, who beg for salvation as their hero stands accused of treason. In the actual court case, numerous witnesses were brought forward in the six hours that followed, but Emmet stopped Peter Burrowes, his leading barrister, from cross-questioning them, and did not allow Burrowes to make a speech in his defense. It was only after another three hours of indictments by William Plunkett, who presented the prosecution's closing statement, and Lord Norbury, who addressed the jury as the presiding judge, that Emmet finally retorted. Although mac Liammóir's depiction of the interrogation of the witnesses is, understandably, condensed to a few pages, his version is still fairly detailed and, in this respect, hearkens back to the prominence of informers in nineteenth-century Irish melodrama.[50] In this episode, John Fleming, who had participated in the rebellion but was quick to make a deal with the prosecution to testify against Emmet, is singled out by the Minstrel as "the betrayer," and the Voices of Women express their wish that "the cries and the curse of the people weigh down on his soul."[51]

This collective indictment marks the end of the courtroom drama proper; after Plunkett gives a brief final statement and the jury finds the young rebel guilty as charged, the lights fade on all the characters except Emmet himself. Knowing that his life was forfeit, Emmet had not attempted to mount a defense but nevertheless decided to look to the future: "It is a claim on your memory, rather than on your candour, that I am making."[52] Mac Liammóir chooses to omit this concise statement in favor of a more lyrical segment, but inserts the word "memory" to compensate for this elision: "I have no hopes that I can anchor my character in the breast of the court, I only wish your lordships may suffer it to float down your memories until it has found some more hospitable harbour to shelter it from the storms with which it is at present buffeted."[53] Although in both Patrick M. Geoghegan's transcript as well as in mac Liammóir's version of the speech, Emmet mostly sought to refute the allegation that he had been conspiring with Napoleon to enable the conquest of Ireland by the French Republic, he also reflected more generally on his legacy by creating a diachronical and teleological structure of rebellion: "When my spirit shall have joined those bands of martyred heroes, who have shed their blood on the scaffold and in the field in defence of their country, this is my hope, that my memory and name may serve to animate those who may survive me."[54]

Emmet compounded this assertion of the insurrectionary potential of his death through a paradox, however. In his closing remarks, he requested the "charity of silence" and decreed that "my memory be left in oblivion and my tomb remain uninscribed, until other times and other men can do justice to my character."[55] This prescriptive memory strategy, which seems to contradict his previous statement, implicitly constructs a national teleology, for Emmet declares that only "when my country takes her place among the nations of the earth, then, and not till then, let my epitaph be written."[56] Emmet's strategy is compellingly paradoxical: by demanding an austere silence that nevertheless implies a future vindication, he simultaneously erects and effaces his own ethereal tombstone, creating a legacy that will be invoked for more than a century to come. *The Ford of the Hurdles* confirms the effectiveness of this idiosyncratic pronouncement: after presenting the seventeenth-century Ballad Seller's defiance in singing Gaelic songs to English soldiers as the inception of Irish nationalism in the previous episode, mac Liammóir here depicts Robert Emmet's speech

from the dock as a mnemonically charged and thereby teleologically constitutive event that paved the way to independence.

With the establishment of the Irish Free State in 1922, the cultivated
immediacy and the political potency of Emmet's martyrdom reached
their logical conclusion. In that case, however, the attainment of Ireland's
freedom should also have marked the end of "the charity of silence" that
had been Emmet's dying wish, even as the traumatic conditions in which
independence was won came to problematize the imperative to finally
write Emmet's epitaph. Denis Johnston provided one possible inscrip-
tion for Emmet's postcolonial tombstone with his first play, *The Old Lady
Says "No!"* (1929), which was written at a time when, as Johnston himself noted, "several years of intermittent and unromantic civil war had
soured us all a little towards the woes of Cathleen ni Houlihan."[57] His
satire was produced by Edwards and mac Liammóir during the Gate's first
season after two earlier drafts—*Shadowdance* and *Symphony in Green*—had
been rejected by the Abbey; indeed, the play's eventual title supposedly
derives from Lady Gregory's dismissive attitude toward Johnston's sarcastic expressionism.[58] Yeats did recognize the quality of Johnston's play, but
since he knew that it would offend the Abbey's audience, he, too, decided
to reject it, although not without offering Johnston fifty pounds toward
staging a production at the Gate Theatre.[59]

*The Old Lady Says "No!"* is undoubtedly the most famous original
play that the Gate produced before the advent of World War II and virtually the only creation to have received sustained critical attention. One of
the most succinct descriptions of Johnston's sprawling satire is Harold Ferrar's description of *The Old Lady Says "No!"* as a collection of "mordant
images of morbid Ireland" that aimed to "ruthlessly expos[e] Ireland's
legions of shortcomings."[60] More recently, Mary Trotter has observed
that the play "deconstructs the central myths, figures, and texts that had
been integral to the construction of early twentieth-century Irish cultural identity," while Chris Morash argues that, during the performances
of Johnston's play, the Gate stage was partially obscured by "the dark
shadows of a modernity with which the play is only half in love."[61] As
Ondřej Pilný states, the play depicts "an Ireland that says 'No!' to both
nationalist heroes and to the current political and cultural leaders."[62] *The*

*Old Lady Says "No!"* indeed offers a total fragmentation of the blinkered attempts at constructing a monolithic national identity that characterized the first postindependence decade, with its clichéd Romantic nationalism, its cultic veneration of martyred rebels and insurrectionary violence, and its stringently conservative politics. More importantly, however, Johnston's play questions the transgenerational memory structures that underlie postcolonial identity formation and ultimately confronts its audience with the debilitating nature of such reverential imperatives so that their stranglehold over the Irish people may be broken.

For a few minutes, though, the spectators that attended the first performance of *The Old Lady Says "No!"* on July 3, 1929, might have thought that they were watching yet another melodramatic depiction of Robert Emmet and Sarah Curran exchanging sentimental affectations in a pastiche of nineteenth-century Irish Romantic poetry.[63] This conventional style is soon abandoned, for when Major Sirr arrives at Rathfarnham and tries to arrest Emmet, one of his soldiers hits the rebel leader over the head rather too sharply: the actor playing Emmet, who is denoted as "the Speaker," loses consciousness, and Major Sirr seemingly breaks character to call for medical assistance. Someone in the audience—the Doctor—gets up and climbs onstage to find that the Speaker has a slight concussion; he dismisses the other actors, who are crowding their colleague, and then also leaves himself to find a rug to cover the Speaker's legs. During the Doctor's absence, the injured actor seems to wake up in a delirium: he believes that he actually *is* Robert Emmet and struggles to recompose himself, muddling his lines—"I am an honored gloriable Nationvoice you Sirrflinthearted Saxons"—while a mass of shadowy figures move behind him and whisper incoherent phrases that slowly become a "clanking, shrieking concatenation."[64] While the Speaker thus seems "ventriloquised by the dead," as Alexandra Poulain notes, his fragmented identity slowly takes form again, and the din resolves itself into the "the throb of petrol engines, the hoot of motor horns, the scream of tram trollies upon overhead wires, the rattle and pounding of lorries, and, above all, the cry of the newsboys" (13): the Speaker finds himself out on the street in 1920s Dublin, and resolves to make his way back to Rathfarnham to rescue Sarah Curran and free the nation.[65]

The delusional actor's pursuit, which serves as a mirror image of Ireland's misguided attempts at constructing a postrevolutionary identity, is, in many ways, incoherent and chaotic. Accordingly, the events that comprise his quixotic quest do not really constitute separate scenes: through innovative sound and lighting effects, the play generally progresses seamlessly from one location to the next. Chris Morash and Shaun Richards interpret these techniques as an illustration of how "the work of producing the space (in Lefebvre's sense of 'production') is transferred from the director and scenic designer to the audience."[66] At the same time, the Speaker's initial absence and sudden disappearance from several settings implies that his dreamscapes are more substantial than his state of delirium would otherwise suggest. *The Old Lady Says "No!"*, then, is a play of discrepancies: the Speaker experiences temporal, physical, emotional, and, above all, moral discords that undermine his sense of time, of place, of duty, and even of self.

Despite these uncertainties, the Speaker's perceived identity remains inextricably yet problematically linked to the nation that he has sworn to liberate, and this struggle is reflected in his initial attempts to find his footing in contemporary Dublin. As he works his way through the bustling crowds, he shouts that "a dark chain of silence is thrown o'er the deep. Silence. . . . silence I say!" (ellipsis in original), while he uses similar images of bondage to address his fellow countrymen and make them understand that "it is still unriven, that clanking chain" (14). These remarks, which are repetitions of lines from poems by William Drennan and Mary "Eva" Kelly that the Speaker had already declaimed in the opening scene, ironically suggest both the paradoxical persistence of the "charity of silence" that Emmet had requested in his speech from the dock, as well as his complete inability to recognize the fact that his beloved country has already achieved independence.[67]

This discrepancy is further accentuated by the anachronism of his rallying cry—"Men of Eire, awake to be blest!"—which he shouts while everyone ignores him; a passerby whom he tries to recruit for his cause brushes him off by saying that he is "in a hurry" (14). For the Speaker, time is not simply out of joint: his failure to acknowledge the realization of the sovereignty that Robert Emmet had fought to attain is not so much a ridicule of "the darling of Erin" as it is an indictment of Irish modernity.[68] To Emmet, the Free State is unrecognizable, even though it should constitute the fulfillment of his ambition, which makes his place in contemporary Ireland virtually untenable. The Speaker's role in the play, then, is a wry application of Karl Marx's famous dictum that "all facts and personages of great importance in world history occur, as it were, twice . . . : the first time as tragedy, the second as farce."[69]

The Speaker's subsequent attempts to find a bus that will bring him to Rathfarnham is an enactment of this farce that further undermines the contemporary cult of nationalist martyrdom, which had accorded Emmet a place of honor in the pantheon of Irish heroes. When the Speaker accosts two girls to ask for directions, they hurl abuse at him, believing him to be a vagrant; a group of passersby rallies in defense of their virtue, but the Speaker staves off their threats by revealing himself as Robert Emmet. The bystanders shout out in joy and an Older Man attempts to formalize the occasion by introducing the Speaker as Emmet, who begins to declaim excerpts from Patrick Pearse's speech at the grave of the Fenian hero Jeremiah O'Donovan Rossa: after stating that "we know only one definition of freedom: it is Tone's definition, it is Mitchell's [sic] definition, it is Rossa's definition," the Speaker goes on to decree the immutability of their martyrdom: "Let no man blaspheme the cause that the dead generations of Ireland served by giving it any other name and definition than their name and their definition."[70]

This speech is a potent example of "heterochronia," the temporal manifestation of a "heterotopia"; both concepts were coined by Michel Foucault and refer to cultural spaces that are characterized by paradoxical confluences in which constituent elements are "represented, contested, and inverted." Indeed, Foucault explicitly identified the stage as an example of a heterotopic site, since it "is capable of juxtaposing in a single real place several spaces, several sites that are in themselves incompatible. Thus it is that the theater brings onto the rectangle of the stage, one after the other, a whole series of places that are foreign to one another."[71] Through Emmet's heterochronic speech, Johnston equates the antiquated, formulaic tropes of Irish nationalism that had littered his prologue in Rathfarnham with the rhetoric of Irish modernity, which is no less stringent, reactionary, and mechanical.

This disparagement extends to the play's audience as well. As the people amuse themselves with Emmet's return and wait for the bus that will lead them to the goal that they have already achieved, a Flower Woman, who speaks mostly in lines taken from Yeats and Gregory's *Cathleen ni Houlihan* (1902) and who is played by the same actor as Sarah Curran, reveals that Emmet is actually an impostor. The Speaker cannot refute her allegations, and the crowd turns hostile in a markedly metatheatrical manner: the Older Man states that Emmet is "not going to be allowed to hold up this country to disgrace and ridicule in the eyes of the world. Throwing mud and dirt at the Irish people," while a Young Man does not "like to see [his] country insulted by indecent plays" (35) either. In this way, Johnston casts his audience as characters in his play, thereby preempting their criticism and holding up a mirror to their notion of sacrilege: the onstage Dubliners turn on their fallen hero, who shoots one of them in self-defense before the curtain drops on the first act, while the Dubliners in the auditorium are confronted with the shallowness of their reverence.

Rather than continue this metatheatrical commentary, the second part of the play opens in a much more straightforward satirical vein by depicting a social gathering where various caricatures of contemporary politicians, generals, and artists are in attendance while the affable Minister for Arts and Crafts presides.[72] The socialites are applauding patriotic art and the introduction of censorship when Emmet rings the doorbell, and, although his appearance is somewhat startling—he is wearing gaudy slippers, his boots having previously been removed by the Doctor—they welcome him in their company nevertheless. After some relatively innocent jabs at these Cumann na nGaedheal politicians and their mindless coterie, however, traumatic collective memories begin to surface when Emmet is asked to "tell us . . . about your wonderful experiences in the trouble" (49). His temporal dislocation and his emotional apprehension are underlined by an insidious stream-of-consciousness Chorus, which voices their hypocritical heroism: "Fighting pay no attention shellshock wonderful to have seen it fighting" (50). After Emmet breaks down and admits that he shot a bystander in the previous scene, the Minister's Wife responds in a frighteningly casual manner: "Well what if you did shoot somebody. Everybody's shot somebody or other nowadays. That's all over now" (50).

This pathological dismissal of the horrors of the recent War of Independence and the Civil War is mirrored by the Minister's gleeful reminiscences about the days that he spent fighting the Black and Tans, which further reveal the traumatic collective memories of violence that the newly independent nation was trying to assimilate. Such morbid celebrations are momentarily suspended when Emmet and a General are invited to sing and recite poetry, which they start to do simultaneously as other characters join in with jarring reflections on recent Irish history. While Emmet regresses into his usual collage of Romantic poetry, the General sings "She Is Far from the Land," even as one of the artists, like the Minister before him, openly embraces the carnage of the previous decade: "And that night, waiting up on the North Circular for word of the executions. Ah, not for all the wealth of the world would I give up the maddening mingling memories of the past" (55). This celebration of paramilitary carnage is rooted in an acknowledgment of violent collective memories as disturbing, convoluted, but ultimately constitutive elements of Ireland's national identity.

By the end of the General's song, the partygoers have all faded from the stage, and the Speaker is left in the Tiresian company of a Blind Man, who tells him that "poor Bob Emmet . . . died for Ireland" (58). As the Speaker tries to reconcile himself with his double identity—"He died for Ireland. I died. I." (58)—they sing "The Struggle Is Over," a nineteenth-century ballad about Emmet, together. In his despair, the Speaker finally hears Sarah Curran's voice again, but when the lights turn up the scene has changed to a tenement house where the Younger and the Older Man from the first act live together with the man whom the Speaker shot earlier, who is now lying on his deathbed. To the Speaker's horror, the voice of Sarah Curran belongs to the old Flower Woman, and the two men believe the Speaker's romantic ravings to be the result of alcohol. The two tenement dwellers get into an argument about the merits of Irish nationalism, which the Older Man disparages even as the Younger Man describes his participation in the republican cause as an eternal katabasis: "I went down into hell shouting 'Up the living Republic,' and I came up out of hell still shouting 'Up the living Republic'. . . . Well, one of these fine days my laddo, you'll wake up and find that the Republic does live after all" (63–64). Despite having witnessed the carnage of the War of Independence and the Civil War, the Younger Man does not attribute the realization of national sovereignty to the violence with which it was attained, but rather to the power of reiterative language, for he believes that "we can make this country—this world whatever we want it to be, by saying so, and keeping on saying so. I tell you it is the knowledge of this that is the genius and glory of the Gael" (64–65).

It is precisely this essential mutability that proves partially redemptive: when the man whom the Speaker shot finally succumbs to his wounds, several socialites from the previous scene show up to pay their half-hearted respects to yet another Irish martyr in a manner that foregrounds both the power of language as well as the pathology of memory. The most prominent mourner in their company is a talking statue of the eighteenth-century Irish politician Henry Grattan, which had previously berated the Speaker both when he woke up in Dublin and when they attended the upper-class get-together.[73] At the wake, however, the Grattan statue ignores the Speaker and only addresses the recently deceased man, but its remarks are no less applicable to Robert Emmet: "A word-spinner dying gracefully, with a text upon his lips. The symbol of Ireland's genius. Never mind. He died well. He knew how to do that" (69). This macabre celebration of impotent eloquence and meaningless death echoes the Blind Man's earlier observation that, in the contemporary Free State, the "land belongs not to them that are on it, but to them that are under it" (67).

The Speaker's visions, then, are dramatic externalizations of Ireland's collective memories: although the newly independent nation was attempting to define its future, it had become mired in discursive reiterations of its conflicted history. In this sense, *The Old Lady Says "No!"* exemplifies the mnemonic practices that Karl Marx described as modernity's sinister cultivation of the heroic dead:

The tradition of all the dead generations weighs like a nightmare on the brain of the living. And just when they seem engaged in revolutionising themselves and things, in creating something that has never yet existed, precisely in such periods of revolutionary crisis they anxiously conjure up the spirits of the past to their service and borrow from them names, battle-cries and costumes in order to present the new scene of world history in this time-honoured disguise and borrowed language.[74]

In *The Old Lady Says "No!"*, the aftermath of the Easter Rising, the War of Independence, and the Civil War is experienced as an ongoing crisis: the most potent collective memories are gruesome venerations of insurrectionary bloodshed. As such, the martyrs of previous generations literally become the living dead in a postcolonial society that knows no common denominator except violence—even the Blind Man can see that Dublin "is no City of the Living: but of the dark and the dead!" (60).

In the final scene, the Speaker, too, comes to realize this terrible truth about the Irish Free State's pathological obsession with the memory of insurrection. As the socialites move to the sides, several Shadows take to the stage, calling for Emmet, who has disappeared, to fulfill his destiny in terms that once again evoke the sacrificial fetishism of *Cathleen ni Houlihan*: "Your Mother Eire is always young" (71). When the Speaker returns, he reaffirms his faith in the nation and his resolution to die for Ireland so that Cathleen ni Houlihan might be rejuvenated. After repeating phrases from the speech from the dock and declaring that "[his] ministry is now ended," he attempts to bring a close to his own legacy by finally formulating a teleological terminus that might redeem the disordered Irish nation:

Strumpet City in the sunset
Suckling the bastard brats of Scot, of Englishry, of Hugenot [*sic*]
Brave sons breaking from the womb, wild sons fleeing from their
    Mother.
Wistful City of savage dreamers
So old, so sick with memories.
Old Mother

Some they say are damned

But you, I think, one day will walk the streets of Paradise, head high,
      and unashamed.

(*His eyes close. He speaks very softly.*)

There now. Let my epitaph be written.[75]

After this final speech, the Speaker falls asleep on an empty stage, and the audience comes to realize that the entire play has comprised no more than a few moments: as the actor lies there in his original pose, the Doctor returns with a rug to cover him.

The question remains, however, as to what exactly constitutes Robert Emmet's epitaph. Is it the play's final speech, which comprises an ambiguous acknowledgment of Ireland's convoluted heritage, its crippling diaspora, and its traumatic memories? Or is it rather the multiplicity of *The Old Lady Says "No!"* as a whole, with its cacophony of visions and voices, its satirical shadows and paradoxical confrontations? Or is Emmet's epitaph actually a blank mnemonic imperative, as personified by the Doctor, who "*looks at the Audience, places his finger to his lips and makes a sign for the front curtains to be drawn*" (77), thereby insinuating that only silence and forgetfulness can deliver the Irish people from their history and harrow the hell of nationalist dogma?

Although most scholars agree that *The Old Lady Says "No!"* is a critique of postcolonial Irish politics and society, Emmet's ultimate assent remains a conundrum. This is also true for the play's initial audiences: the reviewer for the *Irish Times* observed that "Emmet's apostrophe to Dublin which brings down the final curtain possibly gives the play a meaning— but what does old Lady Dublin reject?" While admiring mac Liammóir's acting and Edwards's production, this critic was much less sympathetic to Johnston's message: "There is no coherent, or connected, idea in the work, but there is a good deal of somewhat obvious satire," as "the lash tickles rather than cuts."[76] David Sears's review for the *Irish Independent* was more ambiguous, stating that *The Old Lady Says "No!"* must be "an extraordinary play; I disliked it intensely and admired it enormously." According to Johnston "a remarkable mastery of technique and a powerful imagination," Sears felt that the playwright "lashes the Irish people with

his bitter satire not in a spirit of cheap cynicism or of righteous indignation, but with the cold impersonal detachment of the artist."[77]

In retrospect, scholars have made similar observations about the play's
political stance. Richard Cave, for example, claims that "the grand ambitions for Ireland conceived by her one-time lauded patriots are shown to
have been betrayed, politically, socially, and culturally, while the rhetoric
of the past has become jaded and sentimentalized through constant, mindless reiteration," and Mary Trotter states that "the Speaker ending with
these words [i.e. 'Let my epitaph be written'] points to the long-awaited
establishment of an Irish state."[78] Harold Ferrar interprets Emmet's final
stance as a gesture toward the future, signaling that "the time has come
to let the epitaphs of romance and heroism be written to make way for
Ireland to join the twentieth century," and claims that "there may have
been a historical necessity for Emmet and Emmetism but no nation can
grow up while it shuns the present for the past."[79]

Christopher Murray offers a comparable interpretation, albeit with a
more empowering aspect, for he believes that the Speaker "must take issue
with history and carve a new way out of the scenario of recurring violence
prescribed for him." In doing so, the mythology of Robert Emmet would
perish: "Shibboleths must be abandoned in favour of words imagining a
new, revised and enabling history."[80] Likewise, Nicholas Grene argues
that "the drive of *The Old Lady* is to exorcise that ghost-haunted nightmare of history and to find a new modernised version for Emmet's revolutionary vision of Ireland," while Alexandra Poulain has claimed that
Johnston's play "invents a truly original modernist idiom which revis-
its Ireland's literary heritage 'with critical distance' and makes room for
ambivalence, contradiction and irony."[81] She thus argues that *The Old
Lady Says "No!"* uses "the tropology of the Christian Passion to 'resurrect'
Emmet's utopian dream, and sets out to revitalise the dead language and
theatrical culture which have allowed Emmet's ideals to degenerate into
empty rhetoric."[82]

However, if redeeming the collective memory is the aim of Johnston's play, his finale also serves as an inverted repetition of Emmet's
own pronouncements, which were equally potent in their prescriptive
and prospective ambiguity. Johnston's attempt to engage his audience and

underline their complicity by breaking the fourth wall is most prominent during the play's opening scene, when the actors request the assistance of a doctor from the audience, but the latter's return at the very end of the play is even more revealing. Indeed, the Doctor directs his appeal for silence to the *audience*, which is thus endowed with the agency to reinterpret the meaning of the "charity of silence" that Emmet desired. This has important implications for the Speaker's final lines: the legacy that Robert Emmet instigated cannot take form as a political state that realizes—or fails to realize—the dream of Emmet's nationalism, for it exists only in affective reiterations, in portraits, speeches, and plays. In that sense, each enactment of Emmet's life is part of his tombstone, but the audience itself must be his epitaph.

## The Triumph of the Easter Rising

As Emmet predicted, his legacy would inspire Irish nationalists for over a century to come. One of the young martyr's most devoted posthumous disciples was Patrick Pearse, who established his patriotic school in Rathfarnham and taught there during the six years leading up to the Easter Rising. Likewise, the impact of the Easter Rising—its rhetoric, its ambition, and its failure—on the generation of dramatists and directors that built the Gate Theatre cannot be understated. James Moran has observed that the Easter Rising was "one of the most talismanic moments in Irish history, and exerted a mesmerising effect in the modern Irish state whose very existence it had helped bring about."[83] Moreover, Chris Morash and Shaun Richards consider the 1916 Insurrection to be an example of a historical event that is spatially determined in a way that makes it "already appear theatricalised before it appears on stage," while Roisín Higgins describes the Rising as "an event that had been given poetic form even before it had taken place. . . . Pearse, Connolly and MacDonagh were alert to the theatrical and dramatic potential of what they were about to undertake."[84]

In the decade that followed Irish independence, dramatists engaged with this innate theatricality in various ways. The most controversial staging of the Rising was, of course, Sean O'Casey's *The Plough and the Stars* (1926), which, as Morash notes, treated the Rising with "blatant irreverence" and led to riots in the Abbey auditorium.[85] However, O'Casey's mordant depiction of cowards and prostitutes vis-à-vis Pearse's rallying speeches is a far cry from the account of the Rising that Micheál mac Liammóir portrays in the final episode of *The Ford of the Hurdles* (1929), which would be revived at the Gate as a stand-alone piece titled *Easter 1916* in 1930 and 1932 in a triple bill with *The Singer* by Patrick Pearse and *The Comedy of the Man who Married a Dumb Wife* by Anatole France. The press were ecstatic: the *Irish Times* called it "a powerful piece of symbolism, telling in impressionistic terms the tale of a week that began with bewilderment and anger, and ended in tragedy," while the *Irish Press* found it "hard to write critically" of the play, since it was "a fine, imaginative conception which expresses, not a conventional emotion, but a true comprehension of the event."[86] Likewise, the *Evening Mail* considered *Easter 1916* to embody "the justification of expressionism. In no other technique, one feels, could the events of that week, the aspirations that led up to them and the manner in which they reacted on the people, be so nobly and yet vividly represented."[87]

Indeed, the pageant's conclusion renders the pandemonium of insurrection in the wild colors of expressionism, with various ensembles of offstage voices contesting Ireland's cultural memories as they alternate between articulating and repressing the wrongs that she has suffered. The final episode presents the failed Easter Rising—rather than the successful War of Independence—as the culmination of a conflicted national teleology that spans twelve centuries, leading Elaine Sisson to interpret mac Liammóir's pageant as "a narrative of progression" that encapsulates his belief in "Ireland's manifest destiny."[88] In thus concluding Ireland's insurrectionary history, mac Liammóir employs markedly prospective and prescriptive memory strategies: the Minstrel embodies the revolutionary potential by which collective memories can transcend their traumatic origins to define the shape of Ireland's postcolonial narrative.

At the opening of *Easter 1916*, the Minstrel once again tries to rouse the citizens of Dublin, but this time, he is met not so much with incredulity as with passivity: "We have no wish to wake. . . . Is it not better to sleep? We are happier when we can sleep."[89] Nevertheless, the drums start rolling, and offstage voices declaring their support for Home Rule and the Irish Volunteers contend with cries like "God save Ireland and the King" and "Treason!" (7.1). A single man, identified only as the Strange Voice, stands in silhouette against a backdrop of the Dublin skyline and recites excerpts from the Proclamation of the Irish Republic and Roger Casement's speech at the Old Bailey.[90] However, the Strange Voice is not the only speaker: while shots are being fired and flames begin to rise around him, a cacophony of voices shout out in fear and exchange political statements (and Yeatsian intertexts) such as "Romantic Ireland's dead and gone" versus "Romantic Ireland's in the womb" (7.2–3). Unwaveringly, the Minstrel describes how "flames of black battle are rising, the red fire of war, and the white fire of peace!," and with his ultimate mnemonic appeal—"Forget not these words, forget not these men, children of Ath Cliath"—he finally receives an affirmative answer: "We hear, we will remember" (7.5).

Of course, this ostensible resolution can only be followed by an anticlimax, since the Rising itself was suppressed. Indeed, the Strange Voice recites words from the Surrender while the Minstrel, who, perhaps against his better judgment, still declares that "your dawn is breaking," faces general despair again: the citizens respond that it is merely "a dawn of new torture" (7.6). After the Voice has quoted a few lines from Patrick Pearse's "The Wayfarer," a single shot rings out and his silhouette drops, which incites the Minstrel to berate the Dublin citizens:

> Have you not seen? Have you not heard, oh blind, oh deaf, oh unremembering children of the Gael? Look up. For from this death-ridden glen of blood and of tears and of steel shall spring the birth of a new land, your daughter and your daughter's daughter, and all your bitterness and all your hatred be an evil dream that you have left behind. It is belief that will carry you on from where you have stood in your rags and your shame; and belief has been born in this fire that was lit by the dreams that your freedom will purge of their shadows they held in their hearts; and now, by the light of this, the newest dawn, I see the things that will come and that tell me that your need for me is passing. The flame of my message I have sheltered down the ages, until this time, when its light has been seen by all the peoples. My message is delivered.

Now I am no more than a minstrel who will sing these old songs to the people of my race for their remembering. (7.7)

The Minstrel's final speech thus not only hearkens back to Emmet's closing remarks about the end of his ministry, but also functions as a prospective eulogy. These words comprise a paradoxical reflection on Ireland's subjugation that substantiates the Rising as the hopeful embodiment of the nation's destiny despite its failure: the teleological implications of past catastrophes have finally been acknowledged through the play's performance, which makes a future vindication nothing less than inevitable. In this way, *The Ford of the Hurdles* offers a dramatic rendition of Ian McBride's observation that the Rising "facilitated the retrospective ordering of earlier rebellions into a cumulative sequence of inspirational defeats."[91]

As Elaine Sisson argues, the final episode of mac Liammóir's pageant illustrates that "the point of a re-enactment is not to extract a historical event from its moment of occurrence . . . but to smooth the narrative into an ordered, and easily understood, representation of that moment."[92] Indeed, *The Ford of the Hurdles* ends with an eclectic recital of lines from Thomas MacDonagh's "Marching Song of the Irish Volunteers" that not only articulates what Joan FitzPatrick Dean describes as a "hybrid Irish identity," but also promises an imminent conclusion to Irish history: "We Gael, we Dane, we Norman now / Have heard the word we waited long."[93]

While mac Liammóir's pageant reads like a belated incentive to would-be Irish revolutionaries in the vein of Pearse's drama, Denis Johnston proposed a much more explicitly *post*colonial performance of the Rising in "A National Morality Play" (1932), an article that was published in *Motley* under his pseudonym, E. W. Tocher.[94] Of course, Johnston had already abolished the fourth wall in *The Old Lady Says "No!"* (1929), but, in the second part of his *Motley* essay, he further expanded and problematized the notion of catering to an audience by proposing the yearly production of a massive history play that would have served to reframe Irish national identities each time it was performed anew. To be staged along the full length of O'Connell Street for the enjoyment and edification of thousands, this reenactment of the Rising was suggested to become

Ireland's "National Morality Play," since it "provide[d] a heroic theme as rich in dramatic values as anybody could wish."[95]

However, Johnston's general appeal—quite remarkably, he claimed to be addressing "a theme which is outside the realm of politics" altogether—did not meet with universal approbation: as Clair Wills has noted, the *Leader* immediately published an article to warn its readers that a congregation of the size that Johnston envisaged would lead to an influenza epidemic, to which Mary Manning issued an acerbic response in the subsequent issue of *Motley*.[96] Wills, observing the contentiousness of Johnston's proposal as well as the passivity of the audience that attended the revival of mac Liammóir's *Easter 1916*, argues that such reenactments of the Rising were attempts to "break down the boundary between stage and street, and render the audience actors in the drama, as they had so conspicuously failed to be fifteen years earlier."[97] Mac Liammóir and Johnston's desire for historical interaction and participation has also been interpreted in markedly political terms by Nicholas Allen, who labels Johnston's plan an attempt to "democratise the rising, beginning the process of political redistribution denied by the first years of a Free State obsessed with capital stability and military security."[98]

This communal relevance of historical reenactment is closely related to the nature of pageantry as a cultural phenomenon: in light of Joan Fitz-Patrick Dean's definition in her discussion of Irish pageantry, Johnston's proposal is another example of how such "paratheatrical events provided a vehicle to express identity and even a measure of celebrity to ordinary people."[99] Indeed, Dean has argued that this mode of historical engagement "takes on special importance during periods of momentous change," such as the anxious years that followed the War of Independence and the Civil War, when the Irish government "deployed pageantry to reinforce its legitimacy, to instill pride in its citizens, and to offer the popular imagination an alternative to an oppressive colonial history."[100]

Johnston's plan is especially interesting, however, in its preemptive incorporation of narrative change, which prefigures Emilie Pine's argument about how historical resolution can only be achieved through the "process of repetition that creates a ritual of the performance."[101] Johnston, too, proposed a renegotiation of collective cultural memories, suggesting that "years of patient experiment with constant cutting and alteration would be needed to perfect it as a spectacle."[102] In this sense, Johnston's proposal confirms James Moran's observation that representations of the Rising are often invested with a mode of "Freudian trauma; relating the story over and over again yet never being able to feel that is has been formulated adequately in a final definitive form."[103]

Johnston, then, sought to reinvigorate the articulation of collective memories by drawing on a traumatic episode in recent Irish history, and, more generally, his grand scheme exemplifies the Gate's complex interaction with contested legacies. Such articulations of what Moran, commenting on the different ways in which the Rising has been interpreted and appropriated, has termed "the equivocal and mutable nature of the event" could, in turn, suggest ways of performing the nation's past in the present with the aim of creating a less burdened Irish future.[104] Elaine Sisson corroborates this interpretation in her discussion of the Gate's productions of Pearse's *The Singer* and mac Liammóir's *Easter 1916* by arguing that "the cognitive dissonance involved in looking at a dead person and a live person as one (Mac Liammóir as Pearse) creates a flattening of time" that "presents a shared imaginative past but also an immediately accessible *now*." According to Sisson, the effectiveness of this attempt at exorcism is borne out by contemporary Irish drama, since "Pearse no longer appears a spectral figure in Irish drama, either as demagogue or messiah, although his presence threw a long shadow over the early years of state formation."[105]

Mac Liammóir's pageant and Johnston's proposal thus reveal attitudes toward postcolonial Ireland that are surprisingly constructive; as Chris Morash and Shaun Richards have observed, the unorthodoxy of mac Liammóir's "expansive spatial sense" in stage design and the audacity of Johnston's pageant proposal underwrite the notion that the Gate Theatre "constituted a differently imagined national space."[106] In this respect, Dean's characterization of both postindependence historiography as well as the Civic Week initiatives as attempts "to pose an alternative to the colonial status of Ireland by fashioning—sometimes from whole cloth—a master narrative of Irish achievement" are partially applicable to the Gate Theatre's construction of Ireland's historical teleology as well.[107] Both mac

Liammóir and Johnston carefully avoided the mistake of simply invert-ing Ireland's fixation on its troubled history by instead reinterpreting the nation's past as a deliberate construct that could be addressed through the performance of traumatic memories and infused with a new teleological function through confrontational repetition.

## Revolution and the Cult of Memory

Historicized confrontations also play an important, if not even more problematic, role in David Sears's *Juggernaut* (1929). In 1928, Sears, who had been one of Patrick Pearse's pupils at St. Enda's and became a veteran of both the Easter Rising as well as the War of Independence, won the Tailteann Games Prize in Drama with this three-act tragedy, which was set during the latter conflict. Somewhat surprisingly, the play was not picked up for production by the National Theatre, but became one of the more successful Abbey rejects that Hilton Edwards and Micheál mac Liammóir put on at the Gate. The play proved to be quite popular: the *Irish Independent* recorded a prodigious run despite the Easter Week break, while the *Evening Herald* noted the audience's "enthusiasm, the appearance of the author being clamoured for at the fall of the curtain."[108] According to the reviewer for the *Southern Star*, "The proved merits of Mr. Sears's play are claimant evidence that other than artistic consideration affect the judgment of the Abbey directorate, and in rejecting *Juggernaut* that body committed a mortal sin against the catholicity of Art from which their pretence to be directing a National Theatre cannot survive." Lauding the play's "good stage form" and the Gate actors' performances, this critic interpreted *Juggernaut* as a confirmation of the belief that "where the least spark of national spirit lingers it will burn up in the ultimate appeal."[109]

In his foreword to the play's belated 1952 publication, Maurice Walsh explicitly blamed Lady Gregory for the fact that *Juggernaut* "suffered a strange eclipse" and claimed that this was a grave injustice, for he regarded Sears's tragedy as "a play that should not be lost to Ireland, for it shows Irish life and an Irish family at the most critical time in all Irish his-tory—the year 1920–'21." Walsh backed up his belief in *Juggernaut*'s lasting significance by referring to its title, considering Sears's attempt to address the emotional ramifications of the War of Independence to have been a poignant demonstration of "what a stark thing nationality has to be in a fight to a finish, . . . [and] what gracious things of life have to be crushed under the inexorable wheels of this Juggernaut."[110]

Indeed, the necessity of spiritual—rather than bodily—sacrifice for a national cause constitutes the play's central theme, for *Juggernaut* concerns the tribulations of the Halpins, a middle-class family whose moderate Home Rule sympathies are put to the test when they have to choose between aiding or turning in Dermot Barry, a wounded IRA soldier who is on the run from the British Army. Barry's possession of a list containing the names of British intelligence officers divides the family: Mr. and Mrs. Halpin fear reprisals for either harboring a highly dangerous rebel or undermining the revolutionary cause, while their son Richard becomes inspired by Barry's nationalist zeal; their daughter Margery, however, threatens to expose the fugitive IRA soldier because she is in love with Captain Hardy, a British officer whose name is on Barry's list. With his bleak depiction of how this ethical dilemma tears the Halpin family apart, Sears offers a surprisingly nuanced discussion of various conflicting conceptualizations of Irish nationhood and the cultural memories on which they are based. The historical touchstones that Sears's characters come to internalize are prosthetic memories of an essential and inviolable notion of Irishness that serves to justify the characters' destructive actions. As such, these assimilated memories undermine the redemptive discourse that mac Liammóir and Johnston propagated in their respective plays on the 1803 rebellion and the Easter Rising.

In terms of its dramaturgical structure, *Juggernaut* offers an example of what Nicholas Grene describes as the "stranger-in-the-house" play, which is characterized by its depiction of "a room within a house, a family in the room, who together stand for normality, for ordinary family life; into that room there enters a stranger, and the incursion of that extrinsic, extraordinary figure alters, potentially transforms the scene," often in a way that is "*unheimlich*."[111] In *Juggernaut*, there are actually *three* alien elements in the Halpin household, for Dermot Barry's dramatic entrance is preceded by the arrival of two other visitors: the Frenchman Auriel, who was one of Richard's brothers-in-arms during World War I, and the British officer Hardy, who is seeking an opportune moment to propose to

Margery. Both soldiers make a faux pas during their respective introductions: Auriel, who initially waxes lyrical about how the "gallant nation [of Ireland had] rallied to the aid of her ancient ally, France" during the Great War, goes on to express his "admiration so great" for the IRA's brave struggle against the British Army.[112] His enthusiasm leads to cold reactions from Mrs. Halpin and Margery, who abhor what they consider to be the IRA's killing sprees, but the seemingly naive line of reasoning that explains his fervor—"I knew Ireland was fighting and I knew Richard. He is an Irishman and a soldier" (9)—actually foreshadows the more complex conceptualization of Irish nationalism that Dermot Barry articulates at a later stage.

Captain Hardy, too, is complicit with an overly simplified representation of nationhood at the outset of the play: when he first appears during a British raid of the Halpin household in search of the wanted IRA gunman, his superior officer declares that he will "teach you cursed Irish" a lesson; on being told that they are not harboring a fugitive (which, at that point, is true), he adds that he "wouldn't accept the oath of an Irishman" (14). Likewise, a sergeant in Hardy's company blatantly states that he doesn't "trust you Irish—you're all Shinners" (14). Hardy dismisses the sergeant for his slurs, but he does go on to provide the most explicit stereotype of Irishness himself—albeit one that suggests a sense of empowerment rather than disloyalty—when he reflects on how "everywhere I go I meet some subtle smiling Celt with a fluent tongue who always makes me feel that they regard me as a child to be humoured and amused" (40). Even before the IRA soldier has intruded into the Halpins' lives, then, the play already introduces several conflicting articulations of Irish identities, which serve as contrasting foils to offset the more elaborate discussion that Barry's plight produces.

While Auriel and Hardy characterize the Irish people from their outsiders' perspectives, the ways in which Mr. and Mrs. Halpin fail to differentiate between the opposing forces in the War of Independence and dismiss any suggestion of personal responsibility in the conflict are equally revealing. Mrs. Halpin, for example, calls the IRA "a nasty pack of murdering gunmen [who] have no respect for religion or decency and . . . would rather shoot a policeman—than drink," while her husband describes soldiers of the Auxiliary Division in strikingly similar terms when he talks about how "those blackguardly Black and Tans will get drunk and burn down the whole place" (9, 13). This shifty externalization of personal responsibility is even more clearly articulated when Mr. Halpin claims that "government men are the curse of this country"; he even accords them something tantamount to the status of a military mob by referring to them as "the Castle gang" (12). Likewise, Mrs. Halpin exhibits a paradoxical combination of naïveté and shrewdness when, one the one hand, she claims that she "do[esn't] believe any of the local people knew a thing" about Barry's counterintelligence mission, but, on the other, hopes that the Black and Tans will burn down the house of the Clerys or the Bradys, both of whom are neighbors of the Halpins, rather than their own, because "everybody knows they're Sinn Feiners" (13).

In the second act, these conflicting reflections on Irish nationhood, from Auriel and Hardy's generalizations to Mr. and Mrs. Halpin's dissociation, come together in a protracted discussion between Richard, Margery, and Dermot Barry about performing one's duty to one's country that reveals the revolutionary potential of assimilated memories. This is related to Chris Morash and Shaun Richards's exploration of the spatial implications that the stranger-in-the-house trope engenders with regard to the Old Woman in Yeats and Gregory's *Cathleen ni Houlihan* (1902), since she "enters what is effectively the mimetic onstage place of the stage from an offstage space that is conceptual, not mimetic."[113] In this sense, Barry's role is problematic as well, for he tries to assuage his very real physical presence—he is a wounded fugitive under clear emotional stress who knows that he will be tortured and hanged if he is caught—through a sense of depersonalization that relies on a strong belief in the existence of an essential and inviolable Irish identity. When Barry claims, for example, that he is "[entitled] to the help and protection of every Irish man and woman," the Halpin siblings attempt to refute the validity of this right by asking whether he would make the same demands of a Unionist family, but he counters their argument by stating that personal choice is an illusion in such matters: "There are thousands of years of unbroken national traditions behind me. Do you think you are stronger than the spirit of nationality?" (29–30).

Barry goes on to articulate a sense of transcendent nationhood which requires sacrifices that are spiritual rather than bodily, for he believes that "if freedom were bought with men's lives, it would be cheap enough" (31). Berating the Halpin siblings' complacent belief in fine distinctions, he argues that he is not only willing to give up his life for Ireland, but that he is also sacrificing his spiritual well-being, since the IRA's guerrilla tactics force him to murder collaborators and enemy agents in cold blood (32). His justification for this complete self-sacrifice derives from the "mandate, spoken and unspoken, of the Irish people" that he claims to have been given, since there is no public opposition to the IRA in Ireland. In counterpoint to Mr. and Mrs. Halpin's dissociated outlook on the war, Barry maintains that "the Irish people as a whole share the responsibility for every shot we fire" (32–33).

Ultimately, however, Barry's validation of his actions hinges not merely on the present political situation, but also on his internalization of Irish history. These prosthetic memories—and their prospective counterparts—explain Barry's final attempt at justifying his actions: when Margery pleads with him to at least leave behind the papers that will otherwise doom her beloved, he responds that "ten thousand years look down on you, ten thousand more are waiting expectantly. Who are you that I should sacrifice your nation's hopes for your sake?" (36). Despite this rejection, Margery comes to adopt Barry's line of reasoning as well: when she first confronts Barry with a portrait of an "ancestor of mine . . . [who] was one of O'Connell's chief lieutenants" and "wonder[s] if he found nationality so indifferent to human happiness," a quick glance at that same portrait when she is phoning Captain Hardy to reveal Barry's presence at their house dissuades her from disclosing the secret (35–37).

Her brother experiences a similar personal assimilation of Irish history through a constellation of strongly affective postmemories, leading him to reason that "if any generation of our forefathers had acted towards men like him as you propose to do, history would have condemned them. They say times are changing—conditions altered—but are they?" (43). This conflation of past and present causes him to fear that the current generation of Halpins are becoming "the first renegades of our name" (43) and even convinces him to lend his car to Barry so that the IRA soldier can attempt his escape. Barry's response to the Halpins siblings' help reveals a prospective and prescriptive mode of memory that constitutes a problematic exhortation to the audience, for the IRA soldier presents Cathleen ni Houlihan's song from Yeats and Gregory's eponymous play as an almost biblical imperative that has been decisively formulated in the past, that should therefore be adhered to in the present, and that should be honored without question in the future: "It is written 'They shall be remembered forever'" (52). In this sense, Barry implicitly confirms the fears that Yeats would come to voice in his final years: "I lie awake night after night / And never get the answers right. / Did that play of mine send out / Certain men the English shot?"[114]

In the end, Barry is able to pass through the British Army blockade with Richard's car and a special pass that Margery procures from Hardy; when the British officer finds out that he has been tricked, he bids Margery a bitter farewell, knowing that her choices have doomed him to be targeted by the IRA (54). Margery breaks down and bewails her spiritual sacrifice to the "inexorable Juggernaut," while Auriel tries to comfort her with the assurance that "patriotism is rarely a matter of marching to the sound of a trumpet. It is on such sacrifices as yours that the glory one calls nationhood is built" (55). However, in light of the image of Irish nationalism as a juggernaut, as a majestic but destructive vehicle that requires the individual to sacrifice him/herself to further its progress, Barry's earlier moment of doubt suggests an additional perspective on Irish identity formation. Before the siblings have decided to help him, Barry confides his personal reservations to Auriel, admitting that "if [the Halpins] can bring themselves to betray an Irish soldier to the British—then there is no meaning in nationality—it is a mere horrible illusion" (40). Despite his skepticism about the existence of free will in the face of historical teleologies, Barry's escape is ultimately effected by a tenuous choice—that is, by the whims of individuals who decide to heave and pull the juggernaut forward at great personal risk.

It has become clear, then, that the greater part of the patriotic appeals to memorialization that are posited in these plays are rendered problematic in their execution: in *Yahoo*, Swift's heroic legacy is almost effaced by Irish independence; in *Ascendancy*, Patrick's prosthetic memories lead him to murder his landlord; in *The Old Lady Says "No!"*, Emmet's epitaph can only be written in a violent delirium and constitutes no more than a blank imperative; in *The Ford of the Hurdles* and Johnston's pageant proposal, the destructive historical teleology that resulted in the Easter Rising requires constant reaffirmation; and, in *Juggernaut*, Margery suffers the death of her beloved and her own emotional breakdown as a result of her forced assumption of nationalist martyrdom. In this sense, these characters who attempt to bridge the gap between history and identity do not simply inherit, adopt, or embody memories *of* traumas that have to be reasserted time and again; they also experience these memories *as* traumas.

At the same time, however, the conflicted assimilations of Irish history that Edward Longford, Micheál mac Liammóir, Denis Johnston, and David Sears present in these plays suggest the possibility of exorcism. Women play important—albeit conflicting—roles in this process: in *Yahoo* and *Ascendancy*, Lady Maxwell, Fanny, Stella, and Vanessa undermine male dominance, while in *The Ford of the Hurdles* and *Juggernaut*, the Voices of Women and Margery function as moral compasses. The role of Sarah Curran, who doubles as the Flower Woman in *The Old Lady Says "No!"*, is an amalgamation of both propensities: she not only reveals the Speaker as a fraud and deludes him during his quest, but she also forces him to finally efface his own legacy and thereby breaks the stranglehold of his cult of personality over the modern Irish nation.

In more general terms, the very existence of the Irish Free State also implies the exorcism of traumatic memories: for better or for worse, it constitutes the terminus of a revolutionary teleology that spanned centuries. For the Gate's playwrights, these episodes of armed rebellion and sectarian strife might still demand expression, subsisting as haunting specters and even requiring acknowledgment as constitutive events, but they were also in Ireland's past. What its future would look like was yet to be determined, and this understanding of the formative yet flexible quality of the nation's history was thus accorded an important role in the nation's postcolonial identity formation.

Indeed, if Irish Studies scholars have quoted Stephen Dedalus's maxim that "history . . . is a nightmare from which I am trying to awake" all too often, these Gate playwrights provide a reason for going through the motions again: although their particular brand of historicism cannot resolve Joyce's dichotomy, it does undermine it.[115] Even if it were possible to awake from the nightmare, that act would constitute the denial of history and therefore the rejection of constitutive memories and identities, which would, in a word, entail oblivion—but once the oppressed sleeper becomes aware that his inescapable reverie might be altered and molded with each performative reiteration, he morphs into a lucid dreamer who has the power to change the dream to his liking.

# 6

## Identity after Independence
### Class and Social Geography in Postrevolutionary Ireland

In his "Modern Architecture and National Identity in Ireland" (2005), Hugh Campbell discusses the Irish pavilion building for the 1939 World Fair in New York. Ostensibly, the design by Michael Scott, who had been commissioned by Edwards and mac Liammóir in 1930 to transform the Rotunda Hospital's concert wing into the Gate Theatre, was "a sleek and sinuous form clad in concrete and glass," but there was more to it than met the eye: "Only from the air would it become clear that the building had a shamrock-shaped plan."[1] As Campbell argues, such attempts at "reconciling the imperatives of nationalism and of modernism within a single representative form" were not merely architectural conundrums: more broadly, they illustrated that "once independence had been achieved, the challenge was to make the model of the nation—what Edward Said calls its 'geographical identity'—a reality."[2]

In the wake of the Civil War (1922–23), a wide range of political organizations promoted their visions for realizing this incarnation. Cumann na nGaedheal and Fianna Fáil were the most prominent parties in the democratic arena, while paramilitary groups such as the ACA and the IRA took to the streets. In their various ways, these organizations demonstrated that

Parts of this chapter have previously appeared in Van den Beuken, "'Three cheers for the Descendency!': Middle-Class Dreams and (Dis)illusions in Mary Manning's *Happy Family* (1934)" in *Navigating Ireland's Theatre Archive: Theory, Practice, Performance*, ed. Barry Houlihan (Oxford: Peter Lang, 2019), 141–57. ISBN: 978-1-78707-372-2. Reprinted by permission of the editor and publisher.

their respective "models of the nation" were as conservative as they were irreconcilable. As Chris Morash describes, the cultural climate of the Free State, which was marked by these political confrontations as well as by widespread economic hardship, came to be "dominated by a harsh tone of disappointment, shot through with a resentment that the young should be sacrificed for the ideals and cravings of a previous generation."[3] Richard Pine captures the anxiety that underlies such bitterness with a theatrical metaphor for the state of Ireland during these troubled decades, observing that the Free State was "a persona, a debatable and dangerous entity: three million characters in search of stage directions."[4]

As Morash's reference to an earlier generation already suggests, the default strategy in finding the newly independent nation's bearings was clinging to the past in ways that Denis Johnston's *The Old Lady Says "No!"* literalized: Robert Emmet's wanderings through contemporary Dublin reveal how the playwright portrayed Ireland's historical fixation as a stranglehold on its future development. Johnston's version of Emmet's final soliloquy eschews the monolithic constructions of Irishness that generally problematized the nationalist rhetoric that various parties in the Free State continued to use, thereby undermining the rebel's subsequent martyrdom. Rather, it was the epitaph of silence imposed by Johnston on his audience that might serve to release the Irish nation from its turbulent history. While Johnston's play thus exemplified how the Gate stage facilitated compelling encounters—cathartic or otherwise—with Ireland's past, it also showed the critical potential of staged representations of contemporary Irish society.

As a result of this confluence, many original Gate plays that are set in the Free State and in the years leading up to World War II were equally concerned with the memory structures that also molded the mythological and historical plays analyzed in previous chapters. By holding up a mirror to their audiences, this subset of the Gate's repertoire of original plays reveals how depictions of contemporary Ireland likewise reassessed the cultural memories of rebellion and strife that persisted in Irish society during the 1920s and 1930s. Indeed, the Gate plays that are examined in this chapter underwrite the continuing relevance of history and memory in an independent state that had, by definition, arrived at the end of the teleology that Irish nationalists had outlined and affirmed for generations.

It is ironic, then, that with the birth of the Free State, the political ideals that had been sanctified as the common cause of the Irish people quickly disintegrated, leading to violent disputes between opposing paramilitary factions. Such pervasive discord revealed that the fundamental unanimity professed and enshrined by Irish revolutionaries from Wolfe Tone to De Valera had been illusive at best. Sociologically, this is not surprising: as Joe Cleary observes, the various "axes of Irish socio-cultural division" have been partially complicit with conflicted notions of progress, since "the temporalities and values of the modern and the pre-modern . . . have routinely been mapped in Ireland not only to the topography of the country (the modern identified with the urban, industrial northeast, and the eastern seaboard; tradition or the pre-modern with the country, with agriculture, the West and the islands), but onto the island's religious or sectarian denominations as well."[5] In glossing over such differences, more traditional concepts of class were likewise ignored, leading Michael Pierse to conclude that "class cohesion became an expedient element in consolidating political stability at a time of national crisis, with the major political parties consequently eager to downplay social inequalities and to cement loyalty to the fledgling state."[6]

Onstage, such disregard could be questioned, however, and indeed the dramatic tensions that feature in these contemporary Gate plays derive less from plot-driven conflicts between individual characters than from the fragmented state of postindependence Irish society. Consequently, the most important fault lines in these dramas are caused by issues of class and social geography that either originated from or were exacerbated by the demographic changes that occurred after the signing of the Anglo-Irish Treaty in 1921. Playwrights such as Christine Longford, Mary Manning, T.C. Murray, and Robert Collis addressed the respective standings of the upper, middle, and lower classes in the new Irish state, as well as the contrasts between urban and rural communities, in their attempts to reconfigure various conflicting monolithical notions of Irishness that were current in the 1930s. The plays discussed in this chapter depict the changing fortunes of various social classes in Ireland, and the following three sections are accordingly structured to analyze the ways in which the Ascendancy, the middle class, and the proletariat struggled to come to terms with the political, cultural, and religious reality of an independent nation that was still burdened by collective memories of violence and strife.

## Rebels without a Cause?

However, before discussing various dramatic representations of this three-fold social stratification, Denis Johnston's second Gate play serves to introduce the attendant conflicts between class, social geography, and memory in contemporary Ireland, since it offers a political allegory of the Free State's pathological introspection. First produced in 1933, *A Bride for the Unicorn* was written by a playwright who, in a later preface to his collected works, resigned himself to being perpetually associated with questions of class and national identity, admitting that he had "given up the Augean task of denying that I am a decayed relic of an ascendancy class, or that I am attempting to raise a laugh at the expense of my singularly unfunny country."[7] Of course, such accusations had mostly been directed at Johnston's authorship of *The Old Lady Says "No!"*, which explicitly addresses—and ridicules—key themes in Irish history and contemporary society. *A Bride for the Unicorn*, however, seems much less politically engaged; in a separate preface to the play, Johnston himself claimed that his second Gate production presented "a symbol of Man, himself . . . [,] as a creature that is born, that struggles for its right to Be, . . . and that spends his life seeking for what he conceives to be his Fulfilment, while at the same time professing his fears for the natural denouement of Death."[8] If anything, then, Johnston chose to describe *A Bride for the Unicorn* as a philosophical parable, or even, as Richard Cave observes, "the trauma of a modern psyche," but the play's implicit setting in the Free State—which can be gleaned from various indirect references to Ireland's turbulent history—also invites a reading of Johnston's tragicomedy as a political critique of the collective memories (and associated teleologies) that imbued contemporary conceptualizations of Irish nationhood.[9]

Not unlike *The Old Lady Says "No!"*, Johnston's second Gate play presents a string of episodes that are only linked tangentially and, prefiguring the unstable identities of the cast in *The Dreaming Dust* (1940), features a group of characters who vaguely resemble Jason and the Argonauts but whose names and identities are in constant flux. Johnston's own summary of the play's "Argument" that prefaced the revised 1935 edition serves as well as any plot description:

> This is the story of the strange adventure of John Foss; of the proposal that was made to him one Christmas Eve; of the manner of his acceptance, and of his subsequent transformation; of how he lost his love in the morning and with his seven doughty companions set out in the world to find her once again; of what befel [sic] them there; of his despair at the march of the seasons and his ever-growing fear that death would overtake him while his quest was still unfinished; and how at last, upon another winter's night, he found again the object of his desire and learnt her secret.[10]

The responses to this "strange adventure" were varied. While the critic for the *Irish Times* praised the play's "superb staging, . . . both in the actual construction of sets, and in the lighting and grouping," he found *A Bride for the Unicorn* to be "a very odd affair, indeed," noting that Johnston's "satire is delightful and vigorous on various aspects of life; but, however brilliantly informative these scenes are, they are not fused into a whole, and seem to be more in the nature of isolated sketches than part of a play." All in all, the critic felt that the play was "a courageous experiment, even if it cannot be considered an altogether successful one."[11] In the same newspaper, however, the "Irishman's Diary" labeled *A Bride for the Unicorn* as "something that, if not a really great play, is very close to it" and claimed that "one of these days [Johnston] will write a play which will leave all the O'Caseys, the Eugene O'Neills and the like in the halfpenny place."[12]

At the beginning of the play, John is working as a gentlemen's tailor, when a tailor's dummy—also known as the Drunk Swell—comes alive and introduces him to a Masked Lady. John is seduced by her sensuous bliss, and, after she disappears, he tries to enlist his old school friends (the Argonauts) to find her again. The rest of the play comprises various composite scenes from their adult lives that depict the companions' private and professional achievements and disappointments as John tries to fulfill his desperate quest. This dizzying succession of stock exchanges, living rooms, pubs, and courtrooms, through which the characters wander with varying degrees of understanding and recognition, is further accentuated by moments in which the fourth wall is broken: one of John's friends, for example, starts fishing out into the audience.[13]

Despite *A Bride for the Unicorn*'s seemingly chaotic temporal structure, to which the abrupt changes in the characters' ages and functions testify, the passage of time is one of Johnston's central motifs. Throughout the play, a magical pendulum, which is set in motion by the Drunk Swell in the play's prelude, is suspended above the stage to keep track of John's fateful quest. Although the Swell ostensibly winds this clock to underline the importance of the singular moment—"in the twinkling of an eyelid to-morrow will be sundered from yesterday and out will fly a golden butterfly—the present"—its looming presence and its intrinsic status as a time-keeping instrument serve to create an artificial continuity between the discrepant episodes.[14] No less importantly, the clock's inevitable march toward midnight suggests that this desire for perpetual immediacy is, in fact, strongly inflected by the past and the future.

The play's frequent mythological and historical references illustrate this point: Leonard, one of John's companions, refers to "Niam [*sic*] of the Golden Hair, daughter of the King of Tir na nOg," who was "was stolen away from her lover" (A, 61) and the titles of various scenes (such as "Gods and Fighting Men" [A, 66], a direct reference to Lady Gregory's eponymous book) likewise take their cues from Irish mythology.[15] Recent history is also important to Johnston's argument: Hercules Limited, a sham investment opportunity that "will not only be a national asset, . . . [but also] a national necessity" (A, 93) seeks to once again exploit the financial system that led to the global economic meltdown of 1929, which had occurred only a few years before the play's premiere. The play also features even darker references to Irish history, with one drunkard in a pub exclaiming that "I am Hunger. I am a rending, screeching emptiness. I am the first and last of living. How do you like that?" (A, 120). While this characterization might seem to be a psychological or existentialist statement rather than an oblique reference to the Great Famine, it is historically substantiated by John's subsequent cry of despair, which clearly employs a key trope from accounts of the Famine: "The earth is full of graves. Where can I run?" (125).

However, Johnston's most significant engagements with the darker pages in Irish history are to be found in his references to (and satirical depiction of) recent armed conflicts such as the Easter Rising, the Civil War, and contemporary paramilitary tensions. In the ninth scene of *A Bride for the Unicorn*, a farcical courtroom drama suddenly transforms into a no less ridiculous onstage portrayal of political violence when Bernard "proclaim[s] this Court suspended by Order of the competent military authority. . . . Martial Law has been proclaimed this evening. A state of national emergency has been announced" (A, 142) because the Hercules investment scheme has collapsed. The action segues into a scene titled "The Harvest of the Dragon's Teeth," which, in the revised 1935 version, became "The Scythe and the Sunset"—a phrase that Johnston would reuse in 1958 as the title of a play that engaged with Sean O'Casey's depiction of the 1916 insurrection in *The Plough and the Stars* (1926). Both titles, then, refer to the flag that the Irish Citizen Army used during the Easter Rising, and while the precise nature of the conflict in *A Bride for the Unicorn* remains unspecified, the 1935 version in particular provides copious hints: for example, John observes that "when the world is mad, schoolboys come back into their own" (B, 271)—an unambiguous reference to Patrick Pearse's enlistment of his St. Enda's pupils for the revolutionary cause in 1916. The subsequent discussions between John and his commanding officer nevertheless highlight the cognitive dissonance of Free State politics in the 1930s, for most attempts to dispel the impending threat of widespread paramilitary violence constitute little more than ridiculous quarrels over the exact terms in which the grim circumstances are to be phrased in public: "Headquarters wishes to impress upon all ranks that this force is not engaged upon a War. That word must not on any account be used by the troops or in any official communications. These are merely Precautionary Military Operations for the Preservation of the Peace, abbreviated to P.M.O.P.P." (B, 271).

Johnston does succeed in distilling the Civil War and its lasting effects on Irish society into a single confrontation that reveals the utter senselessness of internecine strife. After John's legacy has been affirmed (he is promised that his name "will be carved by public subscription on the wall of the gymnasium and rhetorically referred to every year at the annual distribution of prizes"), he goes off to battle, where he comes face to face with his old friend Egbert (B, 272). Both soldiers burst out laughing, and John inquires, "What are you doing here?," to which Egbert responds that he is "fighting. I'm the enemy. That's funny, isn't it" (B, 273). When Egbert points out that John was about to kill him, John defends himself rather weakly—"I didn't know you were anybody in particular"—but Egbert's retort is much more revealing: "Isn't everybody someone in particular?"(B, 274). In this way, Johnston articulates a sense of identity that celebrates individualism and diversity rather than mindless conformity to the monolithic yet contradictory constructions of Irishness for which the various warring parties are willing to shed the blood of their countrymen. Indeed, John and Egbert realize how brothers have turned on each other to perpetuate a legacy of political violence that should have become redundant with the establishment of the Free State when, in a conflation of a key episode from the myth of Jason and the Argonauts with the current state of affairs in Ireland, they recoil in horror from their native soil: "Look at these fields sown with dragon's teeth, where only the fortunate are still and silent, and where the luckless lie crying with crooked mouths for sleep. This is a sorry harvest home to mark the autumn of the year."[16] In light of the conventional fetishization of the nation's "four green fields," this grim representation of the Irish countryside as a ghastly, barren wasteland thus illustrates the destructive effects of civil strife.

When Bernard, John's commanding officer, reappears and demands that John executes Egbert, he refuses—"Why should I kill to save the scheme of things for fools to play with?"—and then refers back to an earlier conversation (with the Drunk Swell in the 1933 version, and with Egbert in the 1935 version) about his first sweetheart, to whom he would not pledge undying love: "'Not for ever,' I told her, 'that would not be love. The magic of happiness is that it has beginning and ending'" (B, 277–78). This reiterated declaration has grown in importance over the course of the play, and, when it is first expressed by John in the fifth scene, it is already wedged in between various explicit uses of memory strategies in a way that subtly intertwines cultural memory, historical trauma, and political nationalism to eventually make a powerful statement concerning Ireland's teleology during the play's conclusion.

In that earlier scene, this imbrication is initially articulated through the gradual development of John's stance on memorialization. At the beginning of the scene, John is still following the Swell's advice to embrace the present; when he inquires after his earlier love affairs—"Don't tell me you got through all these years without some little foolishness. . . . There were dances—you were young"—John ignores such reflections on the past: "Why trouble me with memories? . . . That is nothing to me now" (A, 76). The Swell insists, however, and John reflects on the foolishness of his first love, cynically commanding him to "see that it's not allowed to slip the public memory" (A, 78). While this prescriptive statement might seem to be a throwaway remark, John's subsequent reflections on the obsessive yet ultimately irrelevant nature of such misdirected fervor embeds the memory of his earliest passion in a political context. As such, John's diatribe against blind zeal serves to critique the absolutism of nationalist rhetoric: "Other people's grand passions are so supremely ridiculous, but our own are always so serene. . . . What is this thing that moves us all so deeply, and yet is really only fit for laughter?" (A, 78). In this way, Denis Johnston echoes James Joyce's denunciation of aggressive patriotism that Stephen Dedalus voices when he states that he "fear[s] those big words . . . which make us so unhappy."[17]

Ironically, however, it is precisely the expansiveness and grandiloquence of John's outburst (especially in the more strongly accentuated 1935 version) that ultimately reveals the paradox that lies at the heart of Irish nationalism when he tells Doris, his old sweetheart, that he is sick of wooing her: "Enough of clichés. . . . Your flesh is nobler than a struggle with decay. And when the empty years have fled what incense will be offered to your withered chastity?" (B, 221). Doris is appalled by John's harsh words, and her plea for constancy—"But John . . . will you love me always? . . . for ever?"—is debunked by her former lover as a horrifyingly static and inert demand: "God forbid! Not for ever. That would not be love. The magic of happiness is that it must have beginning and ending" (B, 221; ellipses in original). Like Doris, the current incarnations of Irish nationalism suffer from an anti-teleological obsession: even though the cause of Irish nationalism had already been achieved with the establishment of the Free State, its adherents refuse to accept the obsolescence of martyrdom.

To underwrite this statement, John employs an explicit imperative in addressing Doris—"Let me endow you with a memory"—but in a remarkable variation on this strategy, this prescriptive statement undermines its prospective potential. Rather than stipulating a specific object of commemoration that would only serve to perpetuate the fatalistic cult of memory, John claims that Doris—and, by extension, Ireland—"can work miracles beyond the power of prophets" (B, 222–23). Johnston thus accords a significance to Irish national identity formation that exceeds conventional conceptualizations: beyond the hackneyed prospects of everlasting insurrectionary glory that Irish nationalists still espouse lies the real freedom to develop cultural identities that are unfettered by such one-dimensionally infinite historical teleologies.

As has been observed above, John repeats the importance of demarcations when he meets Egbert on the battlefield, and in the play's final scene, the past and the future are likewise stripped of their unconditional validity as the clock approaches midnight. While John is desperate to find the Masked Woman again, his first love, Doris, implores him to forsake his quest. John reveals that he has finally discarded the temporal absolutes that had chained him before: "The past is dead and my children are living. I can do nothing for the dead, and can never owe more to my children than they owe to me" (B, 296). No longer wishing to "worship words" and the conventions that they represent, John ironically declares his desire to martyr himself to experience the ultimate bliss of looking upon the face of the Masked Woman. In the 1935 version, she reveals herself but keeps her back to the audience as John accepts his demise: "I have captured the heart of my dreams! I, who have run screaming from shadows! . . . Nothing could rob me of my love but Death, but if my love, herself, be Death, oh terrors, where are you now!"[18] John thereby experiences a defiant and otherworldly apotheosis similar to the Speaker's death in *The Old Lady Says "No!"*, and in this case, too, the ultimate imperative is a conclusion rather than a continuation. Just as the Doctor silences the audience to finally bring an end to Emmet's violent legacy, Doris uses this play's closing lines to express the necessity of embracing terminations: "Oh save us, Phoebus, from the fear of Endings!" (B, 300).

*A Bride for the Unicorn*, then, exchanges the composite character of Sarah Curran, the Old Flower Lady, and Cathleen ni Houlihan from *The Old Lady Says "No!"* for the combination of Doris and the mysterious Masked Lady to articulate a similar desire for mnemonic catharsis. Despite its faults, the Irish Free State was to be acknowledged as the fulfillment, and therefore the abolition, of the radical national teleology that Irish republicans had espoused for centuries. Therefore, contemporary attempts to perpetuate that line of thinking (as embodied by various paramilitary organizations) were, by definition, paradoxical, if not destructive. Johnston shows how the "august destiny to which [Ireland] is called," in the words of the leaders of the Easter Rising, had become a nebulous construct that was abused by politicians to impose their narrow conceptualizations of Irishness—the words that they worship—on the nation.[19] In this sense, the tensions that Johnston accentuates illustrate Elaine Sisson's observation that "the bitter legacy of the Civil War meant that decolonisation was a painful process, fraught with contradictions and uncertainties as to what type of nation Ireland might be."[20] As such, *A Bride for the Unicorn* is an oblique and a more abstract articulation of the desire to exorcise the ghost of Irish rebellion: while *The Old Lady Says "No!"* offers a direct confrontation with Ireland's past, Johnston's second Gate play makes a no less powerful statement about the country's future.

### The Decline of the Ascendancy

While Johnston represents the vicissitudes of recent Irish history—as well as their political implications for the nation's future—mostly through satirical jests embedded in philosophical discourse, several other contemporary Gate plays were more explicit in their problematization of the issues of class and social geography. This is not meant to imply, though, that *A Bride for the Unicorn* ignores these topics completely. At the end of the 1935 version of the play, for example, John's former schoolteacher, now an old man, articulates the deep division between urban and rural life that supposedly characterizes the Irish state when he declares himself still "anxious to discover a respectable mythology" and observes that "now as the years are fading, I have found peace of mind, and a deeper sense of the mystery of earth and sky, in the care of a quiet, horse-loving Parish in a rural district."[21] This overly mystical turn toward the pastoral makes a playful jab at the ways in which the Anglo-Irish upper classes attempted to identify themselves as unambiguously Irish after their loyalties had been called into question during the recent decade of rebellion and civil strife.

Such issues of social stratification, historical determination, and geographical divide play important roles in two more realistic plays about upper-class life in the Free State: Christine Longford's *Mr. Jiggins of Jigginstown* (1933) and Mary Manning's *Youth's the Season—?* (1931). Both plays depict the decline of the Anglo-Irish aristocracy and their attempts to craft an alternative teleology in the face of their looming obsolescence in the new societal order. Christine Longford's comedy initially lampoons such efforts as calculated affectations of national pride, but the last act of *Mr. Jiggins of Jigginstown* establishes the possibility of bridging the gulfs between various classes and religious groups. While Mary Manning's play features an equally comical representation of the youngest generation of the bourgeoisie, whose nihilistic bohemianism proves to be readily complicit with neoimperialism, the final scene of *Youth's the Season—?* ends on a much darker note as it violently renounces the notion that the Ascendancy has any meaningful legacy in an independent Ireland. In exploring various conflicting conceptualizations of Irishness, Longford and Manning not only address such problematical notions of class and social geography; they also articulate the cultural memories of sectarian violence that reinforced them.

In *Mr. Jiggins of Jigginstown* (1933), three parties struggle to secure their inheritance of a sizeable estate in the Midlands region that is owned by Mr. Jiggins, an elderly and somewhat eccentric bachelor. In the first act, his cousin Georgiana and her two children, Geraldine and Hugo, arrive at Jigginstown from London with high hopes of convincing their aging relative to bequeath them his estate. Their efforts are subtly thwarted by Richard, another of Mr. Jiggins's cousins and a local landowner, who is keen to expand his property. To Richard's delight, Mr. Jiggins soon reveals his utter distaste for the foppish London set and hints at leaving the estate to Richard instead. The young man's candidacy suffers a blow, however, when Reverend Duckworth reveals that Richard has refused to provide aid to a destitute family who are living on his neighboring estate, which causes Mr. Jiggins to become appalled at Richard's lack of charity.

A few days later, Mr. Jiggins's relatives quarrel violently over dinner, and when all of them decide to abandon their pursuits for the time being, Reverend Duckworth swoops in with an alternative solution to Mr. Jiggins's conundrum: he suggests that the estate's funds be employed in due course to establish a school at Jigginstown. While Mr. Jiggins is enthusiastic about this suggestion, it soon becomes clear that Duckworth will not deign to accept Catholics, and the elderly landlord ultimately writes his testament in dejection. The final act is set several months later: shortly after Mr. Jiggins's funeral, his will is read out, which stipulates that the whole estate is not to be inherited by any of the claimants, but will be bequeathed to the Department of Education for the establishment of a school for children of all religions. The claimants (with the exception of Geraldine) bicker over this gross violation of the rights of inheritance and try to convince the executor that Mr. Jiggins was insane. A loud scream by the cook pierces this chaos: a fox has entered the kitchen, suggesting that Mr. Jiggins's prediction that he would be reincarnated as a fox has come true.

Even though Longford's depiction of this testamentary scurry is largely farcical, her play also explores the ways in which Ireland's independence had overhauled the nation's rigid social stratification. In this sense, Mr. Jiggins's childlessness serves as a metaphorical representation of the end of the old order: irrevocably deprived of the authority that had allowed them to dominate Irish politics and society for centuries, the Anglo-Irish upper classes are forced to consider their legacy. Accordingly, the three potential alternatives that Mr. Jiggins entertains are speculative attempts to resolve this issue. Bequeathing the estate to the London set, whose supposedly Irish affectations are shallow efforts to veil the dangers of neoimperialism, is hardly preferable to allowing Richard to expand his lands, which would entail the rampant exploitation of the lower classes by capitalist opportunists. The third scenario—allowing Reverend Duckworth to establish a school for Protestants—would also undermine the local community, since the clergyman's plans represent the dangers of exacerbating sectarian tensions in postindependence Ireland. The popular sentiments as well as various memories of civil strife that underlie the three options that Mr. Jiggins contemplates reveal how Longford's comedy subtly addresses the roles of bogus nationalism, class division, and religious discrimination in the Free State and tries to offer an alternative solution to the decline of the Ascendancy.

The reviewers who attended the play's premiere acknowledged these aspects in varying degrees. After applauding the playwright, the producer and the actors alike in the *Irish Independent*, David Sears somewhat hyperbolically claimed that the play "added a new character to the immortals of the Irish stage." Sears also reflected on Longford's depiction of the Free State, stating that she "writes about Ireland without a trace of self-consciousness. The play is intensely Irish in atmosphere, and though Lady Longford seems to have few illusions about either Irish or English her humour is always good-natured."[22] In the *Irish Times*, however, an anonymous critic described *Mr. Jiggins of Jigginstown* as "a pleasant, though unpretentious study of a harmless eccentric in an Irish setting." Considering the plot to simply be "a convenient peg on which to hang the characters," the critic did praise the actors and observed that "Lady Longford has certainly hit the nail on the head in her study of Georgiana—the Irish-born lady with the Kensington outlook."[23]

Indeed, during the play's opening scene, the snobbish bigotry and neoimperialist collusion that serve to caricature the financially motivated Anglo-Irish absentees become readily apparent through Georgiana's demeanor: she is Mr. Jiggins's cousin and the primary claimant to his estate. Mrs. Georgie Jiggins immediately foregrounds the class disparities that will continue to simmer over the course of the play by endorsing a markedly dichotomous social stratification: "How can you expect anyone to travel on the railways? The upper classes will go by car, and now the lower classes have the buses."[24] Mrs. Jiggins's bafflement is symptomatic of her chauvinism and is shown to resonate on various levels: her elderly cousin's considerations in upgrading his servants' living quarters are completely lost on her, and, on a grander scale, she professes her belief that "the Sweepstake money ought not to be given to the lower classes, who don't know what to do with it. It ought to be divided up among the poor gentry like ourselves" (274).

While Mrs. Jiggins's asinine aloofness is a comic foil for Mr. Jiggins's sensibility, her lack of solidarity is contextualized in much darker historical terms when the butler remarks that "she was nervous of coming since the troubles" (271) of the War of Independence and the Civil War. Likewise, these conflicts resonate during a discussion of recent social unrest in Cyprus when Mrs. Jiggins brusquely observes that "there was some trouble, but it's well over now. There were only a few agitators, and we've clapped them into jail. There's nothing like a firm hand."[25] The naïveté of Mrs. Jiggins's cozy imperialist doctrine echoes widespread British sentiments with regard to the Easter Rising, illustrating how the upper classes have yet to come to terms with the legitimacy of Ireland's autonomy.

No less revealingly, Mrs. Jiggins's struggles to acknowledge Ireland's independence and modernity are shown to be at odds with the Irish nationalism that she feigns in an attempt to secure her inheritance. She is utterly unaware of the introduction of censorship and gun laws in the Free State and betrays her vapid materialism when she remarks that it is awfully "nice . . . to be in an Irish Country House again. Plenty of everything still" (274, 276). Her contrived Irishness is undermined, however, when she unabashedly declares that she "hope[s] we shall be able to wrangle a job for [her son Hugo] in the Colonial Service, if there are any colonies left" (274). This neoimperialism also surfaces when she asks Mr. Jiggins whether he has "turned Sinn Feiner," to which he responds by celebrating inclusiveness over political squabbles: "Are we not all Sinn Feiners nowadays?" (276). Nevertheless, Mrs. Jiggins is appalled at how "this country's going from bad to worse" now that members of the Ascendancy have come to espouse Republican sentiments, and she feels prompted to betray her imperialist sympathies: in an idiosyncratic modification of the German *Dolchstoßlegende*, she affirms her belief that "we gave up Ireland" and bluntly declares herself a "British subject" (276–77).

While this precarious situation is defused for the time being, tensions flare up again during the second act when Mrs. Jiggins undergoes a mock arrest by two philosophical vagabonds who wander around Mr. Jiggins's estate. Grossly offended, the landlord's cousin rages about how "this would never have happened in the old days under the old R.I.C. Such splendid fellows they were, and most obliging" (292). To an Irish audience, of course, such references to the RIC would hardly evoke the image of jovial constables; rather, they serve to recall the war crimes that several infamous subdivisions of the RIC, such as the Auxiliaries and the Black and Tans, committed during the War of Independence, thereby further underscoring Mrs. Jiggins's dangerous ignorance of historical realities. When she confronts Mr. Jiggins with the men's behavior, since she does not dare to believe that he actually "spend[s] [his] time with these natives," Mr. Jiggins once again propounds a more inclusive notion of Irishness: "We are natives ourselves. I was born at Jigginstown and I believe you were born in Dublin, Georgie" (293). Mrs. Jiggins's exasperated response demonstrates how such problematizations of national identities are, in fact, interwoven with issues of social stratification and religious strife: "You have gone back on your class, Horatio. You are letting us down. It's a question of prestige. . . . It's what I've always said about Irish Protestants. United we stand, divided we fall" (293).

In light of Mrs. Jiggins's desire for clear social demarcations, her cousin's reply might seem all too idealistic—"Should not the nation be united?"—but this optimism illustrates that Mrs. Jiggins wants to accept neither an independent nor a pluralistic Ireland: "Nation indeed! How can you call it a nation?" (293). Mr. Jiggins cleverly rebukes this wholesale dismissal by employing an argumentative strategy that is simultaneously celebratory and trivializing. One the one hand, he taps into the pastoral discourse of national identity construction by waxing lyrical that "we were born in the same country, Georgie, you and I and these men. We have watched the light changing on the same lakes and the same mountains. . . . We get our living from the same soil, poor though it is" (293–94). Of course, such rustic sentimentalism is refused by Mrs. Jiggins, to whom this idea is utterly repellent: "Do you mean to say that I have the same habits of mind as the native Irish?" (294). In an effective countermove, Mr. Jiggins then modulates to a very different register by echoing the stereotypes that his cousin would attribute to the Irish lower classes to debunk her bigotry: "The very same my dear. Do you not carry a gun? . . . You are jealous and hot-tempered and ambitious. . . . And you are fond of strong drink" (294). Mrs. Jiggins is forced to concede defeat; at dinner a few days later, she only comes up with a blatantly inappropriate riposte: "We must be going back to London tomorrow. 'Exiles of Erin,' you know."[26]

Mrs. Jiggins's reactionary politics prove rather wearisome to her cousin, and her two children fare little better in offering him encouraging perspectives. If Mr. Jiggins were to bequeath his estate to Hugo, the future owner of Jigginstown would be a dim-witted, fledgling "missionary of British Culture" for whom "studying the properties of the soil, on which depends the crops and the forestry and the stockrearing" (276), as Mr. Jiggins propounds, has very little appeal. Indeed, his mother, who does most of the talking for her morose son, simply dismisses Mr. Jiggins's fixation on agriculture with an offhand remark: "Very wise, I'm sure" (278). While her daughter, Geraldine, is much quicker on the uptake, she mainly revels in self-pity, living as she does "on Mummy's pension in a poky little flat in Kensington," which is "frightfully pathetic"—a view that is summarily dismissed by Mr. Jiggins in a manner that once again suggests a passionate historical awareness on his part, since "they know nothing [of poverty], less than nothing" (279, 290).

Over the course of a week, however, Geraldine claims that she has come to embrace her Irishness. Even though she admits that "I never felt I was Irish before," she has developed a fascination for the time "when the Irish were cave-men"; while walking through the land that inspired such mythological tales as the stories about the children of Lir, she has realized that "in this country I could believe anything" (286). Richard, who doubles as her financial rival as well as her love interest, describes these fancies as "going soft, . . . going native. It's Irish Country life," but Geraldine is oblivious to the meaning of his words and chooses to define her Irishness in highly superficial terms: "I like all this sleeping and eating. Going to bed early and getting up late" (286). Rather than discovering any constitutive (albeit potentially conflicting) elements of a meaningful Irish identity, Geraldine's remarks rather bear the stereotypical hallmarks of a leisurely upper-class life. In that sense, her earlier casual observation about how "the Irish are so disloyal" (281) suggests that Geraldine's ideas about nationalism are more indebted to her mother's opinions than to any burgeoning understanding of Ireland's modernity.

If Hugo, Geraldine, and their mother are all complicit with various modes of neoimperialism, faux nationalism, sectarianism, and elitism, their local rival, Richard, the owner of "a derelict mansion and some land" (279), shares at least the latter of these vices. Obsessed by financial gain, he attempts to woo Geraldine and to set up devious schemes with her to trick Mr. Jiggins into bequeathing the estate to him, but his unabated lack of interest in his tenants is ultimately revealed to the elderly landlord by Reverend Duckworth. Richard refuses to pay a small sum that might provide clothing to the children of a destitute family living on his lands, claiming that "when times are bad I don't see why I should help the undeserving before the deserving" (296). When Mr. Jiggins berates him for his lack of compassion, Richard simply states that "I know I pay quite enough charity when I pay my taxes" (297). In this sense, Richard's heartlessness represents the ways in which the decline of the Ascendancy runs the risk of giving rise to capitalist speculators who seek to take advantage of the looming power vacuum to further exploit the most vulnerable sections of Irish society. As Mary Trotter observes, such sentiments illustrate how many characters in the play "see the land and its assets (ancient oak trees, thoroughbred horses) as moneymaking assets that should be exploited rather than preserved."[27]

A third option remains, however, for Duckworth's kind-hearted intervention ingratiates him with Mr. Jiggins, who starts to consider leaving his estate to the Church of Ireland with the aim of establishing a school that would provide "a sound general education and . . . a training in the principles of domestic architecture, . . . with special reference to the housing of agricultural labourers" (307). While Duckworth is supportive of these plans, some of Mr. Jiggins's convictions trouble him: the old landlord's celebration of "the religion of Swift and Molyneux and the great Bishop Berkeley . . . [and] Wolfe Tone and Emmet, Mitchel and Parnell" includes some names that are offensive to his sentiments, and he blatantly refuses to acknowledge the potency of cultural memories when his potential benefactor reflects on how rational progress has been stunted by violent imperialism: "Come, come, Mr. Jiggins, that's ancient history. It's doesn't do to brood on it" (306). Even though Duckworth seems to offer a relatively reasonable and constructive legacy for the Jigginstown estate, their conversation breaks down when Mr. Jiggins insists on allowing Catholics to attend the school: "It couldn't be done. . . . You're too visionary. You don't face the facts" (308). Should the estate be left to Reverend Duckworth, then, he would merely perpetuate the sectarian tensions that have plagued Ireland for centuries while refusing to acknowledge—let alone unravel—their historical roots. This cul-de-sac serves to illustrate Cathy Leeney's assessment of how Longford's play creates a "layering of comic style over a much darker foundation of social fracture based on bitterness, miscomprehension, damage, and disdain, whether in relation to gender, class, national identity, or religion."[28]

In the final act, Mr. Jiggins's will is revealed to stipulate the bequest of his entire estate to the "Department of Education of the Irish Free State . . . to be used as a free college for the boys of the neighbourhood . . . without distinction of religion" (316). This confirms, as Leeney also notes, that Mr. Jiggins "despises narrowly exclusive national identities and is, *avant la lettre*, multicultural in his values, extending this idea to redefine Irishness as plural and inclusive of all citizens."[29] Of course, Mrs. Jiggins, Richard, and Reverend Duckworth all protest vehemently against this donation; Geraldine is the only character who seems emotionally affected by Mr. Jiggins's death and opposes their attempts to convince the lawyer of his insanity (319). In shedding her cynicism, Geraldine advocates a singular solution to the decline of the Ascendancy: the Irish people are to place their trust in the government. The sheer optimism of this attitude is not without its problems, but, by this stage, the play has already carefully dissected the dangers that bequeathing this power vacuum to the alternative inheritors—British neoimperialists, capitalist exploiters, religious institutions—would entail. Ultimately, Longford's message is self-consciously naïve, to which the final entrance of the fox in the Jigginstown kitchen testifies: the characters' mutual fears and irrational distrust suddenly turn to levity.

The opening scenes of Mary Manning's *Youth's the Season—?* are also written with a sense of frivolity and satirical humor, but the play's resolution strikes a very different note about the future of the Ascendancy. First produced in December 1931, *Youth's the Season—?* depicts three days in the life of a particularly morose group of Dublin upper-class twenty-somethings as they slouch through their Georgian houses and mope in drawing rooms, feigning attempts at escaping their disaffected existence. Desmond, an aspiring yet impotent artist, speaks for his peers in declaring himself "sick of everything, sick of myself, and unutterably sick of Dublin," while his sister Connie, who is torn between her unrequited love for minor poet Terence and the attentions that civil servant Harry bestows on her, sums up the youngsters' general distaste for city and country alike with one of the Wildean aphorisms that litter the play: "I hate tea in Town. It's so suburban and provincial."[30] Small animosities and petty rivalries flare up during an impromptu birthday bash at Desmond's empty atelier—"Nobody works in studios nowadays—they only give parties in them" (324)—and various entanglements result in half-hearted betrothals that leave most socialites even more dejected than before. Ultimately, the dandyish underachiever Terence is driven to a suicidal lucidity in which he can only strive to (dis)embody the futility of their groping existence by shooting himself through the heart, even if this gesture is "just a fad; I've always preferred it to the head" (403).

One of few original Gate plays to receive scholarly attention, *Youth's the Season—?* has been interpreted as a critique of various Free State demographics, including an indictment of the nation itself. In 1968, Robert Hogan described Manning's play as a powerful illustration of how "youth is really not the season of thoughtless joy, but of exacerbating indecision and lacerating self-scrutiny."[31] More recently, Cathy Leeney has argued that the play "cut a swathe through the complacencies of the young state, its insecure self-satisfaction, its isolationism, its narrowness" by implicitly addressing issues of gender and sexuality.[32] Likewise, José Lanters has discussed Manning's depiction of homosexuality and the enforcement of social conformity in a class that "is shown to be repressed, anachronistic and inauthentic, the product of cowardice and lack of independent spirit."[33] Finally, Gerardine Meaney, Mary O'Dowd, and Bernadette Whelan have commented on the play's "fusion of the psychosexual and national," labeling it "a comedy of manners that tries by one decisive act to expose the tragedy of a generation." In their view, Manning exploited "the questioning, dissenting social and cultural space inhabited by the Gate's dramatists" to address issues of class without risking censure: "The depiction of the remnants of the gentry or indeed the Protestant bourgeoisie as drunkards would not have incited any riots in Dublin in 1931; the depiction of peasants as similarly inclined could have been interpreted as a slur on the national character."[34]

Although Manning's choice to depict only upper-class characters might have been a relatively safe one, her ridicule of Ireland's postcolonial modernity lashes out across the board. Targeting conceited pseudointellectuals, asinine Celtic Revivalists, and spineless neoimperialists alike, Manning's dissection of the Free State bourgeoisie and their sycophants offers a vitriolic representation of the collective failure of the upper classes to understand the Free State or contribute to its future. In light of the play's frequent references to Freudian psychoanalysis, the Ascendancy's inevitable collapse is shown to be rooted in a dual impotence. On the one hand, both the upper-class adolescents and their parents seem unable to process the sociocultural upheavals that have attended Ireland's adoption of nationhood, as manifested by their attempts to perpetuate the familiar power relations between urban and rural Ireland, as well as between the postcolonial nation, its former colonizer, and its diaspora. On the other hand, the young gentry are inhibited by the trauma of growing up during the cataclysmic years of the Easter Rising, the War of Independence, and the Civil War, and they show symptoms of being burdened by equally horrific transgenerational memories. This dual impotence in coping with issues of class, social geography, neocolonial complicity, and revolutionary history signals that the disaffected antics performed by Manning's characters are pathological responses to a world in which their social class has become obsolescent.

The resulting emptiness of the Dublin set is illustrated by the ironic way in which James Joyce is featured in *Youth's the Season—?* as a totem of the genuine Irish artist who renounces a mindless acceptance of monolithic identities. Manning's play mocks facile appropriations of this posture through deliberately overemphasized analogies to Joyce's self-exile: for example, Terence, the loner poet, is ironically decried as "hopelessly suburban" (332) by universal go-between Toots for his Joycean *imitatio* of wanting to have a drink at Davey Byrne's. Similarly, when Toots derides the cerebral pretensions with which Connie seeks to charm Terence, Connie retorts by asserting that "I *am* intellectual [*defiantly*]. I've read 'Ulysses' through twice!" (335). Nevertheless, her pathetic posturing is quickly dispelled when Connie tries to win Harry's affections in an attempt to arouse Terence's jealousy: she suddenly claims that she is "not clever, Harry. [*Viciously*.] And I hate highbrows" (337).

Terence, who could not care less about Connie's dallying flirtations, finally articulates this pseudointellectual bravado, declaring himself "mentally constipated. Too much Proust. Too much Joyce" (366) but this does not prevent him from wandering "down to Sandycove" (402), the beach overlooked by the Martello Tower that Joyce (and Stephen Dedalus in *Ulysses*) once inhabited. In those historic surroundings, Terence finds the resolve to take Joyce's self-exile to the defeatist extreme of committing suicide, having always known that he is a "bloody farce" (332) who lacks the genius to back up his pretensions. Such overly exaggerated parallels only serve to reinforce the metafictional quality of Manning's play, and the sterility of Terence's final act of defiance is preemptively stripped of any weight by Toots's snide remark to Terence that "I really believe you thoroughly enjoy imagining yourself some tragic figure in a Chekhov play" (332). Likewise, Desmond, whose frustrated dreams of artistic emigration brand him an equally impotent caricature of Stephen Dedalus, revels in self-consciously gratuitous plot markers, such as his explication that "things are rapidly coming to a climax" (363). In the face of such feeble gestures, Toots has little choice but to admit that "we're not real people, Desmond; we're only imitation" (381).

The play offers a continuous exposition of its characters as lifeless husks, but the historical roots of this existential fatigue remain obscured until the youngsters' repressed traumas are vented in the final act. In the preceding scenes, Manning disparages the upper class's destructive obsession with maintaining the traditional power relations between urban and rural Ireland, as manifested by the introduction of the character of Europa Wrench at Desmond's party. The host himself describes her as "very clever and awfully National" (354) and the stage directions introduce her as "a living, breathing mass of Celtic embroideries and hand-woven tweeds [who] speaks with an extremely cultured Anglo-Irish accent" (356). One of the conveners of a worldwide "Economic Conference, organised by the Women's International League for Open Windows and Closed Doors" (356), Europa combines vague globalist dogma with an ersatz nationalist agenda, her main occupation being the management of a "hand-weaving industry. The workers are peasant girls from all over Ireland—most of them from the Gaeltacht. There are only two at present, but we hope to have many more. We're teaching them hand-weaving, Irish dancing, embroidery, and harp" (365). The necessity to school country girls in traditional skills (rather than the other way around) illustrates Manning's depiction of the Celtic Twilight as a top-down imposition or an obvious prosthesis rather than an authentic stimulation of tradition.

Europa, then, embodies the political and cultural despotism of the Ascendancy, which, as Gregory Castle has argued, continued to seek to wield "discursive power over the Catholic-Irish whose lives and folkways are the subject of a redemptive anthropological discourse over which they have little or no control."[35] Indeed, Europa voices her belief that "it is so vitally necessary to improve the peasant *culturally*" (365; italics in original), thereby exposing how the Revival is actually an invention of the upper classes. Contrary to its ostensible precepts, then, such traditionalism seeks to *inflict* its construction of monolithic Irishness on the general population rather than *derive* its identity from the people. Europa further betrays this calculating approach when she finally leaves the party: wearing "what appears to be a bathrobe of an early Irish Queen," she solicits Terence's "help with my Rural Cultural Organisation. We want to get the Intelligentsia *interested*" (375; italics in original) in an attempt to rally the dispossessed bourgeoisie and have them enforce an ideological simulacrum of Celtic traditions.

While Europa serves to illustrate the Ascendancy's desperate attempts to maintain its cultural supremacy over the lower classes, Harry and Desmond exemplify the neocolonial ramifications of similarly conflicted politics. Self-declaredly "rather a boring sort of chap" (337), Harry was unable to find employment in Dublin and therefore enlisted in the British Colonial Service, much to Terence's irritation. Sarcastically dubbing Harry "the Empire Builder" (365), Terence repeatedly insults his adversary, and the two eventually come to blows at Desmond's dismal party, where Terence tells Harry, who will soon return to his post in Kenya, that he should "waste no more time beating the dead. Go and kick the niggers; it's more profitable" (375). However, despite being accused of neocolonial collaboration and berated as a "loyal servant of the Empire," Harry revels in his affection for the pastoral Irish countryside: when he is on duty, "it's the mountains I miss most," he declares, and, after his retirement, he is "going to buy a house near Rathfarnham. It's first rate country" (397). Harry, then, would gladly switch places with Desmond, who is given a chance to join his father's bureau in Dublin, yet the young artist is hell-bent on leaving the country. Desmond repeatedly stresses that he can only become a respected painter if he works in London, thereby likewise betraying a form of latent neocolonial subjugation: he consistently employs a British frame of reference, decrying Dublin as a mimetic city that comprises no more than "the Imitation Chelsea, the Imitation Mayfair, the Imitation Bright Young People! And such *un*original sin!" (398; italics in original).

These debilitating issues of class, social geography, and neocolonialism underline the malaise experienced by the next generation of the Ascendancy, and the play's ending serves to reveal how their impending obsolescence is rooted in Irish history. The scene for this naturalist finale is already set by the youngsters' garbled mythohistorical references, such as Terence's vague notion of Connie looking "a little like Dolores of the Seven Veils—or was it Sorrows."[36] Terence thus mangles the Celtic myth of Deirdre of the Sorrows—which had been put on stage in many Celtic Twilight incarnations, such as Yeats's *Deirdre* (1907) and Synge's posthumous *Deirdre of the Sorrows* (1910)—with the biblical tales of Salome's lustful Dance of the Seven Veils before her father Herod, and the theological devotion to the life of the mother of Christ as the Lady of the Seven Sorrows. The result is a hazy evocation of thwarted love, blind determination, and overwhelming despair, all of which serve as nebulous labels for an equally indefinite character.

While Terence tries to outline Connie's personality through these seemingly random historical associations, it is her mother, Mrs. Millington, who functions most explicitly as a marker of historical fatalism.

The stage directions accord her "a faded elegance, a certain vague elderly grace" (341): she is a dying remnant of the Ascendancy, embodying Luke Gibbons's observation that "the 'old' order was already shattered, and convulsed by social upheavals to the point of being in a state of anarchy."[37] In that sense, Desmond's description of Europa's uncle might equally be applied to his mother, for she, too, is "something left over from the Eighteenth Century, undergoing a slow process of decay" (382) since that relatively tranquil pre-Union epoch of absolute Ascendancy domination. Incapable of processing recent events in Irish history, she steadfastly believes "the neglect of the spiritual . . . lies at the root of all this modern unrest" (394), and, consequently, she is adamant that people be put on "one of those new diets, Christian Science, or Theosophy . . . [for such philosophy] has been the greatest help to me" (389). The model of respectability, she thoroughly disapproves of interactions between different social classes—for example, berating "Terence's uncle, Edward Killigrew, who wore the kilt and lived in the Blasket Islands in a tent for ten years. He was learning Irish; all the Killigrews were eccentric."[38]

Despite Mrs. Millington's outdated propriety, she cannot avoid mentioning that her unseen husband has revealingly declared his home a "madhouse" (345), leading Cathy Leeney to conclude that "his values are those of the rigid societal structure that, regardless of the recent republican revolution and ensuing independence, still remained in place."[39] With that note of detachment from reality, the play's frequent invocations of Freudian psychoanalysis hint at how "her upbringing—tight lacing, sealed windows, and the Book of Genesis" (394) has induced a pervasive form of repression.[40] This attitude was imparted to the next generation, which was born around 1910 and thus experienced the disruptive years of World War I, the Easter Rising, the War of Independence, and the Civil War as formative childhood traumas.

If, as Oona Frawley has argued, "postcolonial memory tends to be indirect, delayed or secondary—that is, received from a previous generation, with the colonial time/space not necessarily personally experienced except in the major fallout effects of decolonization," that "fallout" extends to the way the Ascendancy experienced the revolutionary decade. Manning's characters youngsters grew up during a sociocultural catastrophe that rendered their historically dominant class obsolescent, depriving them of the teleological security which had been naturally bequeathed upon them for centuries.[41] As Leeney observes, this misalignment also exists vice versa, since Manning's play "dramatizes the failure of the nascent state to exploit the energy of its most privileged youth; furthermore, between the conservatism of the old, ascendancy order, and the tendentious narrowness of nationalist values, there lies no space for lives outside confining notions of masculinity and femininity."[42] Only when the world is breaking down around him does Desmond finally realize that they have, indeed, been "buried alive" (398) all along, while Toots sees the ghostly persistence of the past as a "Living Corpse" (380) whenever she looks in the mirror. Such remarks transcend the mere personal vanity that they might seem to express, for other peculiar remarks betray similar attempts at maintaining this mnemonic repression. For example, when the newspaper boy calls at the house, Toots suddenly reveals that she "hate[s] Stop Presses. They always remind me of wars and rumours of wars" (400), thereby bringing her childhood fear of hushed conversations and suppressed news (as the hostilities grew ever more menacing) back to the surface.

It is Terence, however, who finally articulates the Ascendancy's historical dispossession and the resulting negation of a viable future most directly when he breaks down in front of Horace Egosmith, a character who was incorporated at the suggestion of Manning's friend Samuel Beckett and whose role Hilton Edwards—likewise hinting at the play's repressed memories—described as "a clouded mirror in which the reflection of something more than the surface of things is seen."[43] Terence uses Egosmith's mute powers to reveal his generation's inevitable demise: "Look at us! Take a good look at us. Raised in gunfire. [*He speaks out towards the others.*] . . . one mysterious universe after the other . . . souls lacerated with psychoanalysis . . . censorship of literature . . . people putting their heads in gas-ovens all over Europe . . . the rest living from hand to flask" (370; ellipses in original). Unable to cope with this ambience of repression and stifled conflict Terence implores the others to "take me home and bury me!" (370), desiring to return to the Freudian womb now that he and his peers have been bereft of any meaningful future and are left to be disposed as complicit remnants of (neo)colonial oppression.

Ultimately, this stalemate remains unresolved: Terence kills himself, and Desmond accepts a job as a clerk rather than pursue his dream of becoming a painter, but not before disabling Toots's hopeless attempt to escape her class identity. At a complete loss, Toots declares that "I wish I was a farmer's daughter" (381), thereby turning against her class in despair, but Desmond reminds her that history cannot be so easily defeated. The catastrophe of the Great Famine is shown to lurk in their collective consciousness as well, for Desmond tells her that, if granted her wish, she would have simply "starved on yon green" (381). In light of the destructive power dynamics between (Ascendancy) landlords and tenants that marked the Famine years, Toots's vapid dream thus betrays her class guilt in ways that are even more insidious than the buoyant artificiality of the Celtic Revival: the fantasies they create are only "idyllic in theory" (381).

Despite their cynicism, then, Manning's characters prove themselves unable to adapt to living in the ruins of their tradition: Europa replicates the authoritarian cultural politics of Celtic Revivalism, Desmond and Harry opt for neocolonial collaboration, Mrs. Millington flees into a realm of morbid spirituality, and Terence kills himself. Their repressed historical and transgenerational traumas are thus shown to have determined them—and their class as a whole—in a manner that precludes redemption. The ways in which *Youth's the Season—?* employs paradoxical dramatic modes in articulating these reflections on the contemporary Free State are especially potent, for, as Cathy Leeney has observed, "Manning's glossy comedy bears an ironic relationship to the images of despair and defeat that she presents, resulting in a dramatization of containment, oppression and lost potential."[44]

Contemporary audiences applauded the result: in the *Irish Independent*, David Sears described *Youth's the Season—?* as "an exceedingly clever and very entertaining play" that was well received by the audience, even though he found her amalgamation of comedy and tragedy somewhat unconvincing. Sears did comment favorably on the actors' performances, as well as on Manning's ability to create characters who "are not only superbly natural in the unnaturalness, but [who] are genuinely Irish. . . . She succeeded in each case in giving an Irish nationality to types we are accustomed to think of as foreigners."[45]

While the general public might have admired Manning's tragicomedy, the fact that her upper-class adolescents experience Ireland's postcolonial independence as a progressively debilitating existential condition that has brought about the sheer obsolescence of their class was not universally appreciated by professional critics. The anonymous reviewer for the *Irish Times*, for example, offered a half-hearted review, according the "finely written" and admittedly well-received play "a light wit that should make it acceptable elsewhere" (although "probably nowhere but in Dublin will its loving cruelty be fully appreciated"), yet they also condemned the play's posturing:

> A generation that is born in war may have a thin skin, and may have its nerves indecently exposed, but that, surely, is no excuse for behaving like "The Wild Duck" astray in "The Cherry Orchard." Nothing more serious than self-analysis, or possibly self-expression, in the loudest and most shocking terms can be taken seriously. With a banner bearing the device (old, yet ever new) *pour epater les bourgeois*, neurotic youth hurls defiance at Rathgar and Ballsbridge; but in the end the ranks which shouted loudly come to terms with life and death—one of its leaders in a coffin and the other in a bowler hat. Who will affirm which is the greater sacrifice: to surrender to life or make a suicide's exit?[46]

According to the reviewer, Manning failed to give a satisfactory answer to this question, but the inclusion of a question mark in the title of her play already avoids the kind of reductive finality and pure cynicism that an unaltered adoption of this line from *The Beggar's Opera* would have otherwise suggested.

## Middle-Class Dreams and (Dis)illusions

While Mary Manning's caustic depiction of upper-class morbidity provides an extremely bleak companion piece to Christine Longford's relatively optimistic assessment of the Ascendancy's legacy, their plays are comparable in suggesting that, for better or for worse, the old order had no future in the Free State. The middle classes might have been expected to profit from this power vacuum, but Manning's *Happy Family* (1934) and T. C. Murray's *A Flutter of Wings* (1930) provide no less revealing accounts of the struggles which attended this societal overhaul. In *Happy Family*, Manning satirizes the conformist ambitions of a middle-class family whose blinkered attempts to get on in the world reveal the lingering importance of the old class system and its tangled roots in Irish history. Murray offers a more allegorical representation of middle-class dreams in *A Flutter of Wings*, in which a young girl's desire to break away from her father becomes an emblematic representation of Ireland's struggle to achieve nationhood. Both plays thus construct intricate metaphors of national autonomy that problematize Ireland's future as a postcolonial state by examining the tensions between its social classes as well as between its urban and rural populations.

Manning's third Gate play, *Happy Family* (1934), depicts the trials and tribulations of the middle-class Blake family. Charles, a hypochondriac armchair economist, and Margaret, a fussy housewife, earn their living by hosting paying guests: Miss White, a scatter-brained spiritualist; Donald, a doctor who is secretly in love with Juliet, one of the Blake daughters; and Rory, a communist activist. Mr. and Mrs. Blake are greatly concerned about their children's prospects: Ted has a steady income, but he is much more keen to travel the world; Rachel is an unemployed artist whose boyfriend, Conor, repeatedly proves to be unable to hold a job; Juliet is an aspiring actor without any connections; and their youngest son, Dick, favors repairing cars over going to university. Mrs. Blake's schemes to provide her children with husbands or jobs are prone to failure, and over the course of the play, the family's financial problems grow increasingly worse as Miss White and Donald cancel their residency, Rory is incarcerated, and Mrs. Blake suffers a nervous breakdown. In the final act, however, all turns out for the best: Rory lands a job hours after being released from prison; Donald renounces his travel scholarship and proposes to Juliet; Dick's dream of becoming a mechanic is accepted by his family; and Conor suddenly inherits his great-aunt's fortune, allowing him to invite everyone to come and live with him in a large country house.

At the time, *Happy Family* received mixed reviews: the *Irish Times*, for instance, noted rather dismissively that "no play with such a number of amusing lines as 'Happy Family' can be called a bad play, but Miss Manning's latest contribution to the Gate certainly is one of the most formless dramas which that theatre has presented. It is a comedy of character, but Miss Manning has let her skill in character-drawing get so much the better of her that she has forgotten almost everything else—including the plot."[47] The *Irish Independent* similarly commented that Manning had "assembled the material for a first-class comedy or farce, but she slings it at us like a sheaf of excellent unthreshed wheat." Its reviewer, David Sears, did praise Manning's characterizations, and he went on to laud the "subtle, rather acid, humour" with which she depicted how the Blakes "are sinking to destitution in the morass of the economic depression. . . . With all their faults they are essentially Irish and their problems are familiar to many Dublin householders to-day."[48]

As Sears's review already suggests, the ostensible frivolousness of the Blakes' misfortunes—which is hardly assuaged by the play's hackneyed ending—is offset by its vituperative representation of middle-class life in the Free State, which resonates beyond the immediate setting of its satire. By explicitly problematizing the ubiquitous issues of class conflict and family loyalty in postindependence Ireland, Manning dissects the rigid social stratification of the young state, revealing an intricate web of paradoxical communal ties that are deeply rooted in Irish history. No less importantly, the play's examination of the Free State's social geography exposes major disparities between urban and rural Ireland that likewise betray a conflicted historical awareness and a convoluted mode of Irish temporality that belies the Blakes' (and, by extension, Ireland's) stolidly middle-class ambitions and even prefigures the advent of World War II.

At the beginning of the play, however, calamities occur on a much smaller scale: the first act opens with one of Mr. Blake's bouts of hypochondria, but quickly becomes more serious when the family finds out that their stock bonds have become virtually worthless due to the recent financial crisis.[49] Mrs. Blake tries to take charge of the situation and makes some feeble attempts at cost-cutting, but, by the end of the first act, she wallows in despair—"Such a house, such a family! . . . Do you realise we're ruined?"—even as Ted sings "Who's Afraid of the Big Bad Wolf?" and Rory plays "The Red Flag" on his flute (1.1, 30). These farcical ripostes serve as counterpoints to Mrs. Blake's misery, but, over the course of the play, various characters articulate their concerns in ways that betray a deeper understanding of the historical roots of their poverty. Rachel, for example, exclaims (with an unsteady voice) that "it would be better if we were all lying dead," while her sister Juliet yearns for complete oblivion: "Oh, that I was lying in some cosy little graveyard, with the nice, green grass over me, out of sound, out of hearing."[50] In more ways than one, then, the Blakes are a middle-class mirror image of the waning Ascendancy: "We're just a typical Descendancy class family."[51]

In the face of these troubles, issues of class are repeatedly foregrounded to reveal the deeply ingrained societal stratification that undermines communal cohesion by its perpetuation of mutual mistrust, even if the stereotypes of the lower, middle, and upper classes that Manning's characters voice are shown to be untenable. Mrs. Blake desires nothing more than to secure husbands for her daughters, and she would find it especially "wonderful if Juliet retrieved the family fortunes with a rich marriage" (1.1, 25). Likewise, if her son Ted were to win the lottery, he would "buy Mother a wonderful house in the country with a perfectly planned garden and no stairs," hinting at the obsession with Big Houses that tended to surface in Irish-Anglican families from all classes during the Free State years.[52] Any attempt to challenge this middle-class orthodoxy is met with incredulity: when Dick declares that he would rather become a mechanic than attend university, Mrs. Blake chastises him for not "realis[ing] that we've got our hearts on you carrying on the Blake tradition" (3.1, 28). In his deleted response, however, Dick reveals the narrow-mindedness of his parents' ideals when he observes that "the home market is overcrowded already and the colonies are fast closing up to engineers. I'm damn lucky to get any sort of a job now when thousands of men with first-rate degrees are tramping the streets looking for any sort of work. This is only a start, I tell you, and the only reasons you can put against this are snobbish reasons" (3.1, 29).

Manning's depiction of the plights of the lower classes is similarly intricate. The proletariat is represented by Rory, a lovably roguish character who wants to establish "a republic based on the workers and farmers in whom all the wealth of country shall be vested, and by whom all power shall be exercised" (1.1, 15) and jocularly tells passers-by that they should "go and break the windows of the Mansion House. Tear

up the paving stones. Decapitate the Lord Mayor" (2.1, 29). Unlike Mrs.
Blake, he finds marriage to be "bourgeois bloody nonsense" (1.1, 25) since
"under the present system, parents are compelled to exploit their children in the interests of private property" (1.1, 27). His diatribes against
capitalism and conventional morality provide a strong counterpoint to the
Blakes' middle-class woes, and he frequently expands the play's limited
scope by invoking the unseen presence of the proletariat. For instance,
when Major Gordon, whom Mrs. Blake believes to be one of Juliet's suit-
ors, is forced to admit that he purchased a new car for £2,000, Rory is
quick to abolish the physical boundaries that separate the classes: "Do you
realise that would keep six families in comparative comfort for one year?
Do you know that there are ten people living in one room within a hundred yards of this house?" (1.2, 22). While Rory also embodies a historical awareness of class struggle, singing songs about how "John Mitchell's
[sic] body lies a moulding in the grave / But his soul goes marching on"
(3.1, 38) his ostensibly stereotypical proletarian swagger is complicated by
his upper-class background: as Mrs. Blake observes, Rory actually comes
from "an old country family" and used to live "in the loveliest house,"
which boasted "thirty bedrooms" (1.1, 16). Rory might seem to have broken with his social class, describing his father as "a dirty old man" who has
"cut off my allowance until I renounce my ideas and return to the home"
(1.2, 8) but his very resentment over the fact that he has lost his inherited
wealth only further problematizes his class identity.

The same applies for Rachel's boyfriend, Conor Knox, a Trinity College graduate who has fallen on hard times but nonetheless prides himself
on his perceived social status: "I wish I'd been born a horrible breezy cad,
but I'm a gentleman to my fingertips and that is my tragedy" (3.1, 19).
Wallowing in his self-pity of being "too highly bred" (3.1, 20), Conor,
too, is acutely aware of Ireland's colonial history, tracing his genealogical
roots to the twelfth-century Norman invasion of Ireland: "Do you know
our family is the oldest in Ireland practically? We're descended from Desmond the Unready, a Norman knight. We came over with Strongbow
and settled in Waterford" (2.1, 21). Although Conor brags about having
a "noted duelist" (1.2, 18) for a grandfather, he shows little practical apti-
tude, leading Mrs. Blake to remark that "you can't afford to have all these

finer feelings anymore. They don't pay" (2.1, 19). This pecuniary necessity is removed, however, at the end of the play, when Conor suddenly
inherits his great-aunt's fortune, which allows him to declare all forms of
employment to be "nonsense. Resign at once. Resign from everything.
You can live like a gentleman in the country, dammit" (3.1, 44). As a representative of the upper class, Conor is depicted as being fundamentally
unable to contribute to Irish society in any meaningful way: he regresses
into a life of absolute idleness as soon as the opportunity offers itself.
While Conor might relish this tacit restoration of the traditional class
system, Ted is much more realistic in his assessment of Ireland's social
stratification, responding that he has "no desire to live like a gentleman
anywhere. Gentlemen seem to me to be having a pretty poor time of it
nowadays" (3.1, 44).

In many ways, Ted's sensibility is an exception to the play's farcical depiction of rampant polarization. The gulf between urban and rural
Ireland provides another such instance of profound societal divides in the
Free State. At the beginning of the play, for example, Juliet is staying
in the country with the rich Worthington family for an extended rest.
The perceived gap between the Blakes and the Worthingtons is literalized
when Mrs. Blake comments on the "frightful distance, 200 miles" (1.1, 12)
that separates her from her daughter, even though her husband corrects
this to a mere 80 miles. Likewise, in the letter that announces her return,
Juliet associates country-dwellers with farm animals, stating that she will
"never, never stay in the horsey homes of Ireland again. Too many animals
with threatening faces—horses, dogs and women" (1.1, 4–5). Nonetheless,
class and social geography are shown to be intertwined in paradoxical
ways when Mrs. Blake denounces Mrs. Worthington's alcoholism and her
husband's alleged affairs with his household maids while admitting that
"of course they know everybody and I thought Juliet might possibly pick
up a husband" (1.1, 5). If Mrs. Blake's bigoted belief that "staying with
rich people like the Worthingtons, well, you might be led into anything"
(1.1, 4) only serves to reinforce derogatory stereotypes, Rory's proletarian
perspective fails to provides an alternative: "Those landowners are a lousy
lot. Their utter lack of realisation, their criminal selfishness, their stupid-
ity is overwhelming" (14). The only character to voice an alternative view

of rural Ireland is Miss White, but her observation—"I'm very fond of a country life, you know. Such perfect calm" (3.1, 47)—constitutes no more than an inverted cliché.

*Happy Family*, then, presents a cast of characters whose ingrained views on social stratification along the boundaries of class and geography are polarizing at best, and the play's occasional depiction of sectarian and diasporic divides is equally pessimistic. However, Manning's depiction of traumatic cultural memories provides an important counterpoint to her characters' blinkered dogmas. The resulting reconfiguration of Irish temporalities simultaneously expands and compacts the nation's history in a way that fosters a different perspective on the Free State altogether. An important example of this process occurs when Rachel remarks that Ted "should have lived in the 18th century . . . I could have been a King's mistress, and you would have run away to sea and been a pirate. Ah well, you can always join the Blueshirts or something like that" (1.2, 2). Ted's response to this conflation of the historical quixotism of piracy with the contemporary danger of fascism is to sing a song from Robert Louis Stevenson's *Treasure Island* (1883): "Fifteen men on the Dead Man's chest / Yo-ho-ho, and a bottle of rum!"[53] In Ted's version, however, *sixteen* men are featured, thereby incorporating the executed leaders of the Easter Rising in a powerful mixture of Romanticism, totalitarianism, and insurgency.[54] In this respect, Ted's later remark about Rory is equally revealing, since it finally strips away the young communist's cheeky roguishness: "Don't you realise he'd lay a country waste—for an idea?" (2.2, 7).

Mrs. Blake enables another emergence of a complex sense of Irish temporality when she first states that her "youngest son is a product of the machine age" (1.2, 20), only to articulate her sense of historical disjunction in the final act, when Dick proves steadfast in his determination to become a mechanic rather than attend university: "I'm just trying to cast my mind right back over 17 years and remember, clearly and definitely, if I gave birth to a male child on the 1st October, 1916. And if so, is this the same child? (*she points at Dick*) On the whole, I think not" (3.1, 29). On the date to which Mrs. Blake refers, Greenwich Meridian Time was enforced in Ireland, thereby marking the end of Dublin Time.[55] Whereas Mrs. Blake cannot interpret the present in the terms of the past that she remembers, Donald can only point forward to an even darker future: "There'll be another war soon, and we'll all be smothered under a cloud of poisoned gas. And perhaps it's just as well" (2.1, 26). Likewise, Rory states that "for us living in the 20th century, a fatal hour of history has arrived. There will be a world-wide catastrophe, after which a new era for mankind will begin" (3.1, 39). In this context, Mrs. Blake's observation that "some day you'll look back on all this as the happiest time of your life" becomes a poignant attempt to escape from Ireland's history and its future alike, to which Ted's final exhortation testifies: "Let the bloody old future take care of itself and, judging by the news from Bulgaria, it looks like blood!"[56]

This paradoxical temporality is further accentuated moments later: just before the curtain drops, the cast once again sings "Who's Afraid of the Big Bad Wolf?" as Rory plays "The Red Flag" and Miss White announces that her canary's melodic outburst is to be interpreted as an indication that "all's well with the world" (3.1, 55). Cathy Leeney interprets this scene in a pessimistic way, arguing that "the effect is potentially comic, but also sinister, as the bird's merry chirrups evoke a preface to the threatening catastrophe that had, on mainland Europe in 1934, already begun."[57] However, these extremely contradictory proclamations about Ireland's future derive their final consolidation from Mrs. Blake's metonymical role: throughout the play, most characters consistently refer to her as "Mother Machree," which she describes in almost metafictional terms as a "a horrible stage Irishism" (1.1, 28). At the end of the play, she nevertheless embraces the persona of Cathleen ni Houlihan, complaining that she sees her "children starving and disgracing themselves everywhere . . . and nobody cares, nobody cares" (3.1, 54) only to receive unanimous declarations of affection. Thus vindicated, she accepts her role as an embodiment of the Sean-Bhean Bhocht: "I'm such an old hag and my hair's turned green since I've been in bed. Bless you all, my darlings" (3.1, 55). Ultimately, *Happy Family* resembles Longford's *Mr. Jiggins of Jigginstown*, rather than Manning's first play, *Youth's the Season—?*, in its willfully naïve representation of societal divides as deeply entrenched yet ludicrous—and therefore surmountable—obstacles to Irish national identity formation.

In addressing similar issues in his first (and only) Gate play, T. C. Murray took a somewhat different approach. The Abbey Theatre had already produced seven original plays by Murray since he had made his debut on their stage with *Birthright* (1910), but *A Flutter of Wings* was rejected by the Abbey directorate in September 1930. In one of his letters, Murray described the play as "something on the nature of an experiment," even though he felt that, as such, it was "not a great play in any sense, but a pleasant entertainment."[58] However, when he read the play to a private audience (which included Joseph Holloway) on October 5, 1930, he received a positive response, and Holloway felt that "it was a most interesting piece with the interest well sustained all through."[59] By then, Hilton Edwards had already approached Murray with a view to producing *A Flutter of Wings* at the Gate Theatre, which Murray accepted a few days after his private reading. Capitalizing on this dramatic coup of one of the Abbey's foremost playwrights, the *Daily Express* published the first installment of *A Flutter of Wings* in anticipation of the Gate Theatre's upcoming production on October 13. According to the newspaper, the Abbey's rejection called to mind its controversial denial to stage Sean O'Casey's World War I play *The Silver Tassie* (1929) and thus once again "aroused considerable criticism among drama lovers in Ireland," to which Holloway's outrage also testified.[60]

Holloway's recollection of the play's opening night was—unsurprisingly—very complimentary: "The excellent sketches and clever dialogue piloted the play into the haven of success, and a very critical audience voted it by their generous applause, attention, and hearty laughter, a success."[61] David Sears, writing for the *Irish Independent*, likewise recorded "a verdict in [the play's] favour as an enjoyable night's entertainment," but felt that "the play makes no pretence of being a great play. The theme is obvious" and Murray's power mainly lay in "some very good characterisation," on which the actors capitalized.[62] His lukewarm appraisal is echoed by later assessments: Micheál Ó hAodha thought *A Flutter of Wings* to be an example of a phase in Murray's career in which he pandered too strongly to his critics, resulting in a string of plays that "fail more from a lack of insight than from any lack of craftsmanship."[63] Likewise, Richard Allen Cave argues that *A Flutter of Wings* exemplified "Murray seeking to extend his range and abandoning the peasant idiom altogether; but an appropriate middle-class idiom eludes him to damaging effect."[64]

*A Flutter of Wings* depicts the plight of Tess Luttrell, a middle-class girl who runs away from her overbearing father to pursue an independent life. She is endowed with the characteristics of the Shavian New Woman and thus represents an updated version of the late nineteenth-century developments in the role of women in Irish society that Tina O'Toole has charted: "In their rootlessness, shapeshifting, and alienation from fixed social mores, [Irish New Woman characters] firmly reject the limitations and traps of domesticity, sexual passivity, and a gender-divided patriarchal world."[65] However, *A Flutter of Wings* is thoroughly rooted in Freudian psychoanalysis and displacement, and, as such, Murray's coming-of-age play also offers a postcolonial allegory of Ireland's struggle for independence and subsequent efforts to promote harmony between disparate social strata. By pitting Tess against a domineering father, Murray creates a multifaceted middle-class drama that not only offers a metaphorical representation of the nation's history of armed rebellion, but also explores various perspectives on contemporary tensions between urban and rural Ireland.

From the play's opening scene, Tess's status as a proverbial New Woman is expressed: she tells her brother George that "I've got more brains in my head than twenty like you" and is steadfast in declaring her opposition to traditional gender roles: "It spoils men—this ridiculous fussing over them. They come to expect it as a right."[66] The Freudian aspect of this rebellion is no less explicit, since Tess asserts that she "was born with—what's the jargon—An [*sic*] inferior complex" (1). This psychoanalytic dimension also applies to the relationship between Tess's parents: during a discussion between Mr. and Mrs. Luttrell, the latter exclaims that her husband is "too eaten up with self—self—self" (1, cont.). Her subsequent invective has a double function as emotional introspection in addition to veiled political metaphor: "For thirty years I've given in to you—blindly, unquestioningly, I had no will but yours—my one wish was to please you—to serve you—to make life as easy as I could for you. I asked you for little, and got little, but I was satisfied" (1, cont.).

In the following acts, the play rarely focuses on Mrs. Luttrell; instead, Tess carries the metonymical torch of Ireland's colonial subjugation, observing from the start that "all our life we've floated on the current of his will as if we had no minds of our own. . . . There's no worse superstition than that one's father, right or wrong, must go unquestioned" (1). While her sister Helen believes that this is "the natural law," Tess articulates the political dimension of her opposition to their father: she finds his prerogative to be "no more natural than the divine right of kings" (1). This validation of insurrection develops into a Freudian statement that is equally political: "I've outgrown my silly fears of Dad. My growing pains are over" (1). Mrs. Luttrell's concerns about Tess's state of mind—"What's come over you?"—are answered by a straightforward declaration of independence: "Nothing—only that I've begun to think for myself" (1). Likewise, her father's response is similar to Britain's grudging acceptance of the establishment of the Free State: "Home isn't good enough for her, I suppose. Very well. Let the world teach her. You'll see her returning tomorrow or after sick of herself and ashamed of her folly" (1, cont.).

In a similar vein, Tess's justification of her actions resemble Republican rejoinders to the controversial measures introduced by David Lloyd George during World War I, such as the postponement of Home Rule and the projected imposition of conscription: "It wasn't my fault, really. Dad was just impossible. . . . When I kicked up a dust he ordered that I should take up Minnie's place as the family drudge. That was the last straw" (2.1). While her uncle, Brian Dalton, believes that "it's rather a pity that things should have happened as they did," Tess is adamant about her right to independence—and, by extension, Ireland's right to statehood—even though she knows that the road to autonomy will be harsh: "I'm old enough to think out things for myself . . . I want to take up a post—to be self-supporting like thousands of girls. And I'm quite prepared to rough it a little" (2.1).

While this discourse of imperialism and insurrection functions on a mostly metonymic level, *A Flutter of Wings* very explicitly addresses the tensions between urban and rural communities in the Free State. When Mr. Luttrell attempts to physically intimidate Tess, for instance, his daughter spells out her rural isolation: "I'm not afraid of your stupid threats. The law extends even to Rossallen" (1). Bigoted stereotypes of life outside Dublin abound in the play as well, with Marian Dalton voicing her belief that her husband, "Brian, I fear, will never lose the uncouth manners of his native Cork"; Dalton himself, however, claims that "Cork, my dear woman, is the Athens of Ireland. Everybody knows that," to which Marian responds that this means that "Ireland's in a very sorry plight" (2.1). Conversely, Dubliners are mocked as well, with Dalton commenting that "it's the deuce the way babies multiply in Dublin" (2.1).

The most scathing exchanges of insulting stereotypes, however, occur during conversations between Brian Dalton's wife Marian and Tess, whom she describes as "a little gawkish country girl" and "a little unsophisticated thing from Rossallen" (2.1). When Marian suggests taking Tess to the cinema—because "those country people adore the pictures"—her young niece proves to be much more informed than she expected: Tess has already seen *The Rose Bubble*, since "we're frightfully modern there. Carnegie Library—lectures—cinema—and all that" (2.1). In a desperate effort, Marian tries to regain the upper hand by implicitly asserting the capital's innate superiority: "*(crushingly)* I fear Dublin will seem awfully second-rate to one coming from such a centre of enlightenment," to which Tess replies, "*(with ironic self-pity)*: Yes—only a kind of backwater" (2.1), thereby revealing that she actually reads her prejudiced aunt like a book.

While such mockery serves to illustrate the Free State's geographical divides, the issue of class is only raised when Marian's dim-witted sister Stella remarks that tennis is "tending to became [*sic*] a little *bourgeois*—in Dublin, at least—with shop girls and all that—playing" (2.2). However, Stella plays an important role in foregrounding George Bernard Shaw, whose oeuvre becomes a bone of contention among the Dublin set. Marian, who is seeking to couple Stella and Brian's colleague Frank Harmon, once again tries to vex Tess by suggesting "that Shaw's name has hardly reached as far as Rossallen" (2.2). Her plan backfires when Harmon observes that "the common people are always quick to recognise genius" and grows infatuated with Tess after she reveals that, rather than "turn[ing] your town into a modern Sodom," as Dr. Harold, a family friend, suggests, rural Ireland is more progressive than Dublin: "Rossallen's incorruptible. Shaw was voted as dry and preachy as a book of sermons—nothing *risqué* like the pictures" (2.2). Afraid of losing her intended's interest, Stella tries to chime in with the speech that she memorized to impress Harmon, only to further expose her narrow-mindedness: "[Shaw] shakes us out of our provincial—I, I mean conventional modes of thought" (2.2).

The final act of *A Flutter of Wings*, however, belies this facile dichotomy between urban and rural Ireland and offers a more nuanced assessment of the Free State's social geography. Some nine months after the conclusion of the previous scenes, John Luttrell has moved to a Dublin suburb, where he has retained his servant Minnie, but she cannot get used to metropolitan traffic: "I'll soon be taking a jaunt back to Rossallen. Only for the mistress, all the gold in the world wouldn't keep me here another day" (3). In a surprising counternarrative to the play's earlier depiction of bigoted Dubliners and savvy country dwellers, Murray seems to reinforce the separation of urban and rural Ireland:

> You can't drag the old from their roots, Mr. Dalton. I'd never come to know the people here somehow. They're dark and unneighbourly-like. And a terrible longing comes on me for my own little bit of a house on the side of the road. 'Tis grand to be sitting in the sun darning an old sock or saying a *Pater* an' *Ave* for his own soul maybe, an' having a pleasant word from this one, an' that one and they passing. Ah, Dublin's fearful lonely for the stranger. (3)

Minnie creates explicit and fundamental contrasts between the metropolitan population and the community that she knew in Rossallen: "The people are all for themselves here. At home they're full o' nature" (3). Dalton's opinion on the matter, however, is diametrically opposite to hers: "There's more kindness in the heart of Dublin than in the rest of Ireland put together, I know" (3).

Rather than establish the credentials of both respective groups, Minnie and Dalton reflect on the corrupting influence of social interaction: the servant believes that Dalton's wife is "nice enough, but over-proud and Englified," while she describes herself as "hardly knowing the sound of my own voice since I left Rossallen" (3). The solicitor, conversely, thinks that his brother-in-law John has been corrupted by living in Rossallen: "Those little country towns—they stifle a man's soul. Look what the freer atmosphere of a big city has done for him" (3). While Minnie and Dalton fail to transcend their respective outlooks on social stratification, their mutual respect provides a much more viable conceptualization of Irish identities than their dissimilarities would suggest. In this way, Murray's play serves as a doubly emancipatory assessment of the Free State: not only can *A Flutter of Wings* be read as an allegory of the nation's assertion of independence, but it also presents contrasting views on the differences between urban and rural Ireland without promoting a monolithic idea of Irishness.

## Rural Ireland and the Urban Proletariat

While Mary Manning and T. C. Murray addressed issues of social stratification by depicting the predicaments of the Irish middle classes in the plays discussed above, in *Marrowbone Lane* (1939) Robert Collis focused on the urban proletariat. In his dramatic critique of dilapidated housing conditions in Dublin, Collis introduced a narrative undercurrent that draws strongly on transgenerational memories of the Great Famine of the 1840s. By implicitly referring to traumatic events in Irish history to emphasize a forceful political message, *Marrowbone Lane* uses traditional elements such as songs and mascots in a destabilizing mode that reveals how rural structures of meaning lead to fatal misappropriations in a modern urban context.

The first-nighters were positive about Collis's debut: the critic for the *Irish Times* observed "an audience that seemed genuinely held and moved," resulting in "that unmistakable feeling which only a successful play can make."[67] In the *Irish Monthly*, Gabriel Fallon expressed surprise at this positive reception of what he perceived to be "sociological drama" of another age. Although Fallon agreed with Collis's political message, he was largely dismissive about the play's artistic merit: "Taking them all in all these dwellers in Marrowbone Lane were people without souls. Such dramatised abstractions as they presented cannot be accepted as human beings in any sense. No doubt this is the inevitable result of turning from art to sociology in the theatre."[68] Indeed, Collis was the head pediatrician at the Rotunda Hospital, and his offstage campaign for improved housing conditions included a lecture in the Metropolitan Hall on November 3, 1939, in which he urged for the appointment of a minister of health to address issues of sanitation in dilapidated Dublin tenement housing.[69]

*Marrowbone Lane* is set in such a Dublin slum, where Mary, a newly wed Mayo girl, has been lured by her husband, Jim Kane, who had, in fact, promised her a beautiful house in the suburbs with a garden. Forced to live instead in a dirty, draughty one-room apartment in a tenement hall that also houses her cantankerous mother-in-law, Jim's younger sister, and fifty other people, Mary quickly starts pining for the Irish countryside, which is embodied by her friend Martin, who prudently provides her with five pounds for the bad days to come. However, Jim's friend, fellow laborer and half-hearted communist Joe, plotting with Mary's insolvent in-laws, eventually steals the money. Soon afterward, Mary gives birth to a son, only to be crippled and rendered infertile when she falls down the stairs due to a rotten banister. During a subsequent visit to the doctor with her baby, who suffers from pneumonia, she cannot afford the medical fee, while the thoroughly bureaucratic housing committee repeatedly turns down her requests for less unhealthy lodgings. When her landlord threatens to evict her family because her husband is on strike and cannot pay the rent anymore, Mary takes her baby on a frantic, rain-soaked quest along Dublin's hospitals, all of which suffer an overwhelming shortage of cots and therefore turn away the only child she will ever have. Her infant son does not survive, and the allocation Mary and Jim ultimately do receive from the housing committee is tragically belated. Before breaking down completely, Mary revels in her despair: "I'm glad he's dead. . . . I'm glad I can't have any more children to be born in this city to die in sickness and pain."[70]

This overtly programmatic plot would seem a far cry from the Gate's normal repertoire, and indeed Collis initially offered a first draft of his play to the Abbey. After being rejected by the National Theatre, Collis temporarily shelved the play, only to experience an almost spiritual resurgence a few months later: "Easter came, and I sat down on Good Friday night and commenced to re-write what had already been written. . . . By 2 a.m. on Monday morning it was complete," thereby suggesting a parallel with the Harrowing of Hell and the beginning of a new era with the first shots of the Easter Rising.[71] Collis frankly admits that he aimed to redress the "pain, disease, cold and hunger" that one hundred thousand Dubliners faced daily, and that his play therefore is "propaganda in the same sense as

'The Grapes of Wrath' or 'Love on the Dole' are propaganda, or, for that matter, 'Nicholas Nickleby.'"[72]

Since Collis, as a doctor, addressed these issues from the perspective of a different class, Michael Pierse considers *Marrowbone Lane* to be an example of "dialogical, allegorical inter-class didacticism" that depicts "domestic discord as the microcosmic corollary of macrocosmic inequalities" even as it questions "the closed-shop mentality of sectional interest unions."[73] However, Pierse has also observed that, except for Sean O'Casey's plays, there was little "class-conscious cultural critique" by Irish writers from the working class during the 1920s and 1930s, which he relates to the "moral and political torpor" that characterized both the Free State and Northern Ireland.[74] Collis's position is further complicated by David Convery's analysis of how many conceptualizations of the Irish class system are implicitly predicated on British society despite essential differences between their respective socioeconomic contexts.[75]

Of course, Collis does not problematize his perspective in such terms and his political goal is obvious, but the ways in which his characters are endowed with important cultural memories are much less explicit. Nevertheless, *Marrowbone Lane* obliquely employs various discursive strategies that also characterize nineteenth-century Famine narratives, while transgenerational memories of other traumatic events likewise surface time and again to recontextualize the wrongs of the present, even if many of these troubled episodes in Irish history are referred to in a deliberately mangled way. *Marrowbone Lane* thus relates to the "semiotic system of representations" that Chris Morash describes as the dominant modes of description in accounts of the Famine.[76] This system comprises what Jan Assmann has called "figures of memory": the literary tropes and narrative structures that serve as mimetic substitutes for the traumatic event itself.[77] In *Marrowbone Lane*, such Famine narratives are reconfigured to underscore Collis's political message, thereby illustrating its use of traumatic transgenerational memories to address contemporary social issues. Indeed, as Clair Wills observes, "thoughts of famine were in the air" during the late 1930s and early 1940s, and "the ghosts of the famine of the 1840s were also raised by the sudden return of disease associated with poverty and malnutrition."[78]

While the plot of *Marrowbone Lane*—"made all the more harrowing by its simplicity," according to Robert Hogan—is grounded in Collis's familiarity with the Dublin slums of the 1930s, there are several instances in the play in which established formats of Famine narratives resonate.[79] For example, the familiar story of a destitute cottage family that must appeal to a landlord (or his agent) for mercy is one that has been consolidated by successive waves of self-repeating Famine tales. In *Marrowbone Lane*, this narrative construction is implicitly drawn upon yet also recontextualized in an urban environment, with the mute desolation of a countryside devastated by blight being inverted to become the noisy congestion of Dublin tenement halls. Likewise, although Mary and her child are threatened by illness rather than starvation, in *Marrowbone Lane*, too, hunger always lurks in the background, and many Famine victims actually died of an illness contracted due to malnutrition before they could perish from starvation.[80] Partly because of Jim's participation in a protracted strike, the couple and their child lack the means to adequately feed themselves, and they cannot pay their landlord. This destitution recalls the threat of starvation that marked the 1913 Dublin Lockout, and it also provides a close emplotment parallel with mid-nineteenth-century farmers who were unable to pay their arrears due to the potato crop failure, which simultaneously robbed them of their sole means of sustenance.

Mary and Jim, too, run the risk of being evicted from their miserable home and, like land tenants calling at boarded-up Big Houses, the couple has little choice but to appeal to seemingly immovable institutions such as the Housing Department and the hospitals for sustenance and sanitation, only to be turned away due to entrenched class distinctions: Mary has tried to gain access "time and time again and waited for hours, but they've never even seen me. The porter has orders to keep you out unless you have a special introduction from somebody" (48). Whenever an opportunity for improvement does arise, it becomes clear that the play's ostensible focus on money and health is nevertheless associated with a lack of sustenance. For example, when Mary is told to apply as a cloakroom assistant at "one of those big dance places in O'Connell Street," the fact that she will be allowed to eat the guests' leftovers is more important than the money she will make: "A good meal once a day'll do you more good than anything else" (41), the baby's nurse asserts, revealing that the need for food is the narrative's undercurrent even if the couple's financial problems are more explicitly foregrounded.

Mary does not land this position, however, leading to a situation in which the trope of parents roaming the countryside with their starving children is reconfigured into a quest along the hospitals to which Mary wants to commit her ailing child, even "if it breaks my heart" (78). Despite preparing herself for this emotional sacrifice, Mary, like most of her Famine counterparts, does not receive this bitter consolation. While nineteenth-century narratives tended to depict British or Anglo-Irish indifference to the sufferings of the Irish population, contemporary Ireland is shown to be plagued by stifling politics and bureaucracy in a manner that Michael Pierse identifies as a critique of "bourgeois corruption" which abounds in contemporary working-class literature.[81] Joe's communist propaganda provides a foil for such adversity, but his clumsy and feeble initiatives only exacerbate the problems that he tries to address. In this case, too, Collis's depiction of Mary's predicament suggests a comparison with Famine narratives, since the ruthless bureaucracy of both the Housing Department and the Dublin hospitals is reminiscent of the no less ineffectual Famine committees and aborted relief works. The clerks and doctors remain impervious to Mary's cries for recognition, claiming that there is nothing for her to receive, thereby inviting a parallel with the landlords who failed to support the Irish population during the time of the Famine.

While the play's underlying narrative structures implicitly draw on the horrors of the preceding century, the historical events to which the play explicitly refers are equally characterized by a deliberate sense of incongruity. Joe, who is a workers' union front-runner, is sarcastically described as a new Robert Emmet as well as a second Jim Larkin, the contemporary social reformer who spearheaded the unions during the 1913 Dublin Lockout; evidently, Joe does not compare with either. Likewise, the era of Lord Edward Fitzgerald, who joined Wolfe Tone's United Irishmen rebellion in 1798, is invoked by Maggie: "There's people livin' in this house since the days of Lord Edward and you're the first to say it was dirty," indicating that while housing conditions have not improved in centuries, it is finally becoming possible to criticize such destitution.[82]

More often than not, however, historical references are mangled by Collis's characters, with the absurdity of the resulting analogies revealing the revolutionary potential of the play's memory strategies. When Mary is finally admitted to see the director of the Housing Committee, for instance, he does not quite remember where Marrowbone Lane actually is, only to vaguely observe that Oliver Cromwell, who is generally reviled in the Irish popular consciousness, "quartered his troops" (60) there. Cromwell returns in even more incongruous way when one of the tenants declares that she is "as tough as one of them old cab horses which have been standin' there at Westland Row since Cromwell won the Battle of the Boyne" (87), which, of course, took place between the Protestant king William III and the deposed Catholic monarch James II thirty years after Cromwell's death. Of course, such deliberately garbled references have a comic effect, but they also voice a sense of historical fatalism while simultaneously betraying an awareness of the constructed nature of collective memories on which they are based.

Moreover, the fact that the characters in *Marrowbone Lane* are unaware of their complicity with Famine discourse in articulating their present predicaments does not undermine the relevance of such narrative templates, since, as Nicholas Andrew Miller has argued, "in acts of memory, forgetting must be acknowledged as an instrumental aspect of remembering rather than its opposite."[83] The play's transposition of a Famine narrative from rural devastation to urban degradation underlines Ann Rigney's argument that mnemonic structures are "constantly in process, involving both recollection and forgetting in the light of changing patterns of relevance and shifting social frameworks."[84] While the inversion of the urban/rural dichotomy requires some modifications to the narrative structures that are thus transposed, they nevertheless continue to dominate the expression of similar crises in other spatial and cultural environments.

At the same time, the ways in which *Marrowbone Lane* problematizes the incorporation of rural structures of meaning in an urban context serve to underline the divisive stratification of contemporary Ireland. Maggie, for example, sings the patriotic song "A Little Bit of Heaven" during the play's opening (13), but when Martin travels to Dublin to play the All Ireland Final for Mayo, Maggie demands his mascot—a doll dressed in the Mayo colors—and wears it on her coat. When Joe calls at the house, after having expressed his unequivocal opinion that "all this nationality talk's bloody cod; it's the classes that must be broken down and all the people given a fair chance" (34), he vocally protests against her support for her rural countrymen: "Aye, wearing the Mayo colours. You little blackleg. Can you beat that, Jim, and she a Dublin girl born and bred?" (52). Accused of being a scab (which once again recalls the 1913 Lock-out), Maggie immediately renounces her sympathy: "Are they the Mayo colours? Oh, Joe, I didn't know. (*Sobs.*) He made me take it. . . . I never knew it was a Mayo badge. I thought it was only an old fakey-me-jig. (*Pulls it out of her coat and throws it down on the floor and kicks it.*) I don't want the dirty old thing" (52). This repudiation of a more inclusive Irish national identity is given an ironic touch when Joe and Maggie declare Mary to be "not civilised" (54) while they are plotting to steal her money.

Mary, by contrast, feels stifled in the squalid urban environment of her married life, and when her friend Martin visits, she pleads with him to sing her a song in Irish. He initially refuses—"Not in this place. I couldn't do it *here*" (47; italics in original)—but eventually relents and starts singing "The Mayo Exile," an eighteenth-century ballad made popular in the United States by Famine émigré George Fox. Combined with the earlier image of Mary "clasp[ing] [the bunch of heather] to her bosom, burying her face in the flowers" while the light "[gives] a prison cell-like impression" (29) to her oppressive new home, the fatal incongruence of rural and urban conceptualizations of Irishness is expressed without any reprieve for the main characters.

If Collis's play seems overly pessimistic in its depiction of Dublin's urban dilapidation and Ireland's social stratification, its complex engagement with the nation's traumatic history does suggest the possibility of changing its future for the better. Both the sheer number of mangled historical references and the general pervasion of the present by the past serve to underline that, as Marianne Hirsch has argued, collective

memories are "not actually mediated by recall but by imaginative investment, projection, and creation" from an authorial perspective.[85] As such,
a greater awareness of the persistence of these cultural memories might
help to overcome the ignorance and resignation that Collis's characters
experience. In this sense, the play's articulation of the transgenerational
persistence of the Famine as a formative collective experience that continues to determine the nation's present condition testifies more generally
to the ways in which Gate playwrights attempted to confront their audiences and reconfigure Ireland's history so that a different future might
become possible.

These contemporary plays, then, utilize complex memory strategies
to reveal the historical roots of Ireland's social stratification and criticize
facile assertions of its homogeneity. By addressing the persistence of class
divides, exposing the discrepancies between urban and rural Ireland, and
confronting contested memories of pivotal historical events such as the
Famine, the War of Independence, and the Civil War, these Gate playwrights questioned the monolithic nationalist teleologies that had out-
lasted the establishment of an independent Irish state. In doing so, they
sought to reconfigure Ireland's postcolonial identities in ways that would
transcend the cultural uniformity and political sectarianism that characterized contemporary Irish society.

# Conclusion

*"Another Ireland, in fact"*

The plays that have been discussed in this book cover a period of thirteen seasons, from mac Liammóir's debut with *Diarmuid and Gráinne* on the Peacock's diminutive stage on August 4, 1928, to Robert Collis's *Marrowbone Lane*, which premiered on October 8, 1939, two days after Nazi Germany formally annexed western Poland. A month earlier, the Fianna Fáil government, which had won an outright majority in the Dáil during the 1938 elections, had proclaimed a state of emergency and committed itself to a policy of neutrality.

For Edwards and mac Liammóir, the advent of World War II not only imperiled many of their European friends and relations, but it also had very concrete ramifications for their management of the Gate Theatre. After heated disputes with the Longfords over the Gate's 1936 tour to Cairo and Alexandria led to a permanent rift between both parties, the Boys had come to an arrangement in which Edwards–mac Liammóir Productions and the Longford Players both produced separate seasons at the Gate Theatre each year. To supplement their company's revenue, Edwards and mac Liammóir had toured across the Mediterranean and the Balkans during the off-seasons, performing plays ranging from Shakespearean

Parts of this chapter have previously appeared in Van den Beuken, "'Ancient Ireland comes to Rathmines': Memory, Identity, and Diversity in Micheál macLíammóir's *Where Stars Walk* (1940)," in *The Gate Theatre, Dublin: Inspiration and Craft*, ed. David Clare, Des Lally, and Patrick Lonergan (Dublin: Carysfort Press/Oxford: Peter Lang, 2018), 47–61. Reprinted by permission of the editors.

classics such as *Othello* and *The Comedy of Errors* to George Bernard Shaw's *Don Juan in Hell* and Alberto Casella's *Death Takes a Holiday*.[1] With the outbreak of hostilities on the Continent, however, such tours became impossible, compelling Edwards and mac Liammóir to adopt the Gaiety Theatre (located on South King Street, near St. Stephen's Green) as their secondary base of operations from 1940 onward.

As various (auto)biographers have observed, this partial relocation to the Southside marked the end of an era in the Gate's history. Largely cut off from the cosmopolitan theater scene that had fostered international cultural exchange during the 1920s and 1930s and forced to cater to the crowds that might fill the Gaiety's massive auditorium, Edwards and mac Liammóir had to revise their artistic policy.[2] In *All for Hecuba* (1946), mac Liammóir comments on such wartime strictures, noting that "Dublin, in spite of the return of many wanderers come home to shelter from the storm, remained a small city on a small island; its half-million inhabitants could never support the amount of professional players that the output of work demanded."[3] In light of their financial situation, it is understandable that the Gate's production lists for the 1940s feature a much larger number of mainstream comedies, variety shows, and Shakespearean tragedies: while renting the Gaiety, unproven original Irish plays or new experiments in avant-garde drama were unlikely to attract the large audiences that the Gate needed to stave off bankruptcy.

However, before concluding this book by evaluating the preceding analyses of the Gate's earlier manifestos and original productions in light of its engagement with Irish identity formation, one final play warrants discussion. On February 19, 1940, President Douglas Hyde attended the premiere of the Boys' opening season at the Gaiety as they launched mac Liammóir's *Where Stars Walk*, which would be revived twice during the war (in 1942 and 1945) and once in 1952. In the *Irish Independent*, David Sears described mac Liammóir's drama as "an astonishing play," praising the variety of styles that mac Liammóir employed: "Laughter alternates with eeriness and cynical epigrams with rhythmical poetic prose until the magnificent final scenes recreate the witchery of Gaelic literature."[4] Likewise, the *Irish Times* and the *Evening Herald* waxed lyrical: the former called *Where Stars Walk* "one of the most truly satisfying plays that Dublin has seen for a very long time" and stated that it could boast "almost every quality of appeal," while the latter felt that the play bore the "unmistakable stamp of genius," since mac Liammóir had "contrive[d] by a masterly blending process to bring together two worlds—the legendary past and the Dublin of to-day."[5]

As these quotes already suggest, *Where Stars Walk* is a thematic amalgamation of the three focal points of this study: it addresses the mnemonic potency and postcolonial relevance of mythological tales, the traumatic and contested history of the Irish nation, and the struggle to assert viable collective identities in a newly independent state that suffered from pervasive societal fragmentation. Mac Liammóir's engagement with these interconnected issues reveals an alternative vision of postcolonial Ireland through the play's celebration of cultural diversity, and, in that sense, *Where Stars Walk* provides an overture to more general reflections on the Gate's contribution to cultural identity formation in the Free State and its function as a conduit of avant-garde nationalism.

Not unlike Denis Johnston's *The Old Lady Says "No!"*, the play opens by hoodwinking its audience: during a stylized depiction of the mythological tale of Midhir and Etáin, the lights suddenly come up to reveal a contemporary Dublin drawing room, where a group of Anglo-Irish socialites are rehearsing a play that is to be staged during a charity night. Sophia, an aging actor who in her prime had been a success in London, discusses the play's defects with two amateur actors, Bob and Sheila, as well as Rex, the director, and Tommy, the play's author. As midnight approaches, Tommy and Sophia play planchette in an attempt to communicate with departed spirits, until they are interrupted by Eileen, the new servant girl, who thought that she had been called. Equally abruptly, there is a knock at the door: a man called Martin has come to apply for a position as a houseboy. Surprised at the lateness of his arrival, Tommy and Mary, the other servant, are somewhat apprehensive—all the more so because Martin claims that he had not actually read Sophia's advertisement for the job—but she decides to hire him anyway. After everyone has gone to bed, Eileen enters the darkened room again and stands in the moonlight; she sees Martin's shadow, and he tells her that he has come for her.

The second act takes place the next morning, when Mary accuses Eileen of having gone out with Martin somehow, even though she took the precaution of locking him in his room. Eileen cannot remember what happened the previous night, and when she speaks to Martin again, their memories are blurred and the scene grows progressively mysterious as they slowly begin to recognize each other. A sudden knock on the door brings them back to reality, and when the other characters return, they resume their usual roles. Tommy discusses his play with an English journalist, Brunton, who has come to interview Sophia. As the actor describes to him the contents of the play and comments on the thematic importance of memory loss, Eileen looks at Martin again and suddenly swoons. The final act picks up immediately after the performance of *Midhir and Etáin*; the servants and the upper-class set have just returned from their night out and are reflecting on the virtues and faults of the production. When Sophia and her friends leave the room for supper, Martin and Eileen finally realize their true origins: they are actually reincarnations of Midhir and Etáin. Having fulfilled their destinies by finding each other again, they step into the moonlight and disappear. When Sophia and Tommy enter the room again, they look outside and see two swans flying away—the exact tableau that marked the ending of their own mythological play.

The play's title derives from W. B. Yeats's *The Land of Heart's Desire* (1894), which opens with a girl reading about how Princess Edain was spirited away to "the land of faery," where she has remained, "busied with a dance, / Deep in the dewy shadow of a wood, / (Or where stars walk upon a mountain-top)."[6] Over the course of mac Liammóir's play, both Eileen and Martin repeatedly use this phrase, which implies their true nature as spiritual beings and serves to underscore the acceptance of their shared fate when they look outside during the final scene and see that "the stars are walking over the edge of the world."[7] In this way, various iterations of Yeats's phrase function as markers of the lovers' status as outsiders, which is confirmed by Sophia's indeterminate feeling that "they're really only an incident in this house. They neither of them belong . . ." (34; ellipsis in original). In addition to their emblematic function as interlopers, however, mac Liammóir also uses the couple to hint at the artificiality of his own Irish identity. During a discussion with Tommy about how

Etáin slowly comes to recognize her true nature in the play that they are producing, Sophia muses that "you're alien with your own people too: you're always suspecting they're bogus, or suspecting that they suspect you of being bogus, and one awful day you suspect yourself of being bogus and the fat's in the fire" (11).

Mac Liammóir's veiled insecurity about the authenticity of his Irishness extends to his exploration of how the misalignment of the past and the present determines contemporary attempts at collective identity formation, which is shown to be stratified along temporal, spatial, and social lines. Rex and Bob, for example, self-consciously admit that their play is "badly dated, of course. . . . Celtic Twilight Drama for Cab Horses. It's a period piece" (8) that has little bearing on the exigencies of the modern Irish nation. In this sense, Rex's cynical description of their artistic endeavor as "ancient Ireland comes to Rathmines" (15) encapsulates such discrepancies: in a bourgeois suburb of contemporary Dublin, a group of affluent Protestants are staging a drama set in rural Ireland during mythological times to raise funds for the "Retired Cab Horses' Protection League" (7). While their endeavor at least implies some solidarity between different social classes, Sophia's outlook on Ireland's modernity takes the shape of a reductive dichotomy that is indicative of her historically determined outlook: she feels that "everything in Ireland is either Georgian or Pre-Celtic. Though all the Pre-Celtic things look very Celtic to me" (14).

At the same time, the post-Georgian period is depicted as being strikingly Georgian in its reinforcement of traditional distinctions between English and Irish identities, albeit in ways that also serve to undermine the latent neocolonial power relations. The English journalist Brunton claims that Sophia has "that heavenly Celtic burr (*He pronounces it with a soft 'C'*)," even though the actor prides herself on her London accent: "I speak pure Hammersmith. I was at school there" (54). Indeed, Sophia sardonically professes an anti-patriotic outlook by reminiscing on how "nobody's got any manners" in contemporary Ireland, as opposed to "the old days, you know, when we were oppressed. Grand it was, being oppressed. Only by the English, though. The English oppress one so much better than any other nation could. Sort of firmly unconscious" (12). Such mocking references to the colonial era are made in the same vein as mac Liammóir's sardonic appeal to Mother Ireland in *All for Hecuba* (as discussed in chapter 2): if Cathleen ni Houlihan has become a whining old woman who should stop complaining about her troubled past, the most effective method of liberating Ireland from its history of oppression might be to subject it to ridicule.

In *Where Stars Walk*, Brunton functions as Sophia's foil in facilitating this process: despite his English background, he is thoroughly unaware of both his own country's colonial politics as well as Ireland's cultural identity formation after independence. Claiming that he has "fallen in love with Ireland" after having been in the country for a single day, Brunton makes various inane statements about his appreciation of all things Irish: "Of course you must be prepared to rough it, but if you are, Ireland is quite, quite perfect" (49). He is surprised to learn that Sophia's friends do not speak "Erse," especially because he "saw lots of it written up in the Post Office this morning. Looks a bit of a mess, actually. Still I think it's fun to have one's own language, don't you?"[8] Precisely because Brunton is implausibly clueless about the iconic value of the GPO during the Easter Rising and equally unaware of the disputed position of the Irish language in contemporary politics, his ignorance enables him to transcend his role as a mere clown: allowing a character representing the former colonizer to mock Ireland's traumatic history and its contested postcolonial identity on the Irish stage marks an important step in exorcising the ghosts of the past.

Such possibilities of redemption are not straightforward, however, and the play offers ample reason to believe that waking from Ireland's historical nightmare is a difficult process. The circumstances in which independence was achieved continue to determine the contours of the nation's postcolonial identity: as Sophia remarks, "Life in Dublin is pointless unless you're fighting for something" (7). Furthermore, the fact that she has "no objection to ancient Ireland. It's the new Ireland that's given me the willies" (15) denotes an uneasy belief that monolithic Revivalist conceptualizations of Irishness seem more tenable than their fragmented modern counterparts, which rely on the persistence of violent nationalist rhetoric beyond its teleological terminus.

This problematic Irish temporality is also borne out by Sophia's reflections on how Ireland's struggling economy has caused widespread emigration, leading her to claim that "all the healthy young men of Ireland have left the country. Ireland is a land of adolescence and senility" (18). Similarly, Rex finds life in contemporary Ireland to be oppressive, believing that "the only time you every see unadulterated pleasure on Dublin face is when you announce that you're going away. . . . It isn't rudeness exactly—it's a sort of congratulation on being able to escape" (64). Rex and Bob's subsequent discussion of the Irish propensity toward introspection articulates a paradoxical desire for patriotic exile:

> BOB. Irish people say more and feel more about their country than any
>     other people in the world
> REX. Yes, and live in it less.
> BOB. Of course they live in it less. What has it to offer any of us apart
>     from inspiration, frustration and intoxication?
> REX. You're forgetting annihilation. (64)

While these qualifications are no less stereotypical—as Bob observes, "Every emotion you can feel about this country is bound to be hackneyed" (64)—*Where Stars Walk* also employs such generalizations to undermine the social stratification of contemporary Ireland, to which numerous comical depictions of perceived religious and geographical differences testify. By the end of the play, however, many of these stereotypes are inverted or conflated in ways that reveal their artificiality. Eileen, for example, admits that she has "never seen a play in all my life, only the pictures an odd time" (60)—ironically, as a lower-class Catholic, she is more familiar with modern forms of entertainment than the upper-class Protestants, who spend their time producing outdated plays. More importantly, Eileen destabilizes the very conceptualizations of Irishness that are at the core of Revivalist drama as imperialist constructions: while she describes the play's plot as "some class of an old story . . . , you know, like—like one you'd read—or—something like—you might hear" (59), she finds the rendition to be "very Englishy all right," since everyone "talked terrible queer, mind you . . . 'Treasure of my heart,' and 'pulse of my soul,' and all that" (60). Even Rex, the play's producer, admits that "it just became a dreary Celtic Twilight play in fancy dress," but he is sensitive to the notion that "the real thing is here somehow—here in this house" (65). Brunton simply ascribes this feeling to Rex's "Irish imagination" (65), leading Tommy, the author of the drama, to observe somewhat dolefully that "English people may love the Celtic Twilight still I don't know: but here it reminds people of their nursery days" (66).

This assessment ostensibly reduces Revivalism to an immature cultural pursuit, but it also highlights the vital importance of memory in determining processes of identity formation—and, in this sense, *Where Stars Walk* is, fundamentally, a drama of memory. From the very start of the mythological play-within-the-play, the tenuous but constitutive function of memory is articulated: Midhir's voice is heard in an attempt to awaken Etáin—"Do you not remember that country, Etáin? That smiling country that is beyond the end of the world"—to which she responds that she "can remember so dimly. You are too far away" (5). Mirroring this exchange, Martin problematizes the function of memory during his introduction to Sophia, initially stating that "'tis only my memory is bad," but subsequently developing a more nuanced notion: "I'd not say 'twas exactly bad. But 'tis queer. You see, madam, there's two sets of things to remember. 'Tis like the night and the day" (36).

Martin's composite mode of memory quickly begins to affect Eileen as well, for when Mary scolds her for roaming outside at night—"To think of you forgetting yourself"—Eileen is struck by her words: "Forgetting myself? (*On her lips the phrase has a different meaning*)" (40). Bewildered by her experience, Eileen claims that she "can't remember" (41) what transpired, and when she finally meets Martin, he tells her that she has "forgotten where we met before" (44). Their subsequent exchange reveals the constitutive, if fragile nature of the lovers' memories:

MARTIN. There's two memories in my head. One memory's about a
    dream I had last night, and 'twas of you, and you were standing her
    [*sic*] right enough, and we went walking out of this house together.
EILEEN. That was no dream. I stood here waiting for you, and you told
    me you had come to find me.
MARTIN. And the other memory I have . . .
EILEEN. What is it?

MARTIN. 'Twas a long time ago.

EILEEN. When you were a little lad, is it?

MARTIN. Ages ago. Too far away.

EILEEN. Tell me about your country.

MARTIN. I can't. I can't remember rightly.

EILEEN. You called me by my name last night.

MARTIN. Your name. What is your name?

EILEEN. My name is—(*She stands very proudly.*)

MARTIN. Tell me. (44; ellipsis in original)

At this moment, a knock on the door interrupts their encounter, but its importance is confirmed at the end of the second act, when Sophia tells Brunton that "what fascinates me so much is that non-recognition, that loss of memory" (57) in the play that she is performing. As Sophia describes the dramatic reunion of the mythological couple, Martin and Eileen exchange looks and begin moving toward each other just before the latter faints.

At the very end of the play, Eileen's acceptance of her true identity is likewise enabled by the reintegration of her memories. While watching the mythological play, the servant girl felt that she already "knew it like by heart, and I thought there were bits in it were wrong and that I'd know better myself the way to do it . . . 'Twas like looking in a mirror and seeing everything a touch crooked" (61; ellipsis in original). Martin acknowledges the legitimacy of these discrepancies, which leads him to advocate for the abolition of the cultural simulacra that the upper classes have imposed: "All them fine people and they writing their plays and they acting out other people's lives and making great stories out of other people's words, what can they do at the end of it all when yourself can see what's wrong but leave the likes of you and me together and let the real story live itself out again" (69). In this way, *Where Stars Walk* paradoxically suggests that Revivalist dramatizations have stultified the development of Ireland's cultural identities, even as it readily embraces the form and content of such Twilight productions to make this assertion.

Indeed, Eileen and Martin's characterization serves to underline the importance of this contradiction. While Eileen finally admits that Martin "told me all the things I had forgotten" (70), she becomes afraid of abandoning "this life where 'tis warm and safe and there's things to do and people to talk to" (71). Consequently, the difficulty of truly assimilating memories is confirmed by her *negative* prescriptive strategy, for Eileen pleads with Martin to preserve her ignorance: "Don't make me remember" (71). Martin is relentless, however, and his imperative—"You can't forget! You remember it now" (71)—opens her eyes to the past that she had forgotten: "I remember it now. The night of feasting, the harps and the wine, the battle in the air, your eyes like two candle flames, and I going back in your arms to our own people" (72). At the same time, however, Martin reaffirms the conventional Revivalist trope that the Irish peasantry have somehow eluded the advent of modernity and embody an authentic, living tradition: "What other way would I have found you? Only the poor people have remembered the likes of you and me" (72).

While Eileen and Martin's archaic diction and essentialist rhetoric appear to be readily complicit with the social conservatism that generally characterized the cultural productions of the Celtic Twilight movement, the function of such hackneyed structures of meaning in *Where Stars Walk* is revealed to be self-consciously ironic and ultimately serves to illustrate the play's promotion of multifaceted identities. A few moments after the lovers have disappeared, Sophia and Tommy enter the drawing room, and the latter reflects on his failure as an author by remarking that "in a modern play, you've living people all around you to model your characters on, but in a play about the ancient world where are you to look?" (72). Tommy remains ignorant of the idiosyncratic miracles that happen under his very nose, because his imagination has been stifled: he thinks about replicating standardized modes of expression rather than creating new experiences of Irish life. In so doing, he embodies a debilitating inclination toward normalization, to which Sophia's earlier revelation of "one of the greatest secrets of life" offers a potent contrast: she tells Tommy that "when you're as old as I am you'll discover that [nobody is ordinary], and you'll stop writing plays about people like Midhir and Etán [*sic*], because you'll discover that everyday people and everyday things can be just as mysterious and just as preposterous as anything in ancient legend" (33). At the onset of the blinkered Emergency years, *Where Stars Walk*, too, must have seemed "mysterious" as well as "preposterous," but it is precisely through its contradictory, composite form that an alternative cultural poetics could be formulated: mac Liammóir's play openly embraced *difference*, celebrating multiplicity and incoherence over orthodoxy and uniformity.

Like many original Gate plays, *Where Stars Walk* was well received in the 1940s but has since been largely forgotten. However, as Christopher Murray has asserted in his discussion of several popular plays of this period, the plot of *Where Stars Walk* "serves to represent the very ways plays work, recycling other writers as MacLíammóir recycled Yeats, and showing how a play is no more than an echo from the past which alerts and estranges the present."[9] Indeed, Murray develops this argument about the constitutive temporality of the Irish stage to contend that "writers who strike a chord in their own day, who hit upon a contemporary mood or obsession, set up echoes for later generations to hear, however faintly, in others." If forgotten plays of earlier periods are still "all around us like ghosts," as Murray claims, the contemporary relevance of the Gate's original playwrights, whose intricate engagement with Ireland's postcolonial identity formation has been discussed in the previous chapters, cannot be overstated.[10]

In this sense, Murray's assertion that Irish playwrights of the 1950s "were struggling to define the audience's location between tradition and modernity" is equally applicable as an assessment of the poetics that the Gate's dramatists espoused during the 1920s and 1930s—all the more so in light of Murray's affirmation that Micheál mac Liammóir "showed us all how the question of identity is at bottom a theatrical one."[11] The unruly multiplicity and deliberate artificiality of *Where Stars Walk* illustrates the complex, if not contradictory, ways in which such issues were addressed and thus serves as a prime example of how the Gate's stage, as Chris Morash and Shaun Richards have stated, "had the potential to produce a theatrical space that, rather than reinforcing the inherent limits of space, transcends them."[12]

However, identifying this potential was easier than realizing it, as Edwards and mac Liammóir acknowledged themselves. In December 1951, they produced *God's Gentry*, a comedy in verse that had debuted at the Belfast Arts Theatre a few months earlier. Its author was Donagh

MacDonagh, the son of Thomas MacDonagh, who had directed at the Theatre of Ireland before he was executed as one of the signatories of the 1916 Proclamation of the Irish Republic. In addition to listing the usual information about the actors and their roles, the program for this play featured a reflection on the Gate's commitment to promoting Irish playwrights. After some preliminary comments on the popularity of Maura Laverty's work—*Liffey Lane* and *Tolka Row* had been produced that year, and would soon be followed by *A Tree in the Crescent*—the Gate's directors articulated their avant-garde nationalism of introducing foreign techniques and styles to foster the development of native writers, even as they voiced their awareness of the difficulties in actually staging new Irish drama:

> Although from our very earliest days we have presented first productions by Irish authors, as evidenced by the inclusion in our first seasons at the Peacock Theatre, Micheál Mac Liammóir's *Diarmuid and Grannia* [*sic*] David Sears' *Juggernaut*, An Philibin's *Tristram and Iseult* and Denis Johnston's *The Old Lady Says "No"*; our policy was mainly concerned with the importing of foreign works with a view to showing Dublin the developments of the authors and theatres of other lands thus endeavouring to broaden the theatrical horizon. The results of our work during the past twenty years have led us to believe that this has been achieved.
>
> From our point of view this meant the encouraging of authors to write in a freer and less conventional technique than was their habit, but we realize that this could only be of incidental interest to the public for whom the subject matter rather than the style must always, rightly, be of paramount importance.
>
> We feel that after these twenty years something of this task has been accomplished but there is still much that remains to be done, and we feel that until we can achieve a theatre and fulfil our early ambition of a permanent home for us in this city which has not only greater space and comfort for our audiences but gives us proper facilities and working conditions for our actors and staff, not to mention a certain degree of comfort. The continuation, let alone the development, of our work is in jeopardy; without some degree of permanency development becomes impossible.

Every effort is being made to remedy this state of affairs; meanwhile in thanking you for your support in the past and depending upon it for the future we hope soon to ask you to assist us to be in a position to give you, unhampered by physical and structural limitations, the fruits of our experience during the past.[13]

While Edwards and mac Liammóir only expressed partial satisfaction with their results in cultivating Irish drama and pointed to the architectural issues that might hinder future efforts (and that indeed would force the Gate to close for extensive repairs in 1957), this book has made the case that their endeavors nevertheless merit acknowledgment and scrutiny. By various means, the early Gate Theatre sought to participate in the highly contested processes of cultural identity formation that were taking place in the Free State, thereby embodying, as Morash and Richards have observed, a "sense of openness and possibility" in creating a "stage freed from the demands of narrative realism, thrown from the constraints of place into the freedom and threat of space" in ways that nevertheless have been shown to also extend beyond the realm of dramaturgy and stylistics.[14]

This duality of liberty and danger can be seen in Micheál mac Liammóir's adoptive Irishness and his engagement with prosthetic memories, which illustrate the constructed nature of national identities and the empowering prospect of exorcising traumatic collective memories. A similar awareness of the malleability of historicized identities is also borne out by the manifestos published by Gate directors and affiliates such as Edward Longford, Mary Manning, and Norman Reddin. Moreover, their reflections on Ireland's troubled past expressed a steadfast belief in the Gate's importance in transcending political divides and fostering a cosmopolitan Ireland, which led them to explicitly accord their playhouse the standing of an alternative national theater. Likewise, Hilton Edwards's musings on the debilitating effects of naturalist drama and the dangers of the encroaching cinema provide insights into his attempts to reinvent the Irish stage through a combination of traditional and innovative techniques that acknowledged the audience as a constitutive element of modern theater.

On the Gate stage, these complex dramatic poetics were manifested in several mythohistorical plays, which illustrated the changing function of national epics in postindependence Ireland. While obviously indebted to the plots of their Revivalist precursors, these plays by Micheál mac Liammóir, An Philibín, and David Sears reconfigured several mythological love triangles to function as historicized emblems of imperialist power and anticolonial struggle. By implicitly incorporating recent historical events and adapting revolutionary discourse to a mythological context (and vice versa), these plays problematized various contested cultural memories through simultaneously prospective and prescriptive strategies, allowing audiences to recognize the artificial nature of the collective identities and national teleologies to which contemporary political controversies still appealed.

Likewise, the Gate's repertoire of original history plays depicted various episodes of religious strife and revolutionary upheaval in Ireland's past, revealing engagements with the nation's postcolonial future that exceeded the scope of mere period pieces. By employing provocative expressionist techniques and implying complex historical parallels, playwrights such as Edward Longford, Denis Johnston, Micheál mac Liammóir, and David Sears confronted audiences with the problematic contemporary status of these potent collective memories. While the 1803 rebellion, the Catholic Emancipation campaign, or the War of Independence might have been paramount to fostering Irish nationalism in the years leading up to the establishment of the Free State, their persistent legacy in an independent nation proved destructive, as the mutually exclusive conceptualizations of an essential Irish identity on which they were based led to civil war and paramilitary violence. However, in an attempt to transcend such historically determined antagonisms, these plays challenged the transgenerational memories that served to justify the continued hostilities, instead propounding a more inclusive and pluralistic sense of Irishness.

Similar impulses impelled the Gate plays that were set in the contemporary Free State and offered dramatic reflections on the debilitating social stratification of the newly independent nation. Written by Denis Johnston, Christine Longford, Mary Manning, T. C. Murray, and Robert Collis, these plays revealed how the triumphant teleology of Irish self-determination had, in fact, been undermined by far more tangible societal ills. In various ways, these playwrights illustrated how the pervasive differences between urban and rural Ireland contradicted conventional celebrations of a revitalized, homogenous nation. Moreover, the upheaval of the old class system was shown to have profound ramifications: rendered obsolete by the end of British rule, the Protestant Ascendancy was characterized as having failed to produce a meaningful legacy, while depictions of the urban middle classes featured bigoted misgivings about social climbers and rural compatriots alike. For the proletariat, the establishment of an independent Ireland had not brought any significant change, with their misery being underlined by the persistence of transgenerational memories of deprivation. In addressing such contested issues of class cohesion and social geography, these plays offered fundamental critiques of the Free State as a communal project.

While these engagements with Ireland's conflicted modernity exemplify the ways in which the Gate's directors, associates, and original playwrights espoused an avant-garde nationalist approach to cultural identity formation in the Free State, it is important to avoid a reductive appraisal in this respect and instead recognize the constitutive multiplicity of these endeavors. As a cultural project, the Gate cannot be said to have subscribed to the strictures of any particular political agenda; rather, it thrived precisely on exchanges between opposites and interactions between conflicting strategies. As Richard Pine has observed, the tensions that the Gate thus addressed were myriad: "Stability versus deviance and dissension; reconstruction versus iconoclasm, and above all the issues of identity and purpose, which were divisive and bitterly contested."[15] While this makes it difficult to adequately summarize—let alone assess—the ways in which Ireland's cultural advancement was to be effected, the inclusiveness of Edwards and mac Liammóir's enterprise should be acknowledged as a defining element of their conceptualization of Ireland's modernity.

Edwards and mac Liammóir thus attempted to strip down and confront, rather than simply reject, the exhausted artistic modes and mnemonic legacies that had dominated Irish culture and society, offsetting them with imported overseas aesthetics and innovative memory strategies that they, in turn, reconfigured in an Irish context. In this way, they embodied a spirit of avant-garde nationalism, creating a versatile playhouse that facilitated interactions between strongly divergent theatrical styles and political perspectives, to which their promotion of new Irish playwrights testifies. If anything, their objective was to promote a cosmopolitan Free State that would embrace a wide range of cultural identities and facilitate the free proliferation of ideas and opinions. In so doing, the Gate contributed to the cultural paradigm shift that Declan Kiberd has identified as occurring over the course of the twentieth century: "The seamless garment once wrapped like a green flag around Cathleen ní Houlihan had given way to a quilt of many patches and colours."[16] Edwards and mac Liammóir's motley interpretation of Irish modernity already recognized its conflicted nature, and so they endowed the Gate with an emblematic function that might stimulate the emancipation of contested identities.

Contrary to much of the conventional historiography of twentieth-century Irish theater, then, the Gate, from its very beginnings, presented itself and functioned as an alternative national theater. Ireland's postcolonial condition—historically, culturally, and politically—was an important topic of reflection for its directors and playwrights, while the innovative international repertoire on which the Gate's reputation has mostly been founded did not constitute a mode of aestheticist escapism, but served to confront Irish audiences with innovative dramatic techniques during a particularly conservative period in Irish history. To borrow Christopher Murray's phrase, then, the Gate Theatre held "the mirror up to nation" in ways that have only been partially acknowledged.

Of course, the present attempt to redress this historiographical omission by elucidating some of the processes that informed the Gate's reconfiguration of Irish national identities through its engagement with concepts of tradition, modernity, nationalism, and cultural memory in editorial pieces and original plays only addresses a small part of the Gate's importance to Irish theater and society more generally. The Gate Theatre Research Network (GTRN), which was established in 2018, is exploring other promising avenues of inquiry, including the ways in which the Gate functioned as a cultural ambassador on its tours of mainland Europe, Egypt, and the United States during the 1930s and 1940s, since these might be examined to chart larger infrastructures of cultural exchange.[17]

As such, GTRN employs the Gate as a model for studying how cosmopolitan theaters engage with issues of identity formation in a comparative perspective with other European avant-garde playhouses. In an Irish context, however, Edwards and mac Liammóir's complex relationship with the Abbey directorate and other theater companies—to which their long-standing support of An Comhar Drámaíochta (the Gaelic Players) testifies—still warrants consideration.

GTRN also hopes to stimulate researchers to examine the ways in which the Gate's directors translated foreign avant-garde drama (such as *A Merry Death* by Nikolai Evreinov or *Gas* by Georg Kaiser), as well as stage and costume design, to an Irish context, and, conversely, how they reclaimed Irish playwrights such as Goldsmith, Wilde, and Shaw.[18] No less importantly, scholars might assess to what extent new adaptations of stories and novels such as Sheridan Le Fanu's *Carmilla* (by Edward Longford) or Emily Brontë's *Wuthering Heights* (by Ria Mooney and Donald Stauffer) were influenced by the Gate's expressionist repertoire. Likewise, the contemporary relevance of original Gate plays that depicted foreign historical events—such as the conquest of Melos by Athens in 416 BCE (in *The Melians* by Edward Longford) or the death of Mary, Queen of Scots (in *Three Leopards* by Cecil Monson)—requires further scrutiny.

Moreover, Gerardine Meaney, Mary O'Dowd, and Bernadette Whelan's assertion that "the Gate Theatre was a forum where new and often radical ideas about modern women were presented to a public audience untroubled for the most part by the vigilance of the censor's supervision" and that its "eclectic programming was more conducive to women's participation" underlines the necessity of further study of the role of women playwrights such as Mary Manning, Christine Longford, Dorothy Macardle, Hazel Ellis, Ulick Burke (the pseudonym of Lilian Davidson), M. J. Farrell, Maura Laverty, and H. T. Lowe-Porter.[19] Likewise, female actors such as Coralie Carmichael, Meriel Moore, and Betty Chancellor, as well as the violinist Bay Jellett, who operated as the Gate's musical director, deserve academic attention. Also, with regard to the Gate's offstage influence on Irish society, the general acceptance of Edwards and mac Liammóir's homosexuality and their creation of a tolerant Dublin gay scene would also provide a highly interesting topic for sociological research on the Free State years.[20]

While this book has evaluated the Dublin Gate Theatre's role in engaging with contested collective identities in the Free State during the 1920s and 1930s by analyzing its cultural poetics and its promotion of new Irish playwrights in some detail, the importance that mac Liammóir ascribed to his company's engagement with Ireland's postcolonial development is borne out more concisely by his anthropomorphic representation of the Gate as the feisty embodiment of the Irish nation. Indeed, although mac Liammóir was supposedly getting "sick and tired" of how "everywhere one went people talked about the dear old Gate" during the success of its first seasons, his wistful reflection on the capriciousness of the project on which he had embarked serves to capture the constitutive multiplicity of Ireland's avant-garde national theater:

> Already the wretched thing was acquiring a personality, was becoming a living thing in the imagination, a bully who gave itself airs, a spoilt exacting creature who before it had properly taken shape at all was ruling our lives. It was like having an irresistible and impecunious young mistress whose demands were as outrageous as the power she wielded over one's head, and whose adolescent fascinations were of so subtle a nature that only a few could see them at all, leaving her a small and overworked circle of lovers upon whom she shamelessly battened— another Ireland, in fact.[21]

# Appendix
· · ·
# Notes
· · ·
# Bibliography
· · ·
# Index

# APPENDIX

# Original Irish Plays Staged by Edwards-mac Liammóir Productions, 1928-1940

The following list of original Irish productions at the Gate from 1928, when Edwards and mac Liammóir founded their theater, until 1940, when their artistic policy changed due to their temporary lease of the Gaiety as a secondary playhouse, is largely compiled from *Enter Certain Players: Edwards–MacLiammoir and the Gate 1928–1978* (1978), edited by Peter Luke, 93–104; and the Irish Theatre Institute's database at www.irishplayography.com. New adaptations of literary texts have been excluded, as well as the later plays of Edward and Christine Longford, who directed their own company, Longford Productions, from 1936 onward. All plays listed below, then, are original Irish plays that were staged for the first time by Edwards–mac Liammóir Productions, either at the Gate Theatre or at venues that were temporarily leased by their company. More information can be found in Lally, Clare, and Van den Beuken, "Gate Theatre Chronology (1928–1982)."

## Abbreviations

NLI.   Available as typescript and/or manuscript in the Department of Manuscripts, National Library of Ireland

NU.   Available as typescript and/or manuscript in the Dublin Gate Theatre Archive, Charles Deering McCormick Library of Special Collections, Northwestern University (Evanston, IL)

TCD.   Available as typescript and/or manuscript in the Manuscripts and Archives Research Library, Trinity College Dublin

| Title | Playwright | First production | Availability |
|-------|-----------|------------------|--------------|
| *Diarmuid and Gráinne* | Micheál mac Liammóir | 1928 | NLI, NU |
| *Juggernaut* | David Sears | 1929 | Published, NLI |
| *Tristram and Iseult* | An Philibín (J. H. Pollock) | 1929 | Published |
| *The Old Lady Says "No!"* | Denis Johnston | 1929 | Published, TCD |
| *The Ford of the Hurdles* | Micheál mac Liammóir | 1929 | NLI, NU |
| *A Flutter of Wings* | T. C. Murray | 1930 | Published, NLI |
| *Bride* | Ulick Burke | 1931 | Unknown |
| *The Melians* | Edward Longford | 1931 | Unknown |
| *The Dead Ride Fast* | David Sears | 1931 | NLI (partial) |
| *Youth's the Season—?* | Mary Manning | 1931 | Published, NU |
| *Mogu of the Desert* | Padraic Colum | 1931 | Published, NU |
| *Queens and Emperors* | Christine Longford | 1932 | Unknown |
| *Dark Waters* | Dorothy Macardle | 1932 | Unknown |
| *Storm Over Wicklow* | Mary Manning | 1933 | Unknown |
| *Mr. Jiggins of Jigginstown* | Christine Longford | 1933 | Published, NU |
| *A Bride for the Unicorn* | Denis Johnston | 1933 | Published, NLI, NU, TCD |
| *Grania of the Ships* | David Sears | 1933 | NLI, NU |
| *Yahoo* | Edward Longford | 1933 | Published, NU |
| *Storm Song* | Denis Johnston | 1934 | Published, NU |
| *The New Girl* | Christine Longford | 1934 | NU |
| *Happy Family* | Mary Manning | 1934 | NU |
| *Ascendancy* | Edward Longford | 1935 | Published, NU |
| *Three Leopards* | Cecil Monson | 1935 | NU |
| *When Lovely Woman* | Lennox Robinson | 1936 | Published, NU |
| *Portrait in Marble* | Hazel Ellis | 1936 | NU |
| *Murder, Like Charity,…* | Andrew Ganly | 1937 | NU |
| *Women Without Men* | Hazel Ellis | 1938 | NU |
| *Marrowbone Lane* | Robert Collis | 1939 | Published, NU |
| *Where Stars Walk* | Micheál mac Liammóir | 1940 | Published, NLI, NU |

# Notes

**Introduction**

1. Mac Liammóir, "Problem Plays," 202. See also Richard Pine's discussion of this lecture in "Micheál macLíammóir," 88–89.

2. Mac Liammóir, "Problem Plays," 203.

3. Leerssen, *Remembrance and Imagination*, 4.

4. Kearney, *Transitions*, 9–18.

5. Gibbons, *Transformations in Irish Culture*, 159.

6. Misztal, "Memory and History," 3.

7. Fitz-Simon, *Boys*, 13.

8. Both Christopher Fitz-Simon (*Irish Theatre*, 176) and Chris Morash (*History of Irish Theatre*, 182) use the phrase "director's theatre"; the latter qualification is given by Ben Levitas in "Abbey and the Idea of a Theatre," 56.

9. Likewise, in the postwar years, Edwards and mac Liammóir facilitated the debuts of playwrights such as Maura Laverty, Donagh MacDonagh, Desmond Forristal, and, most prominently, Brian Friel.

10. Edwards, *Mantle of Harlequin*, 3.

11. Manning, "Dublin Has Also Its Gate Theater."

12. Indeed, Paige Reynolds has noted that, "ironically, the remarkable design and direction of the Gate so powerfully dominate its historical narrative that, with the exception of Denis Johnston, few of its plays and playwrights have received sustained attention" ("Design and Direction to 1960," 210). David Clare, Des Lally, and Patrick Lonergan relate the Gate's relative absence in Irish theater scholarship to various methodological and historiographical issues in their introduction to *The Gate Theatre, Dublin: Inspiration and Craft* (2018), which is, rather tellingly, the first scholarly essay collection on the Gate Theatre to ever be published. See Clare, Lally, and Lonergan, "Introduction," 1–4.

13. Kiberd, *Inventing Ireland*, 292.

14. Mac Liammóir, *Theatre in Ireland*, 29–30.

15. Mac Liammóir, 30.

16. Gassner, *Theatre in Our Times*, 387.

17. Mac Liammóir, *All for Hecuba*, 87.

18. Miller, *Modernism, Ireland, and the Erotics of Memory*, 3.

## 1. Cosmopolitan Dublin

1. Mac Liammóir, *Theatre in Ireland*, 7; Ó hAodha, *Theatre in Ireland*, xi.

2. Murray, *Twentieth-Century Irish Theatre*, 3.

3. Morash, *History of Irish Theatre*, 117–18. See also Murray, *Twentieth-Century Irish Drama*, 3–8.

4. Arrington, "Irish Modernism and Its Legacies," 237.

5. Fay, "Irish National Theatre," 391–94.

6. Martyn's manifesto was reproduced and discussed by Ó hAodha in *Theatre in Ireland*, 87–89. See also Morash, *History of Irish Theatre*, 180; and Trotter, *Modern Irish Theatre*, 74.

7. Arrington, *Revolutionary Lives*, 41–46.

8. Robinson, *Abbey Theatre*, 121.

9. Quoted in Katz Clarke and Ferrar, *Dublin Drama League*, 13.

10. Morash, *History of Irish Theatre*, 180.

11. Katz Clarke and Ferrar, *Dublin Drama League*, 13.

12. Katz Clarke and Ferrar, 14–17, 33, 35; Fallon, "Some Aspects of Irish Theatre," 302.

13. Ferrar, *Denis Johnston's Irish Theatre*, 9–11, 14, 17; Katz Clarke and Ferrar, *Dublin Drama League*, 20–21; Morash, *History of Irish Theatre*, 180–81.

14. Ó hAodha, *Theatre in Ireland*, xiii. Shaun Richards makes similar observations in "Unthreatening in the Provincial Irish Air," 394.

15. Mac Liammóir, *All for Hecuba*, 50.

16. Edwards, *Mantle of Harlequin*, 3.

17. For a discussion of the influence of McMaster's acting style on the Gate, see Frazier, "Irish Acting in the Early Twentieth Century," 245–46.

18. Fitz-Simon, *Boys*, 17. For a discussion of Edwards and mac Liammóir's introduction of techniques by Edward Craig, Adolphe Appia, and others, see Reynolds, "Design and Direction to 1960," 207–11.

19. Mac Liammóir, *All for Hecuba*, 50; Fitz-Simon, *Boys*, 49.

20. Mac Liammóir, *All for Hecuba*, 43, 48.

21. Mac Liammóir, 50.

22. Mac Liammóir, 55; see also 18.

23. Mac Liammóir, 55. Hilton Edwards discusses his direction of *The Hairy Ape* in "Production," 25.

24. Mac Liammóir, *All for Hecuba*, 55. Elaine Sisson discusses the New Players (also known as "the Dramick") in "Experimentalism and the Irish Stage," 43–47.

25. Mac Liammóir, *All for Hecuba*, 55. A few years before his death, mac Liammóir reflected on his gastronomical metaphor in a conversation with Richard Pine, during which he praised Synge as "the only man at the time who combined the bacon and cabbage with his own practical ambitions and who had the spirit, the seed and the essence of poetry as well as the crudities of Irish peasant life" (*Dublin Gate Theatre 1928–1978*, 30–31).

26. Mac Liammóir, *All for Hecuba*, 30.

27. Mac Liammóir, 30.

28. Mac Liammóir, 31.

29. Mac Liammóir, 56. For a discussion of the establishment of this theater, see Stafford, "Taibhdhearc na Gaillimhe."

30. Mac Liammóir, *All for Hecuba*, 60–61.

31. Sisson, "Experimentalism and the Free State," 23, 25. Also see Pine, "Micheál macLíammóir," 85.

32. Edwards and Mac Liammóir, "Dublin Gate Theatre Studio" (1928 pamphlet). Courtesy of the National Library of Ireland.

33. Edwards and Mac Liammóir, "Dublin Gate Theatre Studio" (1928 pamphlet). The full list includes plays by the following playwrights: Dymov, Cocteau, Kaiser, O'Neill, Toller, Ibsen, Strindberg, Greensfelder, Hassenclever, Asch, Mohr, Werfel, Vildrac, Evreinov, Gantillon, Andreyev, Goethe, Wilde, Maeterlinck, and mac Liammóir himself.

34. Katz Clarke and Ferrar, *Dublin Drama League*, 20; Fitz-Simon, *Irish Theatre*, 174; Morash, *History of Irish Theatre*, 180–81; Fallon, *Age of Innocence*, 133; and Richards, "Unthreatening in the Provincial Irish Air," 394.

35. Mac Liammóir, *All for Hecuba*, 67.

36. Fitz-Simon, *Boys*, 69–70.

37. Morash, *History of Irish Theatre*, 186.

38. Quoted in Fitz-Simon, *Boys*, 70.

39. "Dramatic Enterprise in Dublin: New Company Floated," *Irish Independent*, October 7, 1929; "Gate Theatre's Venture to Acquire Spacious Hall," *Irish Independent*, June 28, 1929. J.W.G., the *Independent*'s drama critic, had already hailed the Gate's first season as an "experiment . . . [that] has completely justified itself" in his review of Edwards and mac Liammóir's production of Eugene O'Neill's *Anna Christie* (1921). The reviewer stated that "artistically [the Gate] has been the best venture of its kind that has been attempted in Dublin" and that "the new generation is turning out dramatic masterpieces, all of them . . . extraordinarily interesting" ("Play Dickens Would Have Enjoyed: Gate Season Success," *Irish Independent*, January 14, 1929).

40. Hogan and O'Neill, *Joseph Holloway's Irish Theatre*, vol. 1, 41. See also Malone, "Ibsen and the Irish Free State"; "Denis Johnston's Ibsen and Post-revivalist Ireland," 54; and Reynolds, "Design and Direction to 1960," 209.

41. Sisson, "Experimentalism and the Irish Stage," 53–54.

42. Fitz-Simon, *Boys*, 19, 53.

43. Edwards and Mac Liammóir, "Dublin Gate Theatre Studio" (1929 pamphlet).

44. Edwards and Mac Liammóir. The ILT pamphlet is reproduced in Lady Gregory, *Our Irish Theatre*, 8–9.

45. Edwards and Mac Liammóir, "Dublin Gate Theatre Studio" (1929 pamphlet).

46. Edwards and Mac Liammóir.

47. In his untitled contribution to a 1978 commemorative booklet that celebrated the Gate's demicentenary, Michael Scott outlines some of the decisions he made in converting the Rotunda concert hall. Also see Chris Morash's discussion of this reconstruction as a form of exorcism, a "deliberate clearing away of the spectral past so that something new might emerge" (427) in "Places of Performance," 432, 439.

48. Joseph Holloway described how this "first night was attended by all who consider themselves literary and artistic in Dublin. The theatre was cold, although crowded" (Hogan and O'Neill, *Joseph Holloway's Irish Theatre*, vol. 1, 59). While Holloway's initial appraisal of Edwards and mac Liammóir's production was not overly enthusiastic, his second viewing led him to observe that it was "a memorable [performance] in many ways": "Hilton Edwards' 'Mephistopheles' was certainly a weird, masterful creature, and Micheál macLiammóir's 'Faust' was a study of great merit—his delivery was most musical and meaningful. . . . The lighting of the various episodes was ever and always a marvel of colour and harmony, and so perfect and masterfully accomplished. It was almost uncanny how scene followed scene so rapidly, and each and all conveyed exactly what was required to give the proper touch of poetry or weirdness to each episode" (59).

49. Clare, Lally, and Lonergan, "Introduction," 3.

50. Miller, *Independent Theatre in Europe*, 308.

51. Freedley and Reeves, *History of the Theatre*, 493.

52. Canfield, *Plays of Changing Ireland*, 3, xiii. Canfield's additional claims that "the Gate is not set up in opposition to the historic Abbey" and that "the two theatres are complements rather than competitors" seem contradictory and require some explanation. While these statements ostensibly echo Edwards and mac Liammóir's cautious manifestos as well as prefigure the Gate's later reception as a conduit of foreign drama, Canfield described the difference between both theaters in purely stylistic terms. The Abbey and the Gate are equally represented in the anthology with four plays each, and when Canfield referred to how "the Gate stresses the universal and catholic side of the drama rather than its intensely national aspect, which is the Abbey's chief responsibility," he was discussing their respective dramatic techniques, not a supposed aversion to producing original Irish plays (xiii–xiv).

53. Fallon, "Some Aspects of Irish Theatre," 302, 306. For Fallon's discussion of the Gate's commendation by overseas audiences, see 303–4.

54. Fallon, "Some Aspects of Irish Theatre," 303.

55. Fallon, 306.

56. Cole, "Gate Influence on Dublin Theatre," 14.

57. Cole, 7, 14.

58. Cole, 14. Edwards and mac Liammóir would produce Yeats's *The King of the Great Clock Tower* (1935) at the Gaiety Theatre as part of the Summer Harlequinade in May 1942, and *The Countess Cathleen* (1892) at the Gate in April 1953. Mac Liammóir's *Talking About Yeats*, a spiritual successor to his one-man show concerning Oscar Wilde's life and works, premiered at the Shelbourne Hotel in 1965; he also cowrote a (nonfiction) book about his idol, titled *W. B. Yeats and His World* (1971), with the poet Eavan Boland.

59. Gassner, *Theatre in Our Times*, 387.

60. Gassner, 387.

61. Gassner, 389. In this context, Gassner discussed the plays that he presumably saw when one of the Gate's transatlantic tours brought them to Broadway in early 1948; these were George Bernard Shaw's *John Bull's Other Island* (1904) and two original Gate plays: Denis Johnston's *The Old Lady Says "No!"* (1929) and Micheál mac Liammóir's *Where Stars Walk* (1940).

62. Robert Hogan, who dedicated a substantial section of *After the Irish Renaissance* (1968) to original Gate plays, provides a pertinent exception.

63. Quoted in Fitz-Simon, *Boys*, 292, 303.

64. Ó hAodha, *Theatre in Ireland*, 127. Indeed, Ó hAodha's concise list of Gate authors only served to illustrate his claim that Edwards and mac Liammóir's company "failed to attract a steady succession of new playwrights and eventually became a valuable showcase for the classics and international drama, rather than a creative force as far was playwriting is concerned" (125).

65. Fitz-Simon, *Irish Theatre*, 178. Fitz-Simon did admit that Edwards and mac Liammóir's style "naturally attracted younger writers whose work was unlikely to prove acceptable at the Abbey" and discussed a few of these anomalies, ranging from Mary Manning through Maura Laverty to Desmond Forristal.

66. See, for example, Fallis, *Irish Renaissance*, 181, 194–95, 199; and Maxwell, *Critical History of Modern Irish Drama*, 132.

67. Pine and Cave, *Dublin Gate Theatre*, 22. Pine already contributed a comprehensive overview of the Gate's history in *All for Hecuba* (1978), a souvenir catalog for the exhibition celebrating the theater's fiftieth anniversary, which took place a few months after mac Liammóir's death.

68. Pine and Cave, *Dublin Gate Theatre*, 16, 56, 87. In their introduction to *The Gate Theatre, Dublin: Inspiration and Craft* (2008), Clare, Lally, and Lonergan also stress the validity of this term (5, 8).

69. Pine and Cave, *Dublin Gate Theatre*, 31.

70. Pine and Cave, 48.

71. Pine and Cave, 16, 22. Pine's parallel is unambiguous: "The new theatre had in fact so much in common with the Abbey that it is impossible to distinguish absolutely

between 'Abbey' authors and 'Gate' authors" (50). Likewise, he maintains that the Gate playwrights' "ambitions, in terms of a developing Irish drama, would be comparable rather than contrasting" (51).

72. Pine and Cave, *Dublin Gate Theatre*, 24.

73. Pine and Cave, 51. Pine stresses this point again in "Micheál macLíammóir," 90–92.

74. Also, John Cowell's double biography of the Longfords, *No Profit But the Name* (1988), had been published a few years earlier.

75. Brown, *Literature of Ireland*, 90–91.

76. Brown, 91. Richards reassesses precisely this claim in "Unthreatening in the Provincial Irish Air."

77. See, for example, assessments of the Gate's sociocultural importance in Allen, *Modernism, Ireland, and Civil War*, 98–100, 109; Trotter, *Modern Irish Theatre*, 91–93, 99; and Sisson, "Note on What Happened," 144–45.

78. Morash and Richards, *Mapping Irish Theatre*, 62.

79. Morash and Richards, 61.

80. Morash and Richards, 24.

81. Arrington, "Irish Modernism and Its Legacies," 236.

82. Arrington, 248–49.

## 2. Mac Liammóir's Exorcism

1. Fitz-Simon, *Boys*, 130.

2. Fitz-Simon, 302.

3. Walshe, "Sodom and Begorrah," 152–53. Walshe reiterates this argument in his chapter on mac Liammóir in *Oscar's Shadow*, 55–68.

4. Ó hAodha, *Importance of Being Micheál*, 19.

5. Ó hAodha, 18–19.

6. Madden, *Making of an Artist*, 2.

7. Madden, 15.

8. Pine, "Micheál macLíammóir," 73.

9. Ó hAodha, *Importance of Being Micheál*, 190. Madden, too, comments on mac Liammóir's ability to "[blend] seamlessly into whatever setting in which he found himself" (*Making of an Artist*, 2) and repeatedly refers to mac Liammóir as a "chameleon" (2, 3, 15, 327).

10. Ó hAodha, *Importance of Being Micheál*, xvi, 182. Madden also accords mac Liammóir this title in *Making of an Artist*, 2.

11. Ó hAodha, *Importance of Being Micheál*, 190.

12. Mac Liammóir, *All for Hecuba*, 146.

13. Mac Liammóir, 147.

14. Wilde, "Critic as Artist," 43.

15. Kearney, *Transitions*, 17, 14.

16. Leerssen, *Remembrance and Imagination*, 225.

17. Cleary, *Outrageous Fortune*, 59.

18. Eagleton, *Heathcliff and the Great Hunger*, 274.

19. Cleary, "Misplaced Ideas?," 19.

20. Cleary, 45.

21. Morash and Richards, *Mapping Irish Theatre*, 54.

22. Cleary, "Misplaced Ideas?," 21. See also C. L. Innes's reflection on the belated acknowledgment of Ireland's postcolonial status in literary studies in "Modernism, Ireland, and Empire."

23. Kinealy, "Famine Killed Everything," 3–13; "Beyond Revisionism."

24. Whelan, "Pre- and Post-famine Landscape Change," 31.

25. Lloyd, "Memory of Hunger," 215.

26. Lloyd, *Irish Times*, 31.

27. McLean, *Event and Its Terrors*, 150; Eagleton, *Heathcliff and the Great Hunger*, 11.

28. Gibbons, *Transformations in Irish Culture*, 6, 167.

29. For a discussion of the complex societal fragmentation that characterized the Free State's early years, see, for example, Foster, *Irish Civil War and Society*, 225–26.

30. Morash and Richards, *Mapping Irish Theatre*, 23.

31. O'Halpin, *Defending Ireland*, 105–21; "Politics and the State," 124–25; Lee, *Ireland 1912–1985*, 178–84.

32. Gibbons, *Transformations in Irish Culture*, 167.

33. Castle, *Modernism and the Celtic Revival*, 2.

34. Castle, 3.

35. Castle, 11, 3.

36. Huyssen, *After the Great Divide*, 163–64.

37. Kearney, *Transitions*, 28.

38. Kearney, 28.

39. Murphy, *Theorizing the Avant-Garde*, 3.

40. See also Paul Peppis's argument about the patriotic credentials of Vorticism and concurrent avant-garde movements in *Literature, Politics, and the English Avant-Garde* (2000).

41. Miller, *Modernism, Ireland, and the Erotics of Memory*, 5.

42. Miller, 8.

43. Mac Liammóir, *All for Hecuba*, 216–17.

44. Landsberg, *Prosthetic Memory*, 19.

45. Landsberg, 152.

46. Mac Liammóir, *All for Hecuba*, 100.

47. Giddens, *Consequences of Modernity*, 4; mac Liammóir, *All for Hecuba*, 100.

48. Mac Liammóir, 100.

49. Mac Liammóir, 201.

50. Mac Liammóir, 309.

51. Gibbons, *Transformations in Irish Culture*, 179.

52. Kiberd, *Inventing Ireland*, 6; mac Liammóir, *All for Hecuba*, 309.

53. Misztal, "Memory and History," 6.

54. Misztal, 7; Frawley, "Towards a Theory of Cultural Memory," 29.

55. Frawley, 30.

56. Wertsch, *Voices of Collective Remembering*, 62.

57. Mac Liammóir, *All for Hecuba*, 309.

58. Hirsch, "Generation of Postmemory," 107.

59. Hirsch, 110.

60. Grene, *Politics of Irish Drama*, 267.

61. Hirsch, "Generation of Postmemory," 110.

62. Mac Liammóir, *All for Hecuba*, 310–11. The ubiquity of ghosts, specters, and skeletons in Famine literature has been described as an "identifiable discursive formation" by Chris Morash in *Writing the Irish Famine*, 5.

63. Hirsch, "Generation of Postmemory," 111.

64. Mac Liammóir, *All for Hecuba*, 311.

65. Mac Liammóir, 312.

66. Mac Liammóir, *All for Hecuba*, 341. Ellipsis in original.

67. Miller, *Modernism, Ireland and the Erotics of Memory*, 8.

68. Pine, *Politics of Irish Memory*, 4; mac Liammóir, *All for Hecuba*, 341.

69. Mac Liammóir, 66.

70. Mac Liammóir, 52.

## 3. Playing Their Part for Ireland

1. Pine, *Politics of Irish Memory*, 16.

2. Frawley, "Introduction," xv.

3. Pine, *Politics of Irish Memory*, 17.

4. An example of how Irish applications of Carlson's concept tend to focus mostly on postwar drama is found in Paul Murphy's discussion of class conflict in "Ireland's Haunted Stages," where he argues that such specters "re-materialize in the themes, characters and performance accretions of plays in successive decades *since 1949*" (24; italics added).

5. Pine, *Politics of Irish Memory*, 4.

6. Morash and Richards, *Mapping Irish Theatre*, 176.

7. Morash and Richards, 98.

8. Allen, "Imagining the Rising," 168.

9. Holdsworth, "Introduction," 2. See also Ben Levitas, *Theatre of Nation*, 5–6.

10. Holdsworth, "Introduction," 3.

11. Holdsworth, 6.

12. Kruger, *National Stage*, 25.

13. Kruger, 26.

14. Murray, *Twentieth-Century Irish Theatre*, 123. Indeed, Murray considers the Abbey's 1977 revival of *The Old Lady Says "No!"*—which came two years shy of marking the play's demicentenary—to have been the first production of Johnston's masterpiece in the setting "where it properly belongs" (123).

15. O'Faoláin, "Mr. O Faolain's Plea for the Abbey Theatre," *Irish Times*, March 2, 1935.

16. Pilkington, "Abbey Theatre and the Irish State," 231–32.

17. Pilkington, 233, 242.

18. Pilkington, *Theatre & Ireland*, 55.

19. Lonergan, *Theatre and Globalization*, 218.

20. Sisson, "Experimentalism and the Irish Stage," 55. See also Murray, "Irish Theatre," 21.

21. Trotter, *Modern Irish Theatre*, 92.

22. Fallon, *Age of Innocence*, 1–2.

23. Allen, *Modernism, Ireland and Civil War*, 12.

24. Allen, 4.

25. Allen, 2.

26. Fallon, *Age of Innocence*, 13.

27. Allen, *Modernism, Ireland and Civil War*, 61.

28. Allen, 16.

29. Miller, *Modernism, Ireland, and the Erotics of Memory*, 7; Jameson, "Marxism and Historicism," 153; Longenbach, *Modernist Poetics of History*, 13. See also Frawley, "Introduction," xiv–xviii.

30. Morash, *History of Irish Theatre 1601–2000*, 276.

31. Reynolds, *Modernism, Drama, and the Audience*, 11.

32. Reynolds, 32.

33. Heinige, *Buffoonery in Irish Drama*, 92.

34. Murray, "Irish Theatre," 13.

35. Mac Liammóir, *Theatre in Ireland*, 30.

36. Shakespeare, *As You Like It*, 2.7.58–59.

37. Allen, *Modernism, Ireland, and Civil War*, 17, 89.

38. Allen, 101.

39. Allen, 102.

40. Longford, "National Asset," 2.

41. Longford, 2.

42. Longford, "National Theatre at Athens," 6–8. Mary Manning made a similar appeal in a short article titled "Subsidies," 2.

43. Whelan, "Lord Longford's *Yahoo*," 147.

44. Longford, "National Asset," 2.

45. Longford, 2.

46. Allen, *Modernism, Ireland, and Civil War*, 97.

47. Longford, "Preface," 9.

48. Longford, 9.

49. Manning, "Present Position of Irish Drama," 2.

50. Manning, "Gate Theatre," 2. The issue's table of contents lists this article's title as referring to the years 1932–33, corresponding with "the present theatrical season" that Manning was reviewing, but the heading on the page itself erroneously reads "1932–32."

51. Manning, "Still Going Forward," 2.

52. Manning, "Present Position of Irish Drama," 3.

53. Longford, "Preface," 9.

54. Reddin, "National Theatre," 6. Jerry Nolan has commented on Reddin's comparison in "Edward Martyn's Struggle for an Irish National Theater," 103.

55. Reddin, "National Theatre," 6.

56. Reddin, 6.

57. Reddin, 8.

58. Reddin, 8.

59. Longford, "Preface," 10.

60. Edwards, "Why the Dublin Gate Theatre?," 3.

61. Edwards, 4.

62. Edwards, 3.

63. Edwards, 3.

64. Edwards, *Mantle of Harlequin*, 3.

65. Pine and Cave, *Dublin Gate Theatre*, 22.

66. Mac Liammóir, preface to *Mantle of Harlequin*, xv; Edwards, *Mantle of Harlequin*, 4.

67. Edwards, 41.

68. "Future of Gate Theatre," *Irish Times*, January 29, 1936. Edwards had already voiced some of these sentiments (such as observing that "deliberate nationalism is rarely so powerful in art as spontaneous nationality") in a letter to the editor that was published in the wake of the controversy that had occurred after Seán O'Faoláin had attacked W. B. Yeats in the *Irish Times* (discussed above); see Edwards, "To the Editor of the *Irish Times*."

69. Pellizzi, "As Italy Sees Us," 3.

70. Johnston, "National Morality Play," 4. This piece appeared under the pseudonym E. W. Tocher, the name that Johnston, a barrister, initially also employed when publishing and producing his plays.

71. Johnston, 4. In the second part of his essay, Johnston went on to propose a yearly theatrical reenactment of the Easter Rising along the length of O'Connell Street; this scheme will be discussed in chapter 5.

72. Reynolds, *Modernism, Drama, and the Audience*, 21; Sisson, "Experimentalism and the Irish Stage," 54.

73. Manning, "Realism," 3.

74. Allen, *Modernism, Ireland, and Civil War*, 100; Johnston, "Towards a Dynamic Theatre," 4. See also Morash and Richards's discussion of Johnston's manifesto and poetics in *Mapping Irish Theatre*, 59–61; and Richard Cave's discussion of technological and dramaturgical innovations in "Modernism and Irish Theatre," 134–37.

75. Edwards, "Production," 21.

76. Edwards, 21–22.

77. Edwards, 22.

78. Edwards, 26.

79. Morash and Richards, *Mapping Irish Theatre*, 35.

80. Edwards, "Production," 29.

81. Reynolds, *Modernism, Drama, and the Audience*, 32.

82. Edwards, "Production," 30–32. On November 20, 1933, the Gate organized a symposium to debate the proposition "that the Cinema must eventually supersede the Theatre" (Manning, "Processional," *Motley* 2.7, 8). The next issue of *Motley* included a report on this meeting (Manning, "Processional," *Motley* 2.8).

83. Edwards, "Production," 32.

84. Morash and Richards, *Mapping Irish Theatre*, 77.

85. Edwards, "Production," 32–33. Edwards would revisit these issues as well as the rise of the radio play and the television in *Mantle of Harlequin*, 8–10, 24–25, 42.

86. Edwards, "Production," 33, 44.

87. Edwards, 45.

88. Edwards, 45.

89. Edwards, 45.

90. Carlson, "Space and Theatre," 22.

91. Walsh, "Hilton Edwards as Director," 41.

## 4. Mythology Making History

1. Kearney, *Postcolonial Ireland*, 120.

2. Cave, "Dangers and Difficulties," 3.

3. Cave, 9. Italics in original.

4. Whereas the tale of Diarmuid and Gráinne is part of the Fenian Cycle, the Celtic origins of the legend of Tristram and Iseult (or Isolde) are somewhat more complex. For the textual genetics of this myth, see Grimbert, *Tristan and Isolde*, 23–34.

5. Corbett, *Allegories of Union*, 16.

6. Corbett, 53.

7. Hansen, *Terror and Irish Modernism*, 17. See also Robinson, "Marriage against Inclination."

8. Kearney, *Postcolonial Ireland*, 120.

9. Said, "Afterword," 179.

10. McBride, "Memory and National Identity in Modern Ireland," 3.

11. McBride, 12.

12. Morash and Richards, *Mapping Irish Theatre*, 80, 83.

13. Morash and Richards, 85–86.

14. "A Fianna Play," *Irish Times*, November 19, 1928.

15. Hogan and O'Neill, *Joseph Holloway's Irish Theatre*, vol. 1, 42.

16. Mac Liammóir, *Diarmuid and Gráinne*, 3. Courtesy of the National Library of Ireland. The characters' names are spelled in accordance with the program that was distributed during its first run rather than the typescript, which uses Anglicized spellings (e.g., "Finn" for "Fionn").

17. Yeats and Gregory, *Cathleen ni Houlihan*, 86; Kearney, *Postcolonial Ireland*, 113.

18. Morash and Richards, *Mapping Irish Theatre*, 44–45.

19. Yeats, "Easter 1916," 203.

20. Mac Liammóir, *Diarmuid and Gráinne*, 21; Yeats, "Easter 1916," 204.

21. J. W. G., "New Irish Verse Play," *Irish Independent*, June 6, 1929.

22. Hogan and O'Neill, *Joseph Holloway's Irish Theatre*, vol. 1, 47. The songs that were played during the intervals between the three plays were composed by Dr. J. F. Larchet, but Holloway felt that they were sung rather badly (48). However, the play's setting and lighting were to Holloway's liking: "The elongated, celtic-ornamentesque-like figures that filled the panels of the pavilion of 'Tristan's' ship were amongst the weirdest shapes imaginable, and filled the eye with the barbaric splendour of the time. It is marvellous what Edwards can do on such a small stage, and his settings and lighting and dressing of plays leave little to be desired" (48).

23. Mac Liammóir, *Diarmuid and Gráinne*, 16; An Philibín, *Tristram and Iseult*, 12.

24. An Philibín, 33; Yeats, "Rose Tree," 206. Similar imagery is found in Joseph Plunkett's "I See His Blood upon the Rose."

25. Murray, "History Play Today," 273.

26. Although the character's name is spelled "Grania" in the play's title as featured on playbills and programs, the typescript reads "Graine." Throughout this discussion, the typescript versions of names have been maintained to avoid inconsistencies in quotations.

27. A.E.M., "New Play at the 'Gate': *Grania of the Ships*," *Irish Independent*, September 6, 1933. Another reviewer called *Grania of the Ships* "a vigorous, sometimes brilliant drama" and "a finely tempered play." See "Sears Play Success at the Gate Theatre," *Evening Herald*, September 6, 1933.

28. Sears, *Grania of the Ships*, 51. Courtesy of the National Library of Ireland.

29. Yeats and Gregory, *Cathleen ni Houlihan*, 85.

30. Kearney, *Postcolonial Ireland*, 117.

31. Morash and Richards, *Mapping Irish Theatre*, 24.

32. Cave, "Dangers and Difficulties," 15.

33. *"The Ford of the Hurdles*: Pageant Play at the Mansion House," *Irish Times*, September 10, 1929.

34. "City in the Dawn: Peace and Fulfilments of Dreams: Pageant of Dublin," *Irish Independent*, September 10, 1929.

35. Dean, "Rewriting the Past," 34. Dean has expanded on her analysis of *Ford of the Hurdles* in *All Dressed Up*, 118–28.

36. Mac Liammóir, *Ford of the Hurdles*, 1.1. Courtesy of the National Library of Ireland. In the typescript, the page numbers are reset for each episode.

37. Mac Liammóir, 1.6. When the Old Woman leaves the house at the end of Yeats and Gregory's *Cathleen ni Houlihan*, Peter asks Patrick whether he saw "an old woman going down the path," and Patrick answers, "I did not, but I saw a young girl, and she had the walk of a queen" (88).

38. Yeats and Gregory, 83. These deaths, too, will be violent, for "they that have red cheeks will have pale cheeks for my sake, and for all that, they will think they are well paid" (86).

39. Dean, *All Dressed Up*, 123.

40. One of the phrases that the ballad seller uses is "Go dteachta an diabhal thu" ("May the devil choke you"). For the etymology of "Sean/Seón Buidhe," see Joep Leerssen, *Mere Irish & Fíor-ghael*, 255.

41. McIvor and O'Gorman, "Devising Ireland," 13–14; Reynolds, "Design and Direction to 1960," 214.

42. Dean, "Pageants, Parades, and Performance Culture," 618.

43. Gilbert and Tompkins, *Post-colonial Drama*, 126.

44. Gilbert and Tompkins, 136.

45. Holdsworth, "Introduction," 8.

## 5. From History to Identity

1. This 1897 pamphlet is reproduced in Gregory, *Our Irish Theatre*, 8–9.

2. Gregory, 12.

3. Eglinton, "What Should Be the Subjects of National Drama?," 411.

4. Kiberd, *Inventing Ireland*, 644.

5. Murray, "History Play Today," 269.

6. Swift, "Drapier's Letter I": "Mr WOOD made his HALFPENCE of such *base* metal, and so much smaller than the English ones, that the *brazier* would not give you above a *penny* of good money for a *shilling* of his; so that the sum of *fourscore* and *ten thousand pounds* in good gold and silver, must be given for TRASH that will not be worth above *eight* or *nine thousand pound* real value" (423–24). For an explanation of this controversy and its historical roots, see Fabricant, "Swift the Irishman," 56–57; and the notes to the Drapier's Letters in Swift, *Major Works*, 669–71.

7. Swift, "Swift to Lord Carteret" (April 28, 1724), 431.

8. McMinn, "Swift's Life," 25.

9. Fabricant, "Swift the Irishman," 57.

10. Richard Allen Cave discusses all three plays in "Dramatising the Life of Swift." For further discussions of Johnston's play, see Morash, "Denis Johnston's Swift Project," 56–59; Girel-Pietka, "Winds of Change," 84–99; Girel-Pietka, "Denis Johnston at the Gate," 127–29; and Pilný, "Doing Justice to Swift," 88–92. Also, Elizabeth Mannion discusses how earlier Swift plays at the Abbey "reflect the evolution that the Dean's status as a nationalist icon underwent in Ireland" (163) in *Getting Personal*, 158–63.

11. Canfield, *Plays of Changing Ireland*, 7.

12. Trotter, *Modern Irish Theatre*, 100.

13. Whelan, "Lord Longford's *Yahoo*," 149–53.

14. Sears, "A Portrait of Dean Swift: Lord Longford's Play," *Irish Independent*, September 20, 1933.

15. D.M., "*Yahoo* at the Gate Theatre: Lord Longford's Play on Dean Swift," *Irish Press*, September 20, 1933. Joseph Holloway believed the play was "fantastic commentary on the life of Dean Swift" and recorded how "Lord Longford made a speech and said Dean Swift was the first of the great Irish Nationalists" (Hogan and O'Neill, *Joseph Holloway's Irish Theatre*, vol. 2, 26).

16. For a discussion of Swift's romantic relationships, see Doody, "Swift and Women," 87–111.

17. Longford, *Yahoo*, 156. For a description of the political upheavals (and the subsequent downfall of the Tories) that had forced Swift to retire to Dublin, see McMinn, "Swift's Life," 21–23. However, Caroline Fabricant has argued that "the popular view of Swift living out his years in Ireland as a disgruntled exile, filled with bitterness at his entrapment in a hateful land and constantly obsessing about his 'glory days' in England, requires drastic modification"; see "Swift the Irishman," 51.

18. Longford, *Yahoo*, 156. Stella's remark refers to Swift's *Proposal for the Universal Use of Irish Manufacture* (1720).

19. Longford, *Yahoo*, 157. Similarly, when Stella asks Swift to "stand forth as Ireland's defender against tyrants," Swift states that "they are all Yahoos, vermin, ingrates, tyrant and slave alike" (158).

20. Barnett, *Jonathan Swift in the Company of Women*, 40.

21. Swift, "Drapier's Letter IV," 440, 442.

22. Canfield, "Note on *Yahoo*," 150.

23. Swift's servant remarks that "he is so changed does naught now but write and write, and write, like a madman in Bedlam" (Longford, *Yahoo*, 179). Longford adapted the chronology of Swift's life for his own purposes: while the play covers a period of only a few months, Swift had already returned to Ireland by 1714; he published the Drapier's Letters in 1724, became incapacitated due to dementia by 1742, and died in 1744. Also,

as Louisa Barnett observes in *Jonathan Swift in the Company of Women* (40), Swift's alleged marriage to Stella is conventionally said to have taken place in 1716, with St. George Ashe presiding over the ceremony rather than George Berkeley, while Vanessa died in 1723. Both events, then, actually occurred *before* the Drapier's Letters controversy.

24. Pine, *Politics of Irish Memory*, 16–17.

25. By 1933, bowdlerized versions of *Gulliver's Travels* had indeed become a staple of children's literature. In his will, Swift decreed the establishment of "an hospital large enough for the reception of . . . idiots and lunatics" ("Dr Swift's Will," 519). This mental asylum, St. Patrick's Hospital, still exists today.

26. Whelan, "Lord Longford's *Yahoo*," 157.

27. The crowd's version stresses their steadfast devotion to the Dean: "Can we the Drapier then forget? / Is not our nation in his debt? / Two kingdoms by a faction led, / Had set a price upon his head. / But not a traitor could be found / To sell him for six hundred pound!" (185).

28. Longford, *Yahoo*, 188. Ironically, he is unable to pronounce the alternative road name that he tries to propose: "I can't read this, it's in Irish" (188).

29. Sears, "New Play at the Gate Theatre," *Irish Independent*, January 30, 1935. Sears also claimed that "in the author's anxiety to show that they were Irish, and regarded themselves as such, he rather gave the impression that the cause of their downfall was drunkenness which, at the period, was a European, not merely an Irish Protestant, vice. Their acceptance of the support of British bayonets . . . was the real cause of their downfall."

30. "A New Lord Longford Play," *Irish Press*, January 30, 1935. Joseph Holloway found the play to be "a very poor effort indeed, but splendidly staged and dressed, and on the whole well played." According to Holloway, the play failed because it was "crudely melodramatic in situation and dialogue, and the characters [are] all strongly marked types rather than human beings" (Hogan and O'Neill, *Joseph Holloway's Irish Theatre*, vol. 2, 44).

31. Longford, *Ascendancy*, 8.

32. Geoghegan, *King Dan*, 187–247.

33. Geoghegan, 248–70.

34. Longford, *Ascendancy*, 48. As Geoghegan notes in *King Dan*, O'Connell frequently received death threats from 1824 onward (205).

35. During the party, the First Gentleman foreshadows the Earl of Clonave's death by remarking that he will decline membership of the William Society because has "no intention of risking a stab in the back from an indignant tenant" (43).

36. Pine, *Politics of Irish Memory*, 16

37. Pine, 17.

38. "Proclamation of the Irish Republic."

39. Geoghegan, *Robert Emmet*, 266–69.

40. Hawkins, "Playing Both Ends against the Middle"; Poulain, *Irish Drama, Modernity, and the Passion Play*, 122–24.

41. Mannion, *Getting Personal*, 147–54.

42. Quoted in Geoghegan, *Robert Emmet*, 24. For a discussion of Sarah Curran's life after Emmet's death, see 30–37.

43. Geoghegan, 286–87. See also Geoghegan's discussion of Emmet's poetry (67–68, 95–96).

44. Geoghegan, *Robert Emmet*, 266.

45. Davies, *Crucified Nation*, 68–69.

46. Dean, *All Dressed Up*, 125.

47. Mac Liammóir, *Ford of the Hurdles*, 6.1.

48. Quoted in Geoghegan, *Robert Emmet*, 228.

49. Quoted in Geoghegan, 296.

50. Morash, *History of Irish Theatre*, 112–14; Dean, "Rewriting the Past," 34.

51. Mac Liammóir, *Ford of the Hurdles*, 6.4.

52. Quoted in Geoghegan, *Robert Emmet*, 247. The version of Emmet's speech that is quoted here is Geoghegan's; for his approach in reconstructing this version, see 244–47.

53. Mac Liammóir, *Ford of the Hurdles*, 6.8–9. Geoghegan's version is slightly different: "I do not hope that you will let my vindication ride at anchor in your breasts. I only ask you, to let it float upon the surface of your recollection, till it comes to some more friendly port to receive it, and give it shelter against the heavy storms with which it is buffeted" (*Robert Emmet*, 247).

54. Mac Liammóir, 6.9. Geoghegan's text is identical except for the comma after "heroes" (*Robert Emmet*, 250). With regard to the alleged French conspiracy, Emmet was adamant: "Let no man attaint my memory by believing I could have been engaged in any cause but of my country's liberty and independence" (252). Mac Liammóir's version is identical, except for omitting "been" (*Ford of the Hurdles*, 6.12).

55. Mac Liammóir, 6.15. Geoghegan's version is identical except for adding "its" to "its silence" in reference to "this world" (*Robert Emmet*, 253–54).

56. Geoghegan, *Robert Emmet*, 254. Mac Liammóir's version is identical (*Ford of the Hurdles*, 6.15).

57. Johnston, "Opus One," 16.

58. For an analysis of the play's textual genesis, see Christine St. Peter's "*Old Lady*," 10–23; the introduction to her 1992 edition of *The Old Lady Says "No!"*; and Ferrar, *Denis Johnston's Irish Theatre*, 22–26.

59. Maxwell, *Critical History of Modern Irish Drama*, 115; St. Peter, "Denis Johnston, the Abbey, and the Spirit of the Age," 197; Murray, *Twentieth-Century Irish Drama*, 120–21; Morash, *History of Irish Theatre*, 181; Trotter, *Modern Irish Theatre*, 96. When Johnston tried to acquire the sponsorship that he had been promised, Yeats happened to be out of the country, leaving the Abbey's affairs in the hands of Lennox Robinson, who was much less keen to provide funding to the Gate Theatre; in the end, Johnston received only £15 (Adams, *Denis Johnston*, 102).

60. Ferrar, *Denis Johnston's Irish Theatre*, 17.

61. Trotter, *Modern Irish Theatre*, 96; Morash, *History of Irish Theatre*, 182.

62. Pilný, *Irony and Identity in Modern Irish Drama*, 97.

63. For an overview of Johnston's dense intertextuality, see Canfield's appendix in *Plays of Changing Ireland*; and the play's edition in Owens and Radner's *Irish Drama 1900–1980*.

64. Johnston, *Old Lady Says "No!"*, 13. Courtesy of the Board of Trinity College Dublin. All references are to the 1929 typescript, which documents the play's first production. Johnston made various revisions in future productions and publications.

65. Poulain, *Irish Drama, Modernity, and the Passion Play*, 133.

66. Morash and Richards, *Mapping Irish Theatre*, 60.

67. Johnston, *Old Lady Says "No!"*, 6. William Drennan (1754–1820) was a doctor and member of the United Irishmen. Mary "Eva" Kelley (1825–1910) was a Romantic poet whose poems appeared in the *Nation*.

68. "The darling of Erin" is a phrase from "Bold Robert Emmet," a popular ballad by Tom Maguire.

69. Marx, "Eighteenth Brumaire of Louis Bonaparte," 93.

70. Johnston, *Old Lady Says "No!"*, 30. For Pearse's speech, see O'Rourke Murphy and MacKillop, *Irish Literature Reader*, 225–27.

71. Foucault, "Of Other Spaces," 24–25.

72. The three artists are called O'Cooney, O'Rooney, and O'Mooney, who are caricatures of Sean O'Casey, Liam O'Flaherty, and Patrick Touhy, respectively. See Owens and Newlon, eds., *Irish Drama 1900–1980*, 379. These three names, without their patronymic prefixes, also occur in "The Luckpenny," where they refer to three local ruffians; see O'Connor, *Turf-Fire Stories and Fairy Tales of Ireland*, 187–97.

73. For analyses of the discussions between the Speaker/Robert Emmet and the statue of Henry Grattan, see Ferrar, *Denis Johnston's Irish Theatre*, 32–33; and Hogan, *After the Irish Renaissance*, 136.

74. Marx, "Eighteenth Brumaire of Louis Bonaparte," 93. Declan Kiberd relates Marx's argument to the cultural poetics of the Easter Rising in *Inventing Ireland*, 202, 206–7.

75. Johnston, *Old Lady Says "No!"*, 77. John O'Brien has argued that Johnston might have been inspired by Josef Čapek's *The Land of Many Names* (1926) in drafting this speech; for a discussion of its genealogy, see "Expressionism and the Formative Years," 41–44.

76. "An Irish Review: *The Old Lady Says 'No!'*," *Irish Times*, July 4, 1929.

77. Sears, "An Extraordinary Play: Mr Tocher's Work," *Irish Independent*, July 4, 1929. Sears observed an "impressed and delighted" audience and praised the performances by Micheál mac Liammóir (the Speaker) and Meriel Moore (Sarah Curran) as well as Hilton Edwards's staging and direction.

78. Cave, "Modernism and Irish Theatre," 133; Trotter, *Modern Irish Theatre*, 98.

79. Ferrar, *Denis Johnston's Irish Theatre*, 39.

80. Murray, *Twentieth-Century Irish Drama*, 124–25.

81. Grene, *Politics of Irish Drama*, 155; Poulain, *Irish Drama, Modernity, and the Passion Play*, 135.

82. Poulain, 126.

83. Moran, *Staging the Easter Rising*, 1.

84. Morash and Richards, *Mapping Irish Theatre*, 8–9; Higgins, *Transforming 1916*, 157–58. See also Kiberd, *Inventing Ireland*, 203–7; and Allen, "Imagining the Rising," 156–58.

85. Morash, *History of Irish Theatre*, 164.

86. "Tragedy and Comedy in Triple Bill," *Irish Times*, March 29, 1932; D.M., "Prophetic Play by Pearse," *Irish Press*, March 29, 1932.

87. "Review of the Week's Amusements: The Gate," *Evening Mail*, March 29, 1932.

88. Sisson, "Dublin Civic Week and the Materialisation of History," 141.

89. Mac Liammóir, *Ford of the Hurdles*, 7.1. The Minstrel's repeated cry to "wake, wake from your sleep" is a motif that occurs in many exhortations to the Irish people. In *Yahoo*, Stella pleads with Swift to "cry aloud and wake" his countrymen, and in *The Old Lady Says "No!"*, Emmet uses a similar phrase: "Men of Eire, awake to be blest." This phrase also features in Emmet's own poetry: the poem "Genius of Erin" features the lines "Erin's sons, awake!—awake! / Oh! too long, too long, you sleep; / Awake! Arise! Your fetters break, / Nor let your country bleed and weep" (quoted in Geoghegan, *Robert Emmet*, 284–85). The Young Ireland leader Thomas Davis would popularize the phrase in his rebel poem "The West's Asleep."

90. Interestingly, in an unmarked and incomplete draft located in the Gate Theatre Archive at Northwestern University, the Voice's lines are divided among the seven signatories of the Proclamation, who feature as separate characters; in the final version, however, none of the characters are named.

91. McBride, "Memory and National Identity in Modern Ireland," 35.

92. Sisson, "Dublin Civic Week and the Materialisation of History," 140–41.

93. Dean, "Rewriting the Past," 38; mac Liammóir, *Ford of the Hurdles* 7.7.

94. This essay was republished nine years later in Seán O'Faoláin's magazine the *Bell*. See Johnston, "Public Opinion."

95. Johnston, "National Morality Play," 5.

96. Wills, *Dublin 1916*, 151–55. For the editor's response, see Manning, "An Open Letter to *The Leader*," 13.

97. Wills, *Dublin 1916*, 154–55. Wills refers to a rather mordant observation that appeared in the second issue of *Motley*, in which the audience's passive reaction to both patriotic plays was lambasted: "The crowded house listened to Pearse and MacLiammoir with the closest attention. When *Easter 1916* is produced next year one would like to see an audience in vocal collaboration. But this is perhaps too much to expect from an Irish

public which has forgotten 'Let Erin Remember' and has never learned the National Anthem" (C.P.C., "Notes on Recent Productions," 6).

98. Allen, *Modernism, Ireland, and Civil War*, 98.

99. Dean, "Pageants, Parades, and Performance Culture," 621.

100. Dean, "Rewriting the Past," 20–21. Likewise, Dean's use of examples of earlier (non-Irish) cultural events that attempted "to create community through the re-theatricalization of theater" (20) is reminiscent of Johnston's pronouncement that "the Theatre should be theatrical" ("National Morality Play," 4).

101. Pine, *Politics of Irish Memory*, 4.

102. Johnston, "National Morality Play," 5.

103. Moran, *Staging the Easter Rising*, 1.

104. Moran, 1.

105. Sisson, "Appeasing Pearse's Ghosts," 171–72.

106. Morash and Richards, *Mapping Irish Theatre*, 24.

107. Dean, "Rewriting the Past," 23.

108. "Great Success of *Juggernaut*," *Irish Independent*, April 2, 1929; "*Juggernaut*: New Play Produced with Success in Dublin," *Evening Herald*, March 20, 1929.

109. "An Irish Problem Play: *Juggernaut* a Popular Success at the Dublin Gate Theatre," *Southern Star*, April 6, 1929. Indeed, the reviewer went on to claim that "from [Sears's] conclusion many an Irishman and woman will lay the flattering unction to their hearts that had opportunity served them, . . . they would have made the same sacrifice without hope of reward to an inevitable idea which Mr. Sears, somewhat harshly, perhaps, likens to the juggernaut."

110. Walsh, "Foreword," 4–5.

111. Grene, *Politics of Irish Drama*, 52.

112. Sears, *Juggernaut*, 7.

113. Morash and Richards, *Mapping Irish Theatre*, 44.

114. Yeats, "Man and the Echo," 393.

115. Joyce, *Ulysses*, 34.

## 6. Identity after Independence

1. Campbell, "Modern Architecture and National Identity in Ireland," 285.

2. Campbell, 293.

3. Morash, *History of Irish Theatre*, 172.

4. Pine, "Micheál macLíammóir," 83.

5. Cleary, "Introduction," 8.

6. Pierse, *Writing Ireland's Working Class*, 14.

7. Johnston, "Preface to the *Collected Plays*," 6.

8. Johnston, "Concerning the Unicorn," 13–14.

9. Cave, "Modernism and Irish Theatre 1900–1940," 133.

10. Johnston, *Bride for the Unicorn* (1935 ed.), 157. In the 1933 typescript, John's last name is Phosphorus.

11. "Mr. Johnston's New Play: *A Bride for the Unicorn*: Expressionism at the Gate," *Irish Times*, May 10, 1933.

12. "The Irishman's Diary," *Irish Times*, May 19, 1933.

13. Johnston, *Bride for the Unicorn* (1933 typescript), 89. Virginie Girel-Pietka discusses Johnston's experimental dramaturgy in this regard in "Denis Johnston at the Gate," 124–27.

14. Johnston, *Bride for the Unicorn* (1933 typescript), 9. For a discussion of the play's indebtedness to *Peer Gynt* in this respect, see Malone, "Denis Johnston's Ibsen and Post-revivalist Ireland," 55–59.

15. In parenthetical references, the 1933 typescript, which was used during the first production, has been indicated as version A; the published 1935 edition, which featured various changes, is version B.

16. Johnston, *Bride for the Unicorn* (1935 ed.), 276. In the Greek myths of Cadmus and Jason, fully armed warriors grow magically from the dragon's teeth; in both stories, they immediately begin to fight each other to the death.

17. Joyce, *Ulysses*, 31.

18. Johnston, *Bride for the Unicorn* (1935 ed.), 298. In the 1933 version, the Lady turns around so that the audience, too, can see "the face of Death" (184).

19. "Proclamation of the Irish Republic."

20. Sisson, "Experimentalism and the Irish Stage," 48.

21. Johnston, *Bride for the Unicorn* (1935 ed.), 291–92.

22. Sears, "Brilliant New Play by Lady Longford," *Irish Independent*, March 29, 1933.

23. "A Good Play at the Gate Theatre," *Irish Times*, March 29, 1933. In his diary, Joseph Holloway noted that, although "a friendly first night audience" applauded Catherine Longford after the "strangely talky" play, "there was too much casual conversation and too little drama to make the piece popular." Holloway did observe that "it is extraordinary how they get the weird and the uncanny over at the Gate. Both Edwards and MacLiammóir have a genius for this sort of thing" (Hogan and O'Neill, *Joseph Holloway's Irish Theatre*, vol. 2, 24).

24. Longford, *Mr. Jiggins of Jigginstown*, 272.

25. Longford, 275. In October 1931, riots broke out in Cyprus, and proponents of unification with Greece burned down the British governor's mansion in Nicosia.

26. Longford, 299. The phrase "exiles of Erin" conventionally refers to destitute Irishmen and women who emigrated to escape poverty and famine during the nineteenth century. The poem "The Exile of Erin," which has been variously ascribed to Thomas Campbell and George Nugent Reynolds, was a popular inclusion in Michael Barry's hugely successful anthology *The Songs of Ireland*.

27. Trotter, *Modern Irish Theatre*, 101.

28. Leeney, "Class, Land, and Irishness," 72.

29. Leeney, 168.

30. Manning, *Youth's the Season—?*, 326, 337.

31. Hogan, *After the Irish Renaissance*, 120.

32. Leeney, "Not-So-Gay-Young-Things," 157. Leeney expanded her analysis of this play in *Irish Women Playwrights*, 138–58.

33. Lanters, "Queer Creatures, Queer Place," 59. Lanters has also analyzed the autobiographical nature of some aspects of *Youth's the Season—?* in "Desperationists and Ineffectuals," 105–10.

34. Meaney, O'Dowd, and Whelan, *Reading the Irish Woman*, 206–7.

35. Castle, *Modernism and the Celtic Revival*, 11.

36. Manning, *Youth's the Season—?*, 350. *Dolores* is Latin for *sorrows*, further compounding the repetition and confusion.

37. Gibbons, *Transformations in Irish Culture*, 167. The name Millington alludes to John Millington Synge, the Abbey playwright and scion of an Ascendancy family.

38. Manning, *Youth's the Season—?*, 342; This "Timon of Aran" (332), who is much less of an embarrassment to Terence himself, serves as another reference to Synge, who wrote *The Aran Islands* (1907) after an extended stay in the west of Ireland.

39. Leeney, "Not-So-Gay-Young-Things," 162.

40. In their biography of W. B. Yeats, Micheál mac Liammóir and Eavan Boland note that the increasing popularity of Freudian psychoanalysis during the 1920s and 1930s "created a new society in which the terror of 'repression' became the order of the day" (*W. B. Yeats and His World*, 96).

41. Frawley, "Towards a Theory of Cultural Memory," 30.

42. Leeney, "Not-So-Gay-Young-Things," 165.

43. Edwards, "Production," 38.

44. Leeney, *Irish Women Playwrights*, 158.

45. Sears, "Dublin Lady's Play: *Youth's the Season?* at the Gate," *Irish Independent*, December 9, 1931.

46. "*Youth's the Season—?*: Gate Theatre New Play," *Irish Times*, December 9, 1931.

47. "*Happy Family*, by Mary Manning," *Irish Times*, April 25, 1934. Joseph Holloway likewise dismissed the play as "a thin, formless farce with the material of a one-act farce, stretched out unduly into three acts" (Hogan and O'Neill, *Joseph Holloway's Irish Theatre*, vol. 2, 3).

48. Sears, "Mary Manning's New Comedy: *Happy Family* at the Gate Theatre," *Irish Independent*, April 25, 1934.

49. Manning, *Happy Family*, 1.1, 19.

50. Manning, 2.1, 12; 3.1, 39. The phrases that follow the word *graveyard* have been deleted in the play's typescript, suggesting that Juliet's death wish is too oppressive to communicate.

51. Manning, 1.2, 24. This phrase is repeated twice during the play's final act: "I'm going to put on a funeral march. Dirge for the Descendancy" (3.1, 39); and "Three cheers for the Descendancy!" (3.1, 54). David Fitzpatrick also employs this term to characterize the decline of Irish-Anglican dominion in *Descendancy*.

52. Manning, *Happy Family*, 1.1, 18. See also David Clare's discussion of this phenomenon in *Bernard Shaw's Irish Outlook*, 39–40.

53. Stevenson, *Treasure Island*, 9.

54. Manning, *Happy Family*, 1.2, 5. Yeats had written about their spectral power over Irish nationalism in "Sixteen Dead Men" (1920).

55. Bartky, *One Time Fits All*, 176.

56. Manning, *Happy Family*, 2.1, 39; 3.1, 55. Ted is probably referring to the Bulgarian coup d'état of 1934.

57. Leeney, *Irish Women Playwrights*, 134.

58. Quoted in Hogan and O'Neill, *Joseph Holloway's Irish Theatre*, vol. 1, 65.

59. Hogan and O'Neill, 67. Holloway's record of this controversy includes transcripts of several letters that were written by Murray at the time (62–71). Albert J. DeGiacomo discusses these letters and other documents pertaining to the Abbey's rejection of *A Flutter of Wings*, which he regards as a flawed transitional piece, in *T. C. Murray, Dramatist*, 122–26.

60. D. E. S. Maxwell did not feel that *A Flutter of Wings* was "of any durable interest" (*Critical History of Modern Irish Drama*, 132).

61. Hogan and O'Neill, *Joseph Holloway's Irish Theatre*, vol. 1, 69.

62. Sears, "*A Flutter of Wings*: First Night Success," *Irish Independent*, November 11, 1930.

63. Ó hAodha, "T. C. Murray and Some Critics," 191.

64. Cave, *Selected Plays of T. C. Murray*, xx. For similar assessments, see Maxwell, *Critical History of Modern Irish Drama*, 132; Hogan, *After the Irish Renaissance*, 29; and Hogan, Burnham, and Poteet, *Abbey Theatre*, 258.

65. O'Toole, *Irish New Woman*, 151.

66. Murray, *Flutter of Wings*, act 1. The play's publication in the *Daily Express* complicates bibliographical references, since none of the surviving copies of the *A Flutter of Wings* as a newspaper publication in the National Library of Ireland (NLI) or the Northwestern University Library are paginated. Incidentally, the autograph manuscript in the NLI (MS 24849/1) does feature page numbers, but the first act is missing.

67. "*Marrowbone Lane*: New Play at the Gate Theatre," *Irish Times*, October 11, 1939. Joseph Holloway, on the other hand, detested the "almost unintelligible lingo" of the actors as well as the play's "pathetic story" (Hogan and O'Neill, *Joseph Holloway's Irish Theatre*, vol. 3, 37).

68. Fallon, "Those Dwellers in Marrowbone Lane," 841, 844–45.

69. "Housing Needs of Dublin," *Irish Times*, November 4, 1939.

70. Collis, *Marrowbone Lane*, 95.

71. Collis, 10.

72. Collis, 9, 11.

73. Pierse, *Writing Ireland's Working Class*, 83, 90, 18.

74. Pierse, "Introduction," 18.

75. Convery, "Writing and Theorising the Irish Working Class," 49–54.

76. Morash, *Writing the Irish Famine*, 4.

77. Assmann, "Collective Memory and Cultural Identity," 129. In this respect, James V. Wertsch's concept of "schematic narrative templates" (*Voices of Collective Remembering*, 65), which organize how a group recounts its past, and Eviatar Zerubavel's notion of how cultural communities employ mnemonic tropes and "emplotment" (*Time Maps*, 15) to give shape to collective memories, have provided a pertinent discourse.

78. Wills, *That Neutral Island*, 257. Wills goes on to note that *Marrowbone Lane* was an example of "good social-realist propaganda" (260) against these conditions.

79. Hogan, *After the Irish Renaissance*, 122.

80. Mokyr and Ó Gráda, "What Do People Die of During Famines," 339–63.

81. Pierse, *Writing Ireland's Working Class*, 218.

82. Collis, *Marrowbone Lane*, 17. Fitzgerald, Wolfe Tone, and Emmet are all referenced in Yeats's famous poem "September 1913" (1914), which was written during the Lockout. Incidentally, the poem also includes the line "You have dried the marrow from the bone" (121).

83. Miller, *Modernism, Ireland, and the Erotics of Memory*, 8.

84. Rigney, "Divided Pasts," 93.

85. Hirsch, "Generation of Postmemory," 107.

## Conclusion

1. Richard Pine discusses the Longford split and the Gate's tours abroad in "Gate—Home and Away," 161–77.

2. For accounts of this period in the Gate's history, including reflections on its financial situation and its changing artistic policy, see Mac Liammóir, *All for Hecuba*, 343–48; Pine and Cave, *Dublin Gate Theatre*, 62–65, 84–86; Ó hAodha, *Importance of Being Micheál*, 109–10, 129–41; and Fitz-Simon, *Boys*, 121–42.

3. Mac Liammóir, *All for Hecuba*, 346.

4. Sears, "*Where Stars Walk*: Dublin Sees New Play," *Irish Independent*, February 20, 1940.

5. "*Where Stars Walk*: MacLiammoir Play at the Gaiety," *Irish Times*, February 20, 1940; "*Where Stars Walk*: MacLiammóir Play at the Gaiety," *Evening Herald*, February 20, 1940. Joseph Holloway recorded that "all save the boxes were well filled [on May 3] to

witness macLiammóir's strange mixture of chatty comedy and weird, legendary-lore, celtic twilight stuff"—an amalgamation that Holloway as well as the audience mostly appreciated (Hogan and O'Neill, *Joseph Holloway's Irish Theatre*, vol. 3, 44).

6. Yeats, *Land of Heart's Desire*, 55. At the end of the play, which takes place on a May Eve—a time associated with witches and demons—during the late eighteenth century, the girl herself falls prey to a faery child, who succeeds in tempting her to forsake her religion and travel to the mythical Land of Heart's Desire.

7. Mac Liammóir, *Where Stars Walk*, 72.

8. Mac Liammóir, 51. His understanding of the insurrectionary years is equally limited: when Bob says that Sophia "belongs to the Countess Markiewiez period," Brunton wonders, "What was that? Arm chairs?" (63). Bob tries to explain—"No, revolutions"—which is much to Brunton's surprise: "I say! Real ones?" (63).

9. Murray, "Where Are They Now?," 59. Likewise, Katherine Anne Hennessey has argued that mac Liammóir's *Diarmuid and Gráinne* and *Where Stars Walk* were "critical successive steps in the evolution of contemporary theatrical adaptations of Irish myth and legend" (95). See "Memorable Barbarities and National Myths," 85–95.

10. Murray, "Where Are They Now?," 70.

11. Murray, 71, 60.

12. Morash and Richards, *Mapping Irish Theatre*, 23.

13. *God's Gentry* program, 3.

14. Morash and Richards, *Mapping Irish Theatre*, 61.

15. Pine, "Micheál macLíammóir," 93.

16. Kiberd, *Inventing Ireland*, 653.

17. More information about this project can be found on the GTRN website at www.ru.nl/gatetheatre (accessed May 21, 2020).

18. See, for example, David Clare's observations in "Goldsmith, the Gate."

19. Meaney, O'Dowd, and Whelan, *Reading the Irish Woman*, 196–97. Sadly, a disproportionate number of plays written by women dramatists in the 1920s and 1930s have not survived.

20. See, for example, Helen Heusner Lojek's discussion of Frank McGuinness's 2002 play *Gates of Gold*, which is partially inspired by Edwards and mac Liammóir's relationship, in "Negotiating Differences in the Plays of Frank McGuinness," 512–13; and Des Lally's examination of how the Boys were parodied in "Fictionalisation of Hilton Edwards and Micheál macLíammóir."

21. Mac Liammóir, *All for Hecuba*, 86–87.

# Bibliography

A.E.M. "New Play at the 'Gate': Grania of the Ships." *Irish Independent*, September 6, 1933, 6.

Allen, Nicholas. "Imagining the Rising." In *The Oxford Handbook of Modern Irish Theatre*, edited by Nicholas Grene and Chris Morash, 156–68. Oxford: Oxford Univ. Press, 2016.

———. *Modernism, Ireland, and Civil War*. Cambridge: Cambridge Univ. Press, 2009.

Arrington, Lauren. "Irish Modernism and Its Legacies." In *The Princeton History of Modern Ireland*, edited by Richard Bourke and Ian McBride, 236–52. Princeton, NJ: Princeton Univ. Press, 2016.

———. *Revolutionary Lives: Constance and Casimir Markievicz*. Princeton, NJ: Princeton Univ. Press, 2016.

Assmann, Jan. "Collective Memory and Cultural Identity." *New German Critique* 65 (1995): 125–33.

Barnett, Louise. *Jonathan Swift in the Company of Women*. Oxford: Oxford Univ. Press, 2007.

Bartky, Ian R. *One Time Fits All: The Campaigns for Global Uniformity*. Stanford, CA: Stanford Univ. Press, 2007.

Brown, Terence. *The Literature of Ireland: Culture and Criticism*. Cambridge: Cambridge Univ. Press, 2010.

Campbell, Hugh. "Modern Architecture and National Identity in Ireland." In *The Cambridge Companion to Modern Irish Culture*, edited by Joe Cleary and Claire Connolly, 285–303. Cambridge: Cambridge Univ. Press, 2005.

Canfield, Curtis. *Plays of Changing Ireland*. New York: Macmillan, 1936.

Carlson, Marvin. "Space and Theatre." In "Interfaces between Irish and European Theatre," special issue, *FOCUS: Papers in English Literary and Cultural Studies* (2012): 13–23.

Castle, Gregory. *Modernism and the Celtic Revival*. Cambridge: Cambridge Univ. Press, 2001.

Cave, Richard Allen. "The Dangers and Difficulties of Dramatising the Lives of Deirdre and Grania." In *Perspectives of Irish Drama and Theatre*, edited by Jacqueline Genet and Richard Allen Cave, 1–16. Gerrards Cross: Colin Smythe, 1991.

———. "Dramatising the Life of Swift." In *Irish Writers and the Theatre*, edited by Masaru Sekine, 17–31. Gerrards Cross: Colin Smythe, 1987.

———. "Modernism and Irish Theatre 1900–1940." In *The Oxford Handbook of Modern Irish Theatre*, edited by Nicholas Grene and Chris Morash, 121–37. Oxford: Oxford Univ. Press, 2016.

———, ed. *The Selected Plays of T. C. Murray*. Washington, DC: Catholic Univ. of America Press, 1998.

"City in the Dawn: Peace and Fulfilments of Dreams: Pageant of Dublin." *Irish Independent*, September 10, 1929, 8.

Clare, David. *Bernard Shaw's Irish Outlook*. London: Palgrave Macmillan, 2016.

———. "Goldsmith, the Gate, and the 'Hibernicising' of Anglo-Irish Plays." In *The Gate Theatre, Dublin: Inspiration and Craft*, edited by David Clare, Des Lally, and Patrick Lonergan, 239–59. Dublin: Carysfort/Peter Lang, 2018.

Clare, David, Des Lally, and Patrick Lonergan. "Introduction." In *The Gate Theatre, Dublin: Inspiration and Craft*, edited by David Clare, Des Lally, and Patrick Lonergan, 1–9. Dublin: Carysfort/Peter Lang, 2018.

Cleary, Joe. "Introduction: Ireland and Modernity." In *The Cambridge Companion to Modern Irish Culture*, edited by Joe Cleary and Claire Connolly, 1–21. Cambridge: Cambridge Univ. Press, 2005.

———. "'Misplaced Ideas'?: Colonialism, Location, and Dislocation in Irish Studies." In *Ireland and Postcolonial Theory*, edited by Clare Carroll and Patricia King, 16–45. Notre Dame, IN: Univ. of Notre Dame Press, 2003.

———. *Outrageous Fortune: Capital and Culture in Modern Ireland*. Dublin: Field Day/Keough-Naughton Institute of Irish Studies, Univ. of Notre Dame, 2006.

Cole, Alan. "The Gate Influence on Dublin Theatre." *Dublin Magazine* 28, no. 3 (1953): 6–14.

Collis, Robert. *Marrowbone Lane*. Dublin: Runa, 1943.

Convery, David. "Writing and Theorising the Irish Working Class." In *A History of Irish Working-Class Writing*, edited by Michael Pierse, 37–56. Cambridge: Cambridge Univ. Press, 2017.

Corbett, Mary Jean. *Allegories of Union in Irish and English Writing, 1790–1870.* Cambridge: Cambridge Univ. Press, 2000.

Cowell, John. *No Profit but the Name: The Longfords and the Gate Theatre.* Dublin: O'Brien, 1988.

CPC. "Notes on Recent Productions." *Motley* 1, no. 2 (1932): 5–6.

Davies, Alan. *The Crucified Nation: A Motif in Modern Nationalism.* Brighton: Sussex Academic Press, 2010.

Dean, Joan FitzPatrick. *All Dressed Up: Modern Irish Historical Pageantry.* Syracuse, NY: Syracuse Univ. Press, 2014.

———. "Pageants, Parades, and Performance Culture." In *Modern and Contemporary Irish Drama,* edited by John P. Harrington, 613–22. New York: Norton, 2009.

———. "Rewriting the Past: Historical Pageantry in the Dublin Civic Weeks of 1927 and 1929." *New Hibernia Review* 13, no. 1 (2009): 20–41.

DeGiacomo, Albert J. *T. C. Murray, Dramatist: Voice of Rural Ireland.* Syracuse, NY: Syracuse Univ. Press, 2003.

DM. "Prophetic Play by Pearse." *Irish Press,* March 29, 1932, 5.

———. "*Yahoo* at the Gate Theatre: Lord Longford's Play on Dean Swift." *Irish Press,* September 20, 1933, 3.

Doody, Margaret Ann. "Swift and Women." In *The Cambridge Companion to Jonathan Swift,* edited by Christopher Fox, 87–111. Cambridge: Cambridge Univ. Press, 2003.

"Dramatic Enterprise in Dublin: New Company Floated." *Irish Independent,* October 7, 1929, 8.

Eagleton, Terry. *Heathcliff and the Great Hunger: Studies in Irish Culture.* London: Verso, 1995.

Edwards, Hilton. "To the Editor of *The Irish Times.*" *Irish Times,* March 19, 1935, 4.

———. *The Mantle of Harlequin.* Dublin: Progress House, 1958.

———. "Production." In *The Gate Theatre,* edited by Bulmer Hobson, 21–45. Dublin: Gate Theatre, 1934.

———. "Why the Dublin Gate Theatre?" *Motley* 1, no. 1 (1932): 3–4.

Edwards, Hilton, and Micheál mac Liammóir. "The Dublin Gate Theatre Studio." 1928. Pamphlet. Ir 3919 d 2. National Library of Ireland, Dublin.

———. "The Dublin Gate Theatre Studio." 1929. Pamphlet. Ir 3919 d 2. National Library of Ireland, Dublin.

Eglinton, John. "What Should Be the Subjects of National Drama?" 1899. In *Modern Irish Drama*, 2nd ed., edited by John P. Harrington, 410–12. New York: Norton, 1991, 2009.

Fabricant, Carole. "Swift the Irishman." In *The Cambridge Companion to Jonathan Swift*, edited by Christopher Fox, 48–72. Cambridge: Cambridge Univ. Press, 2003.

Fallis, Richard. *The Irish Renaissance: An Introduction to Anglo-Irish Literature*. Syracuse, NY: Syracuse Univ. Press, 1977.

Fallon, Brian. *An Age of Innocence: Irish Culture, 1930–1960*. New York: St. Martin's, 1998.

Fallon, Gabriel. "Some Aspects of Irish Theatre." *Studies: An Irish Quarterly Review* 36, no. 143 (1947): 296–306.

———. "Those Dwellers in Marrowbone Lane." *Irish Monthly* 67, no. 798 (1939): 841–45.

Fay, Frank J. "An Irish National Theatre." 1901. In *Modern Irish Drama*, edited by John P. Harrington, 391–94. New York: Norton, 1991.

Ferrar, Harold. *Denis Johnston's Irish Theatre*. Dublin: Dolmen, 1973.

"A Fianna Play." *Irish Times*, November 19, 1928, 4.

Fitzpatrick, David. *Descendancy: Irish Protestant Histories since 1795*. Cambridge: Cambridge Univ. Press, 2014.

Fitz-Simon, Christopher. *The Boys: A Biography of Micheál MacLíammóir and Hilton Edwards*. London: Nick Hern, 1994.

———. *The Irish Theatre*. London: Thames & Hudson, 1983.

"*The Ford of the Hurdles*: Pageant Play at the Mansion House." *Irish Times*, September 10, 1929, 5.

Foster, Gavin M. *The Irish Civil War and Society: Politics, Class, and Conflict*. New York: Palgrave Macmillan, 2015.

Foucault, Michel. "Of Other Spaces." 1984. Translated by Jay Miskowiec. *Diacritics* 16, no. 1 (1986): 22–27.

Frawley, Oona. "Introduction." In *Memory Ireland, Vol. 1: History and Modernity*, edited by Oona Frawley, xiii–xxiv. Syracuse, NY: Syracuse Univ. Press, 2010.

———. "Towards a Theory of Cultural Memory in an Irish Postcolonial Context." *Memory Ireland, Vol. 1: History and Modernity*, edited by Oona Frawley, 18–34. Syracuse, NY: Syracuse Univ. Press, 2010.

Frazier, Adrian. "Irish Acting in the Early Twentieth Century." In *The Oxford Handbook of Modern Irish Theatre*, edited by Nicholas Grene and Chris Morash, 231–47. Oxford: Oxford Univ. Press, 2016.

Freedley, George, and John A. Reeves. *A History of the Theatre*. New York: Crown, 1941.

"Future of Gate Theatre: Mr. H. Edwards Interviewed." *Irish Times*, January 29, 1936, 12.

Gassner, John. *The Theatre in Our Times: A Survey of the Men, Materials, and Movements in the Modern Theatre*. New York: Crown, 1954.

"Gate Theatre's Venture to Acquire Spacious Hall." *Irish Independent*, June 28, 1929, 5.

Geoghegan, Patrick M. *King Dan: The Rise of Daniel O'Connell 1775–1829*. Dublin: Gill & Macmillan, 2008.

———. *Robert Emmet: A Life*. Montreal: McGill-Queen's Univ. Press, 2002; Dublin: Gill & Macmillan, 2004.

Gibbons, Luke. *Transformations in Irish Culture*. Cork: Cork Univ. Press, 1996.

Giddens, Anthony. *The Consequences of Modernity*. Cambridge: Polity, 1990.

Gilbert, Helen, and Joanne Tompkins. *Post-colonial Drama: Theory, Practice, Politics*. New York: Routledge, 1996.

Girel-Pietka, Virginie. "Denis Johnston at the Gate: A Groundbreaking yet Neglected Writer." In *The Gate Theatre, Dublin: Inspiration and Craft*, edited by David Clare, Des Lally and Patrick Lonergan, 111–30. Dublin: Carysfort/Peter Lang, 2018.

———. "'Winds of Change' in *The Moon in the Yellow River* and *The Dreaming Dust* by Denis Johnston: Staging Identity in a Crisis." *Journal of Franco-Irish Studies* 3, no. 1 (2013): 84–99.

*God's Gentry* program. 1951. 1820_MPG_0001. Gate Theatre Digital Archive, James Hardiman Library, National Univ. of Ireland Galway.

"A Good Play at the Gate Theatre." *Irish Times*, March 29, 1933, 4.

"Great Success of *Juggernaut*." *Irish Independent*, April 2, 1929, 8.

Gregory, Lady Augusta. *Gods and Fighting Men*. London: John Murray, 1905.

———. Excerpts from *Our Irish Theatre: A Chapter of Autobiography*. 1913. In *Modern Irish Drama*, edited by John P. Harrington, 377–86. New York: Norton, 1991.

Grene, Nicholas. *The Politics of Irish Drama: Plays in Context from Boucicault to Friel*. Cambridge: Cambridge Univ. Press, 2002.

Grimbert, Joan Tasker. *Tristan and Isolde: A Casebook*. New York: Routledge, 2002.

Hansen, Jim. *Terror and Irish Modernism: The Gothic Tradition from Burke to Beckett*. Albany, NY: State Univ. of New York Press, 2009.

"*Happy Family*, by Mary Manning." *Irish Times*, April 25, 1934, 4.

Hawkins, Maureen S. G. "Playing Both Ends Against the Middle: Boucicault's Political Positions in *Robert Emmet*." In *Ritual Remembering: History, Myth and Politics in Anglo-Irish Drama*, edited by C. C. Barfoot and Rias van den Doel, 41–50. Amsterdam: Rodopi, 1995.

Heinige, Kathleen. *Buffoonery in Irish Drama: Staging Twentieth-Century Post-colonial Stereotypes*. New York: Peter Lang, 2009.

Hennessey, Katherine. "Memorable Barbarities and National Myths: Ancient Greek Tragedy and Irish Epic in Modern Literature." PhD diss., Univ. of Notre Dame, 2008.

Heusner Lojek, Helen. "Negotiating Differences in the Plays of Frank McGuinness." In *The Oxford Handbook of Modern Irish Theatre*, edited by Nicholas Grene and Chris Morash, 497–514. Oxford: Oxford Univ. Press, 2016.

Higgins, Roisín. *Transforming 1916: Meaning, Memory and the Fiftieth Anniversary of the Easter Rising*. Cork: Cork Univ. Press, 2012.

Hirsch, Marianne. "The Generation of Postmemory." *Poetics Today* 29. no. 1 (2008): 103–28.

Hogan, Robert. *After the Irish Renaissance: A Critical History of the Irish Drama since The Plough and the Stars*. London: Macmillan, 1968.

Hogan, Robert, Richard Burnham, and Daniel P. Poteet. *The Abbey Theatre: The Rise of the Realists, 1910–1915*. Dublin: Dolmen, 1978.

Hogan, Robert, and Michael J. O'Neill, eds. *Joseph Holloway's Irish Theatre*, vol. 1. Gerrards Cross: Colin Smythe, 1968.

———. *Joseph Holloway's Irish Theatre*, vol. 2. Gerrards Cross: Colin Smythe, 1969.

———. *Joseph Holloway's Irish Theatre*, vol. 3. Gerrards Cross: Colin Smythe, 1970.

Holdsworth, Nadine. "Introduction." In *Theatre and National Identity: Re-imagining Conceptions of Nation*, edited by Nadine Holdsworth, 1–16. New York: Routledge, 2014.

"Housing Needs of Dublin." *Irish Times*, November 4, 1939, 11.

Huyssen, Andreas. *After the Great Divide: Modernism, Mass Culture, Postmodernism*. Bloomington: Indiana Univ. Press, 1986.

Innes, C. L. "Modernism, Ireland, and Empire: Yeats, Joyce, and Their Implied Audiences." In *Modernism and Empire*, edited by Howard J. Booth and Nigel Rigby, 137–55. Manchester: Manchester Univ. Press, 2000.

"Irishman's Diary." *Irish Times*, May 19, 1933, 4.

"An Irish Problem Play: *Juggernaut* a Popular Success at the Dublin Gate Theatre." *Southern Star*, April 6, 1929, 5.

"An Irish Review: *The Old Lady Says 'No!'*" *Irish Times*, July 4, 1929, 4.

Jameson, Fredric. "Marxism and Historicism." 1979. In *The Ideologies of Theory: Essays 1971–1986, Vol. II: Syntax of History*, 148–77. London: Routledge, 1988.

Johnston, Denis. *A Bride for the Unicorn*. In *Storm Song and A Bride for the Unicorn: Two Plays*, 153–301. London: Jonathan Cape, 1935.

———. *A Bride for the Unicorn*. 1933. Typescript. MS 10066/3/1. Manuscripts and Archives Research Library, Trinity College Dublin.

———. "Concerning the Unicorn." In *The Dramatic Works of Denis Johnston*, vol. 2, 13–15. Gerrards Cross: Colin Smythe, 1979.

———. "The Making of the Theatre." In *The Gate Theatre*, edited by Bulmer Hobson, 11–20. Dublin: Gate Theatre, 1934.

———. "A National Morality Play." *Motley* 1, no. 1 (1932): 4–5.

———. *The Old Lady Says "No!"* In *Plays of Changing Ireland*, edited by Curtis Canfield, 37–102. New York: Macmillan, 1936.

———. *The Old Lady Says "No!"* 1929. Typescript. MS 10066/2/7. Manuscripts and Archives Research Library, Trinity College Dublin.

———. "Opus One." In *The Dramatic Works of Denis Johnston*, vol. 1, 15–18. Gerrards Cross: Colin Smythe, 1977.

———. Preface to the *Collected Plays*. 1960. In *The Dramatic Works of Denis Johnston*, vol. 2, 5–10. Gerrards Cross: Colin Smythe, 1979.

———. "Public Opinion: A National Morality Play." *Bell* 1, no. 6 (1941): 89–91.

———. "Towards a Dynamic Theatre." *Motley* 2, no. 4 (1933): 3–6.

Joyce, James. *Ulysses*. 1922. Oxford: Oxford Univ. Press, 1998.

"*Juggernaut*: New Play Produced with Success in Dublin." *Evening Herald*, March 20, 1929, 3.

J.W.G. "New Irish Verse Play." *Irish Independent*, June 6, 1929, 9.

———. "Play Dickens Would Have Enjoyed: Gate Season Success." *Irish Independent*, January 14, 1929, 6.

Katz Clarke, Brenna, and Harold Ferrar. *The Dublin Drama League, 1918–1941*. Dublin: Dolmen, 1979.

Kearney, Richard. *Postcolonial Ireland: Politics, Culture, Philosophy*. London: Routledge, 1997.

———. *Transitions: Narratives in Modern Irish Culture*. Manchester: Manchester Univ. Press, 1988.

Kiberd, Declan. *Inventing Ireland: The Literature of the Modern Nation*. London: Vintage, 1996.

Kinealy, Christine. "Beyond Revisionism: Reassessing the Great Irish Famine." *History Ireland* 3, no. 4 (1995): 28–34.

———. "'The Famine Killed Everything': Living with the Memory of the Great Hunger." In *Ireland's Great Hunger: Silence, Memory, and Commemoration*, edited by David A. Valone, 3–13. Lanham, MD: Univ. Press of America, 2002.

Kruger, Loren. *The National Stage: Theatre and Cultural Legitimation in England, France, and America*. Chicago: Univ. of Chicago Press, 1992.

Lally, Des. "The Fictionalisation of Hilton Edwards and Micheál macLíammóir in the Novel *Stravaganza!* (1963), by Paul Smith." In *The Gate Theatre, Dublin: Inspiration and Craft*, edited by David Clare, Des Lally and Patrick Lonergan, 193–207. Dublin: Carysfort/Peter Lang, 2018.

Lally, Des, David Clare, and Ruud van den Beuken. "Gate Theatre Chronology (1928–1982): The Edwards–macLíammóir and Longford Directorates." In *The Gate Theatre, Dublin: Inspiration and Craft*, edited by David Clare, Des Lally, and Patrick Lonergan, 341–85. Dublin: Carysfort/Oxford: Peter Lang, 2018.

Landsberg, Alison. *Prosthetic Memory: The Transformation of American Remembrance in the Age of Mass Culture*. New York: Columbia Univ. Press, 2004.

Lanters, José. "Desperationists and Ineffectuals: Mary Manning's Gate Plays of the 1930s." In *The Gate Theatre, Dublin: Inspiration and Craft*, edited by David Clare, Des Lally and Patrick Lonergan, 97–110. Dublin: Carysfort/Peter Lang, 2018.

———. "Queer Creatures, Queer Place: Otherness and Normativity in Irish Drama from Synge to Friel." In *Irish Theatre in Transition: From the Late Nineteenth to the Early Twenty-First Century*, edited by Donald E. Morse, 54–67. New York: Palgrave Macmillan, 2015.

Lee, Joseph. *Ireland, 1912–1985: Politics and Society*. Cambridge: Cambridge Univ. Press, 1989.

Leeney, Cathy. "Class, Land, and Irishness: Winners and Losers: Christine Longford (1900–1980)." In *The Gate Theatre, Dublin: Inspiration and Craft*, edited by David Clare, Des Lally and Patrick Lonergan, 161–79. Dublin: Carysfort/Peter Lang, 2018.

———. *Irish Women Playwrights, 1900–1939: Gender and Violence on Stage*. New York: Peter Lang, 2010.

———. "Not-So-Gay-Young-Things: Mary Manning's *Youth's the Season*—? as Staged in 1930s London." In *Irish Theatre in England*, edited by Richard Cave and Ben Levitas, 157–68. Dublin: Carysfort, 2007.

Leerssen, Joep. *Mere Irish & Fíor-ghael: Studies in the Idea of Irish Nationality, Its Development, and Literary Expression prior to the Nineteenth Century*. Philadelphia: John Benjamins, 1986.

———. *Remembrance and Imagination: Patterns in the Historical and Literary Representation of Ireland in the Nineteenth Century*. Notre Dame, IN: Univ. of Notre Dame Press/Field Day, 1996.

Levitas, Ben. "The Abbey and the Idea of a Theatre." In *The Oxford Handbook of Modern Irish Theatre*, edited by Nicholas Grene and Chris Morash, 41–57. Oxford: Oxford Univ. Press, 2016.

———. *The Theatre of Nation: Irish Drama and Cultural Nationalism, 1890–1916*. Oxford: Oxford Univ. Press, 2002.

Lloyd, David. *Irish Times: Temporalities of Modernity*. Dublin: Field Day, 2008.

———. "The Memory of Hunger." In *Loss: The Politics of Mourning*, edited by David L. Eng and David Kazanjian, 205–28. Berkeley: Univ. of California Press, 2003.

Lonergan, Patrick. *Theatre and Globalization: Irish Drama in the Celtic Tiger Era*. New York: Palgrave Macmillan, 2009.

Longenbach, James. *Modernist Poetics of History: Pound, Eliot, and the Sense of the Past*. Princeton, NJ: Princeton Univ. Press, 1987.

Longford, Christine. *Mr. Jiggins of Jigginstown*. In *Plays of Changing Ireland*, edited by Curtis Canfield, 269–320. New York: Macmillan, 1936.

Longford, Edward. *Ascendancy*. Dublin: Hodges Figgis, 1935.

———. "A National Asset." *Motley* 1, no. 1 (1932): 2.

———. "The National Theatre at Athens." *Motley* 2, no. 5 (1933): 6–8.

———. "Preface." In *The Gate Theatre*, edited by Bulmer Hobson, 9–10. Dublin: Gate Theatre, 1934.

———. *Yahoo*. In *Plays of Changing Ireland*, edited by Curtis Canfield, 153–91. New York: Macmillan, 1936.

Mac Liammóir, Micheál. *All for Hecuba: A Theatrical Autobiography*. Rev. ed. Dublin: Progress House, 1961.

———. *Diarmuid and Gráinne*. 1928. Typescript. MS 41,247/1. National Library of Ireland, Dublin.

————. *The Ford of the Hurdles*. 1929. Typescript. MS 24,562. National Library of Ireland, Dublin

————. Draft of *The Ford of the Hurdles*. 1929. Typescript. Miscellany J, Box 1, Folder 12. Dublin Gate Theatre Archive, Charles Deering McCormick Library of Special Collections, Northwestern Univ., Evanston, IL.

————. "Problem Plays." In *The Irish Theatre: Lectures Delivered during the Abbey Theatre Festival Held in Dublin in August 1938*, edited by Lennox Robinson, 199–227. London: Macmillan, 1939.

————. Preface to Hilton Edwards, *The Mantle of Harlequin*, xiii–xvi. Dublin: Progress House, 1958.

————. *Theatre in Ireland*. 2nd ed. Dublin: Three Candles, 1964.

————. *Where Stars Walk*. In *Selected Plays of Micheál mac Liammóir*, edited by John Barrett, 1–73. Gerrards Cross: Colin Smythe, 1998.

Mac Liammóir, Micheál, and Eavan Boland. *W. B. Yeats and His World*. London: Thames & Hudson, 1971.

McBride, Ian. "Memory and National Identity in Modern Ireland." In *History and Memory in Modern Ireland*, edited by Ian McBride, 1–42. Cambridge: Cambridge Univ. Press, 2001.

McIvor, Charlotte, and Siobhán O'Gorman. "Devising Ireland: Genealogies and Contestations." In *Devised Performance in Irish Theatre: Histories and Contemporary Practice*, edited by Charlotte McIvor and Siobhán O'Gorman, 1–32. Dublin: Carysfort, 2015.

McLean, Stuart. *The Event and Its Terrors: Ireland, Famine, Modernity*. Stanford, CA: Stanford Univ. Press, 2004.

McMinn, Joseph. "Swift's Life." In *The Cambridge Companion to Jonathan Swift*, edited by Christopher Fox, 14–30. Cambridge: Cambridge Univ. Press, 2003.

Madden, Tom. *The Making of an Artist: Creating the Irishman Micheál MacLiammóir*. Dublin: Liffey, 2015.

Malone, Irina Ruppo. "Denis Johnston's Ibsen and Post-revivalist Ireland." In *Ibsen and Chekov on the Irish Stage*, edited by Ros Dixon and Irina Ruppo Malone, 51–60. Dublin: Carysfort, 2012.

————. "Ibsen and the Irish Free State: The Gate Theatre Company Productions of *Peer Gynt*." *Irish Univ. Review* 39, no. 1 (2009): 42–64.

Manning, Mary. "Dublin Has Also Its Gate Theater." *Boston Evening Transcript*, January 17, 1935.

————. "The Gate Theatre, 1932–33." *Motley* 2, no. 4 (1933): 2–3.

———. *Happy Family*. 1934. Typescript. P.93, Box 42. Dublin Gate Theatre Archive, Charles Deering McCormick Library of Special Collections, Northwestern Univ., Evanston, Illinois.

———. "An Open Letter to *The Leader*." *Motley* 1, no. 2 (1932): 12–13.

———. "The Present Position of Irish Drama." *Motley* 1, no. 6 (1932): 2.

———. "Processional." *Motley* 2, no. 7 (1933): 6–9.

———. "Processional." *Motley* 2, no. 8 (1933): 10–12.

———. "Realism." *Motley* 1, no. 7 (1932): 2–3.

———. "Still Going Forward." *Motley* 2, no. 5 (1933): 2–3.

———. "Subsidies." *Motley* 1, no. 3 (1932): 2.

———. Untitled. In *Enter Certain Players: Edwards–MacLiammoir and the Gate 1928–1978*, edited by Peter Luke, 35–39. Dublin: Dolmen, 1978.

———. "A Word about the Audience." *Motley* 1, no. 4 (1932): 2.

———. *Youth's the Season—?* In *Plays of Changing Ireland*, edited by Curtis Canfield, 321–404. New York: Macmillan, 1936.

Mannion, Elizabeth. *Getting Personal: The Urban Plays of the Early Abbey Theatre*. Syracuse, NY: Syracuse Univ. Pres, 2014.

"Marrowbone Lane: New Play at the Gate Theatre." *Irish Times*, October 11, 1939, 6.

Marx, Karl. "The Eighteenth Brumaire of Louis Bonaparte." 1852. In *Selected Works*, by Karl Marx and Friedrich Engels, 93–171. London: Lawrence & Wishart, 1968.

Maxwell, D. E. S. *A Critical History of Modern Irish Drama, 1891–1980*. Cambridge: Cambridge Univ. Press, 1984.

Meaney, Gerardine, Mary O'Dowd, and Bernadette Whelan. *Reading the Irish Woman: Studies in Cultural Encounter and Exchange, 1714–1960*. Liverpool: Liverpool Univ. Press, 2013.

Miller, Anne Irene. *The Independent Theatre in Europe, 1887 to the Present*. New York: R. Long & R. R. Smith, 1931.

Miller, Nicholas Andrew. *Modernism, Ireland, and the Erotics of Memory*. Cambridge: Cambridge Univ. Press, 2002.

Misztal, Barbara A. "Memory and History." In *Memory Ireland, Vol. I: History and Modernity*, edited by Oona Frawley, 3–17. Syracuse, NY: Syracuse Univ. Press, 2010.

Mokyr, Joel, and Cormac Ó Gráda. "What Do People Die of During Famines: The Great Famine in Comparative Perspective." *European Review of Economic History* 6, no. 3 (2002): 339–63.

Moran, James. *Staging the Easter Rising: 1916 as Theatre.* Cork: Cork Univ. Press, 2005.

Morash, Chris. "Denis Johnston's Swift Project: 'There Must Be Something Wrong with the Information.'" *Canadian Journal of Irish Studies* 33, no. 2 (2007): 56–59.

———. *A History of Irish Theatre, 1601–2000.* Cambridge: Cambridge Univ. Press, 2002.

———. "Places of Performance." In *The Oxford Handbook of Modern Irish Theatre,* edited by Nicholas Grene and Chris Morash, 425–42. Oxford: Oxford Univ. Press, 2016.

———. *Writing the Irish Famine.* Oxford: Oxford Univ. Press, 1995.

Morash, Chris, and Shaun Richards. *Mapping Irish Theatre: Theories of Space and Place.* Cambridge: Cambridge Univ. Press, 2013.

"Mr. Johnston's New Play: *A Bride for the Unicorn*: Expressionism at the Gate." *Irish Times,* May 10, 1933, 6.

Murphy, Paul. "Ireland's Haunted Stages." FOCUS: *Papers in English Literary and Cultural Studies,* special issue, "Interfaces between Irish and European Theatre" (2012): 24–36.

Murphy, Richard. *Theorizing the Avant-Garde: Modernism, Expressionism, and the Problem of Postmodernity.* Cambridge: Cambridge Univ. Press, 1999.

Murray, Christopher. "The History Play Today." In *Cultural Contexts and Literary Idioms in Contemporary Irish Literature,* edited by Michael Kenneally, 269–89. Gerrards Cross: Colin Smythe, 1988.

———. "The Irish Theatre: The First Hundred Years, 1897–1997." In *Irish Theatre in Transition: From the Late Nineteenth to the Early Twenty-First Century,* edited by Donald E. Morse, 13–30. New York: Palgrave Macmillan, 2015.

———. *Twentieth-Century Irish Drama: Mirror up to Nation.* Manchester: Manchester Univ. Press, 1997.

———. "'Where Are They Now?': Plays of Significance in the 1940s and 1950s." In *Players and Painted Stage: Aspects of the Twentieth-Century Theatre in Ireland,* edited by Christopher Fitz-Simon, 57–72. Dublin: New Island, 2004.

Murray, T. C. *A Flutter of Wings.* Serialized in *Daily Express,* October 13–23, 1930.

"A New Lord Longford Play." *Irish Press,* January 30, 1935, 5.

Nolan, Jerry. "Edward Martyn's Struggle for an Irish National Theater, 1899–1920." *New Hibernia Review* 7, no. 2 (2003): 88–105.

O'Brien, John. "Expressionism and the Formative Years: Insights from the Early Diaries of Denis Johnston." *Canadian Journal of Irish Studies* 15, no. 1 (1989): 34–57.

O'Connor, Barry. *Turf-Fire Stories and Fairy Tales of Ireland*. New York: P. J. Kenedy, 1890.

O'Faoláin, Sean. "Mr. O Faolain's Plea for the Abbey Theatre: An Open Letter to Dr. W. B. Yeats." *Irish Times*, March 2, 1935, 7.

O'Halpin, Eunan. *Defending Ireland: The Irish State and Its Enemies since 1922*. Oxford: Oxford Univ. Press, 1999.

———. "Politics and the State, 1922–1932." In *A New History of Ireland, Vol. VII: Ireland, 1921–84*, edited by J. R. Hill, 86–126. Oxford: Oxford Univ. Press, 2003.

Ó hAodha, Micheál. *The Importance of Being Micheál: A Portrait of MacLiammóir*. Dingle: Brandon, 1990.

———. "T. C. Murray and Some Critics." *Studies: An Irish Quarterly Review* 47, no. 186 (1958): 185–91.

———. *Theatre in Ireland*. Totowa, NJ: Rowman & Littlefield, 1974.

O'Toole, Tina. *The Irish New Woman*. New York: Palgrave Macmillan, 2013.

Owens, Cóilín, and Joan Newlon Radner, eds. *Irish Drama 1900–1980*. Washington, DC: Catholic Univ. of America Press, 1990.

O'Rourke Murphy, Maureen, and James MacKillop. *An Irish Literature Reader: Poetry, Prose, Drama*. Syracuse, NY: Syracuse Univ. Press, 2006.

Pellizzi, Camillo. "As Italy Sees Us: Literary Men of Ireland—The Poet Æ." *Motley* 3, no. 4 (1934): 3.

Peppis, Paul. *Literature, Politics, and the English Avant-Garde: Nation and Empire, 1901–1918*. Cambridge: Cambridge Univ. Press, 2000.

Pierse, Michael, "Introduction." In *A History of Irish Working-Class Writing*, edited by Michael Pierse, 1–36. Cambridge: Cambridge Univ. Press, 2017.

———. *Writing Ireland's Working Class: Dublin after O'Casey*. London: Palgrave Macmillan, 2011.

An Philibín (J. H. Pollock). *Tristram and Iseult*. Dublin: Talbot, 1924.

Pilkington, Lionel. "The Abbey Theatre and the Irish State." In *The Cambridge Companion to Twentieth-Century Irish Theatre*, edited by Shaun Richards, 231–43. Cambridge: Cambridge Univ. Press, 2004.

———. *Theatre & Ireland*. Basingstoke: Palgrave Macmillan, 2010.

Pilný, Ondřej. "Doing Justice to Swift: Denis Johnston's Solution in Diverse Modes." In *Beyond Realism: Experimental and Unconventional Irish Drama since the Revival,* edited by Joan FitzPatrick Dean and José Lanters, 77–92. Amsterdam: Rodopi, 2015.

———. *Irony and Identity in Modern Irish Drama.* Prague: Litteraria Pragensia, 2008.

Pine, Emilie. *The Politics of Irish Memory: Performing Remembrance in Contemporary Irish Culture.* Basingstoke: Palgrave Macmillan, 2011.

Pine, Richard. *All for Hecuba: An Exhibition to Mark the Golden Jubilee of the Edwards–mac Liammóir Partnership and of the Gate Theatre, 1928–1978.* Dublin: Hugh Lane Municipal Gallery of Modern Art, 1978. Exhibition catalog.

———. "The Gate—Home and Away." In *Irish Theatre on Tour,* edited by Nicholas Grene and Chris Morash, 161–77. Dublin: Carysfort, 2005.

———. "Micheál macLíammóir: The Erotic-Exotic and the Dublin Gate Theatre." In *The Gate Theatre, Dublin: Inspiration and Craft,* edited by David Clare, Des Lally, and Patrick Lonergan, 63–96. Dublin: Carysfort/Peter Lang, 2018.

Pine, Richard, and Richard Allen Cave. *The Dublin Gate Theatre, 1928–1978.* Teaneck, NJ: Chadwych-Healey, 1984.

Poulain, Alexandra. *Irish Drama, Modernity, and the Passion Play.* London: Palgrave Macmillan, 2016.

"The Proclamation of the Irish Republic." 1916. In *Dublin 1916: The Siege of the GPO,* by Clair Wills, ii. London: Profile Books, 2009.

Reddin, Norman. "A National Theatre." *Motley* 1, no. 1 (1932): 6–8.

"Review of the Week's Amusements: The Gate." *Evening Mail,* March 29, 1932, 7.

Reynolds, Paige. "Direction and Design to 1960." In *The Oxford Handbook of Modern Irish Theatre,* edited by Nicholas Grene and Chris Morash, 201–16. Oxford: Oxford Univ. Press, 2016.

———. *Modernism, Drama, and the Audience for Irish Spectacle.* Cambridge: Cambridge Univ. Press, 2007.

Richards, Shaun. "'Unthreatening in the Provincial Irish Air': Ireland's Modernist Theatre." *Irish Studies Review* 26, no. 3 (2018): 390–405.

Rigney, Ann. "Divided Pasts: A Premature Memorial and the Dynamics of Collective Remembrance." *Memory Studies* 1 (2008): 89–97.

Robinson, Lennox. *The Abbey Theatre: A History, 1899–1951.* London: Sidgwick & Jackson, 1951.

Robinson, Nicholas. "Marriage Against Inclination: The Union and Caricature." In *Acts of Union: The Causes, Context, and Consequences of the Act of*

*Union*, edited by Daire Keogh and Kevin Whelan, 140–58. Dublin: Four Courts, 2001.

Said, Edward, "Afterword: Reflections on Ireland and Postcolonialism." In *Ireland and Postcolonial Theory*, edited by Clare Carroll and Patricia King, 178–85. Notre Dame, IN: Univ. of Notre Dame Press, 2003.

Scott, Michael. Untitled. In *Enter Certain Players: Edwards–MacLiammoir and the Gate 1928–1978*, edited by Peter Luke, 19–20. Dublin: Dolmen, 1978.

Sears, David. "Brilliant New Play by Lady Longford." *Irish Independent*, March 29, 1933, 6.

———. "Dublin Lady's Play: *Youth's the Season?* at the Gate." *Irish Independent*, December 9, 1931, 10.

———. "An Extraordinary Play: Mr Tocher's Work." *Irish Independent*, July 4, 1929, 6.

———. "*A Flutter of Wings*: First Night Success." *Irish Independent*, November 11, 1930, 8.

———. *Grania of the Ships*. 1933. Typescript. MS 19,765. National Library of Ireland, Dublin.

———. *Juggernaut*. Birr: Midland Tribune, 1952.

———. "Mary Manning's New Comedy: *Happy Family* at the Gate Theatre." *Irish Independent*, April 25, 1934, 10.

———. "New Play at the Gate Theatre." *Irish Independent*, January 30, 1935, 9.

———. "A Portrait of Dean Swift: Lord Longford's Play." *Irish Independent*, September 20, 1933, 9.

———. "*Where Stars Walk*: Dublin Sees New Play." *Irish Independent*, February 20, 1940, 7.

"Sears Play Success at the Gate Theatre." *Evening Herald*, September 6, 1933, 6.

Shakespeare, William. *As You Like It*. In *The Oxford Shakespeare: The Complete Works*, edited by Stanley Wells and Gary Taylor, 655–80. Oxford: Clarendon, 1986, 2005.

Sisson, Elaine. "Appeasing Pearse's Ghost: History, Memory, and Theatre." In *Patrick Pearse and the Theatre*, edited by Eugene McNulty and Róisín Ní Ghairbhí, 161–72. Dublin: Four Courts, 2017.

———. "Dublin Civic Week and the Materialisation of History." In *Making 1916: Material and Visual Culture of the Easter Rising*, edited by Lisa Godson and Joanna Brück, 138–45. Liverpool: Liverpool Univ. Press, 2015.

———. "Experimentalism and the Free State: Mrs Cogley's Cabaret and the Founding of the Gate Theatre 1924–1930." In *The Gate Theatre, Dublin:*

*Inspiration and Craft*, edited by David Clare, Des Lally and Patrick Lonergan, 11–27. Dublin: Carysfort/Peter Lang, 2018.

———. "Experimentalism and the Irish Stage: Theatre and German Expressionism in the 1920s." In *Ireland, Design, and Visual Culture: Negotiating Modernity 1922–1992*, edited by Linda King and Elaine Sisson, 39–55. Cork: Cork Univ. Press, 2011.

———. "'A Note on What Happened': Experimental Influences on the Irish Stage, 1919–1929." *Kritika Kultura* 15 (2010): 132–48.

Stafford, Seán. "Taibhdhearc na Gaillimhe: Galway's Gaelic Theatre." *Journal of the Galway Archaeological and Historical Society* 52 (2002): 183–214.

Stevenson, Robert Louis. *Treasure Island.* 1883. New York: Harper & Brothers, 1915.

St. Peter, Christine. "Denis Johnston, the Abbey, and the Spirit of the Age." *Irish Univ. Review* 17, no. 2 (1987): 187–206.

———. Introduction to *The Old Lady Says "No!"*, by Denis Johnston, 1–45 Washington, DC: Catholic Univ. of America Press, 1992.

———. "The Old Lady: In Principio." In *Denis Johnston: A Retrospective*, edited by Joseph Ronsley, 10–23. Gerrards Cross: Colin Smythe, 1981.

Swift, Jonathan. "Drapier's Letter I." 1724. In *Jonathan Swift: The Major Works*, edited by Angus Ross and David Woolley, 422–31. Oxford: Oxford Univ. Press, 2003.

———. "Drapier's Letter IV." 1724. In *Jonathan Swift: The Major Works*, edited by Angus Ross and David Woolley, 434–47. Oxford: Oxford Univ. Press, 2003.

———. "Dr Swift's Will, with the Codicil Annexed." In *The Works of Jonathan Swift*, vol. 1, edited by Sir Walter Scott, 516–27. Edinburgh: Archibald Constable, 1824.

———. "Swift to Lord Carteret." April 27, 1724. In *Jonathan Swift: The Major Works*, edited by Angus Ross and David Woolley, 431–32. Oxford: Oxford Univ. Press, 2003.

"Tragedy and Comedy in Triple Bill." *Irish Times*, March 29, 1932, 4.

Trotter, Mary. *Modern Irish Theatre.* Cambridge: Polity, 2008.

Van den Beuken, Ruud. "'Ancient Ireland Comes to Rathmines': Memory, Identity, and Diversity in Micheál macLíammóir's *Where Stars Walk* (1940)." In *The Gate Theatre, Dublin: Inspiration and Craft*, edited by David Clare, Des Lally, and Patrick Lonergan, 47–61. Dublin: Carysfort/Oxford: Peter Lang, 2018.

———. "'A Lament for the Fianna in a Time When Ireland Shall Be Changed': Prospective/Prescriptive Memory and (Post-)Revolutionary Discourse in Mythological Gate Plays." *Études irlandaises* 43, no. 2 (2018): 197–208.

———. "MacLiammóir's Minstrel and Johnston's Morality: Cultural Memories of the Easter Rising at the Dublin Gate Theatre." *Irish Studies Review* 23, no. 1 (2015): 1–14.

———. "Remembering the Drapier and King Dan: The Sectarian Legacies of Swift and O'Connell in Edward Longford's *Yahoo* (1933) and *Ascendancy* (1935)." In *Irish Studies and the Dynamics of Memory: Transitions and Transformations*, edited by Marguérite Corporaal, Christopher Cusack, and Ruud van den Beuken, 19–39. Oxford: Peter Lang, 2017.

———. "'Three Cheers for the Descendancy!': Middle-Class Dreams and (Dis) illusions in Mary Manning's *Happy Family* (1934)." In *Navigating Ireland's Theatre Archive: Theory, Practice, Performance*, edited by Barry Houlihan, 141–57. Oxford: Peter Lang, 2019.

Walsh, Ian R. "Hilton Edwards as Director: Shade of Modernity." In *The Gate Theatre, Dublin: Inspiration and Craft*, edited by David Clare, Des Lally and Patrick Lonergan, 29–45. Dublin: Carysfort/Peter Lang, 2018.

Walshe, Éibhear. "Sodom and Begorrah, or Game to the Last: Inventing Michael Mac Liammóir." In *Sex, Nation and Dissent in Irish Writing*, edited by Éibhear Walshe, 150–69. Cork: Cork Univ. Press, 1997.

———. *Oscar's Shadow: Wilde, Homosexuality, and Modern Ireland*. Cork: Cork Univ. Press, 2011.

Walshe, Maurice. Foreword to *Juggernaut*, by David Sears, 4–5. Birr: Midland Tribune, 1952.

Wertsch, James V. *Voices of Collective Remembering*. Cambridge: Cambridge Univ. Press, 2002.

Whelan, Feargal. "Lord Longford's *Yahoo*: An Alternative Myth from an Alternative National Theatre." In *The Gate Theatre, Dublin: Inspiration and Craft*, edited by David Clare, Des Lally, and Patrick Lonergan, 147–59. Dublin: Carysfort/Peter Lang, 2018.

Whelan, Kevin. "Pre- and Post-famine Landscape Change." In *The Great Irish Famine*, edited by Cathal Póirtéir, 19–34. Dublin: Mercier Press, 1995.

"*Where Stars Walk*: MacLiammoir Play at the Gaiety." *Irish Times*, February 20, 1940, 5.

"*Where Stars Walk*: MacLiammóir Play at the Gaiety." *Evening Herald*, February 20, 1940, 6.

Wilde, Oscar. "The Critic as Artist." 1890. In *Oscar Wilde: Plays, Prose Writings, and Poems*, 1–67. London: David Campbell/Everyman's Library, 1991.

Wills, Clair. *Dublin 1916: The Siege of the GPO*. London: Profile Books, 2009.

———. *That Neutral Island: A Cultural History of Ireland During the Second World War*. London: Faber & Faber, 2007.

Yeats, William Butler. *Cathleen ni Houlihan*. 1902. In *The Collected Plays of W. B. Yeats*, 2nd ed., 73–88. London: Macmillan, 1952.

———. "Easter 1916." 1921. In *The Collected Poems of W. B. Yeats*, 2nd ed., 202–5. London: Macmillan, 1950.

———. *The Land of Heart's Desire*. 1894. In *The Collected Plays of W. B. Yeats*, 2nd ed., 51–72. London: Macmillan, 1952.

———. "The Man and the Echo." 1939. In *The Collected Poems of W. B. Yeats*, 2nd ed., 393–95. London: Macmillan, 1950.

———. "The Rose Tree." 1921. In *The Collected Poems of W. B. Yeats*, 2nd ed., 206. London: Macmillan, 1950.

———. "September 1913." 1914. In *The Collected Poems of W. B. Yeats*, 2nd ed., 120–21. London: Macmillan, 1950.

"*Youth's the Season*—?: Gate Theatre New Play." *Irish Times*, December 9, 1931, 6.

Zerubavel, Eviatar. *Time Maps: Collective Memory and the Social Shape of the Past*. Chicago, IL: Univ. of Chicago Press, 2003.

# Index

**Ruud van den Beuken** is assistant professor of English literature at Radboud University Nijmegen (The Netherlands) and the assistant director of the NWO-funded Gate Theatre Research Network. He received the 2015 Irish Society for Theatre Research (ISTR) New Scholars' Prize and held a Visiting Research Fellowship at the Moore Institute (National University of Ireland Galway) in 2018.

Lightning Source UK Ltd.
Milton Keynes UK
UKHW012131040521
383126UK00002B/195